E. Moore

COMPASSION FATIGUE

Coping with Secondary

Traumatic Stress Disorder

in Those Who Treat the

Traumatized

Brunner/Mazel Psychosocial Stress Series
Charles R. Figley, Ph.D., Series Editor

1. *Stress Disorders among Vietnam Veterans*, Edited by Charles R. Figley, Ph.D.
2. *Stress and the Family Vol. 1: Coping with Normative Transitions*, Edited by Hamilton I. McCubbin, Ph.D., and Charles R. Figley, Ph.D.
3. *Stress and the Family Vol. 2: Coping with Catastrophe*, Edited by Charles R. Figley, Ph.D., and Hamilton I. McCubbin, Ph.D.
4. *Trauma and Its Wake: The Study and Treatment of Post-Traumatic Stress Disorder*, Edited by Charles R. Figley, Ph.D.
5. *Post-Traumatic Stress Disorder and the War Veteran Patient*, Edited by William E. Kelly, M.D.
6. *The Crime Victim's Book, Second Edition*, By Morton Bard, Ph.D., and Dawn Sangrey.
7. *Stress and Coping in Time of War: Generalizations from the Israeli Experience*, Edited by Norman A. Milgram, Ph.D.
8. *Trauma and Its Wake Vol. 2: Traumatic Stress Theory, Research, and Intervention*, Edited by Charles R. Figley, Ph.D.
9. *Stress and Addiction*, Edited by Edward Gottheil, M.D., Ph.D., Keith A. Druley, Ph.D., Steven Pashko, Ph.D., and Stephen P. Weinstein, Ph.D.
10. *Vietnam: A Casebook*, By Jacob D. Lindy, M.D., in collaboration with Bonnie L. Green, Ph.D., Mary C. Grace, M.Ed., M.S., John A. MacLeod, M.D., and Louis Spitz, M.D.
11. *Post-Traumatic Therapy and Victims of Violence*, Edited by Frank M. Ochberg, M.D.
12. *Mental Health Response to Mass Emergencies: Theory and Practice*, Edited by Mary Lystad, Ph.D.
13. *Treating Stress in Families*, Edited by Charles R. Figley, Ph.D.
14. *Trauma, Transformation, and Healing: An Integrative Approach to Theory, Research, and Post-Traumatic Therapy*, By John P. Wilson, Ph.D.
15. *Systemic Treatment of Incest: A Therapeutic Handbook*, By Terry Trepper, Ph.D., and Mary Jo Barrett, M.S.W.
16. *The Crisis of Competence: Transitional Stress and the Displaced Worker*, Edited by Carl A. Maida, Ph.D., Norma S. Gordon, M.A., and Norman L. Farberow, Ph.D.
17. *Stress Management: An Integrated Approach to Therapy*, By Dorothy H.G. Cotton, Ph.D.
18. *Trauma and the Vietnam War Generation: Report of the Findings from the National Vietnam Veterans Readjustment Study*, By Richard A. Kulka, Ph.D., William E. Schlenger, Ph.D., John A. Fairbank, Ph.D., Richard L. Hough, Ph.D., B. Kathleen Jordan, Ph.D., Charles R. Marmar, M.D., Daniel S. Weiss, Ph.D., and David A. Grady, Psy.D.
19. *Strangers at Home: Vietnam Veterans Since the War*, Edited By Charles R. Figley, Ph.D., and Seymour Leventman, Ph.D.
20. *The National Vietnam Veterans Readjustment Study: Tables of Findings and Technical Appendices*, By Richard A. Kulka, Ph.D., William E. Schlenger, Ph.D., John A. Fairbank, Ph.D., Richard L. Hough, Ph.D., B. Kathleen Jordan, Ph.D., Charles R. Marmar, M.D., and Daniel S. Weiss, Ph.D.
21. *Psychological Trauma and the Adult Survivor: Theory, Therapy, and Transformation*, By I. Lisa McCann, Ph.D., and Laurie Anne Pearlman, Ph.D.
22. *Coping with Infant or Fetal Loss: The Couple's Healing Process*, By Kathleen R. Gilbert, Ph.D., and Laura S. Smart, Ph.D.
23. *Compassion Fatigue: Coping with Secondary Traumatic Stress Disorder in Those Who Treat the Traumatized*, Edited by Charles R. Figley, Ph.D.

COMPASSION FATIGUE

Coping with Secondary
Traumatic Stress Disorder
in Those Who Treat the
Traumatized

Edited by

Charles R. Figley, Ph.D.

Routledge
Taylor & Francis Group
New York   London

Routledge
Taylor & Francis Group
270 Madison Avenue
New York, NY 10016

Routledge
Taylor & Francis Group
2 Park Square
Milton Park, Abingdon
Oxon OX14 4RN

© 1995 by Taylor & Francis Group, LLC
Routledge is an imprint of Taylor & Francis Group, an Informa business

International Standard Book Number-13: 978-0-87630-759-5 (Hardcover)
Library of Congress catalog number: 94-49230

Library of Congress Cataloging-in-Publication Data

Catalog record is available from the Library of Congress

Visit the Taylor & Francis Web site at
http://www.taylorandfrancis.com

and the Routledge Web site at
http://www.routledgementalhealth.com

Editorial Note

This volume is the latest in a series of books that have focused on the immediate and long-term consequences of highly stressful events. The first volume, *Trauma and Its Wake*, published in the Psychosocial Stress Series in 1985, provided the initial historical, theoretical, and empirical grounding and included several treatment chapters. The second volume, *Trauma and Its Wake*, Volume II, published the next year, was even more treatment oriented. Both volumes are credited with advancing the field through the publication of theoretical and clinical innovations, along with a comprehensive review of the emerging literature. In 1988 the third book in the series that focused on trauma and treatment, *Post-traumatic Therapy and Victims of Violence*, edited by Frank Ochberg, was published. The fourth book, published in 1989, was edited by John P. Wilson: *Trauma, Transformation, and Healing: An Integrative Approach to Theory, Research, and Post-traumatic Therapy*. The fifth book, *Treating Stress in Families*, published the same year, was edited by this author.

This volume attempts further to define and clarify the field of psychotraumatology. It, however, is only the latest in a series of books with a similar goal. The present volume follows the earlier, two-volume series, *Trauma and Its Wake* (TAW) (Figley, 1985, 1986). The first volume of that series (Figley, 1985), which was also the first to focus specifically on the concept of post-traumatic stress disorder (PTSD), included chapters on treatment. The second volume (Figley, 1986) was more treatment oriented. Volume III in the TAW series, originally planned for publication in 1988, was superseded by the *Journal of Traumatic Stress*, which featured several of the chapters originally destined for TAW as the initial articles in its premier issue. Now, after more than six volumes of the journal, more than a decade of experience with the concept of PTSD, and the emergence of a new field of study, it is time for another volume in the TAW tradition that will once again move the field ahead. This time our focus is secondary traumatic stress.

Charles R. Figley, Ph.D.
Series Editor

Table of Contents

Acknowledgments

This project is a product of the efforts of many, many people, in addition to the eight scholars who contributed chapters. First were my students who were sufficiently interested in this topic to sustain my own interest. Several of them—Jeff Todahl, Mike Barnes, Jerry Solomon, David Mackey, Lynn Marzoni, Cindy Lee, and Brian Bride—formed a research team that assisted me in selecting the most promising chapter proposals. Other students served as my editorial assistants at different stages of development, and in the peer review process, a cumbersome and complex task. Kim Shurliff was especially helpful as an enthusiastic and creative assistant who carefully read many of the chapters. To my students, I express my deepest appreciation and the hope that they one day will be involved in further extending this area of the field of psychotraumatology, as have a number of my former students.

Members of the Series Editorial Board reviewed all of the chapters, blind to authorship. Assisting them in this task were a number of scholars who specialize in one or more areas of psychotraumatology and are among the few dozen, worldwide, who are experts on STSD. Other reviewers were Gail Walker, Ann Burgess, Susan Roth, Evelyn Gislin, Joanne E. McIntyre, Zahava Solomon, Frank Ochberg, Arthur Blank, Larry Rapp, Carolyn Kauffman, Denis Donovan, Conner Walters, Sharon Krantz, Jeffery Mitchell, Christine Dunning, Terry Trepper, Mary Jo Barrett, Lisa McCann, Susan Solomon, C. Denning, Christine Courtois, and Matthew J. Friedman.

Staff members at the Florida State University's Marriage and Family Therapy Center deserve special recognition. Because this volume was peer reviewed and each chapter required numerous revisions, correspondence and phone calls were rather overwhelming at times, and Mike Barnes and Jeff Todahl were very cordial and efficient in their contacts with both authors and reviewers. Barb Myers, center manager, deserves special recognition for her work in coordinating her staff, and for her diplomacy in dealing with authors and reviewers. Also at the center, Kathy Vanlandingham and Michele Smith provided useful support toward the end of the project. Lorrie Guttman did an excellent job as editorial consultant.

No less important are the administrators who have the responsibility of keeping the professors on task and within budget. Dr. Ray Bardill, Dean of the School of Social Work, provided the administrative leadership to ensure that I could focus my energy on this project and encouraged me to get it done. The support of Dr. Penny Ralston, dean of our Interdivisional Program in Marriage and Family, also was vital.

My faculty colleagues offered constant support and encouragement, and, in part, were responsible for the completion of this book. They include Professors Mary Hicks, Tom Cornille, Dianne Montgomery, Carol Darling, Joyce Carbonell, Ron Mullis, Nick Mazza, and Ron and Anne Mullis, among others.

But it was my family that provided the most support and inspiration. My wonderful daughters, Jessica and Laura, frequently illustrated compassion fatigue when dealing with the trauma of completing this project. And they were very effective in sharing their love as well. My mother, Geni, and my sister, Sandy, were a constant source of love and support. And my wife, Dr. Marilyn Reeves, is responsible, in large part, not only for my professional productivity, but also for my personal happiness and satisfaction.

Together with the thousands of people I have worked with over the two decades of my career, these people have made this book possible. I am very grateful for their contributions.

Contributors

E. Jackson Allison, Jr., M.D., M.P.H.
Department of Emergency Medicine, East Carolina University, Greenville, North Carolina

Randal D. Beaton, Ph.D.
School of Nursing, University of Washington, Seattle, Washington

Don R. Catherall, Ph.D.
The Phoenix Institute, Chicago, Illinois

Mary S. Cerney, Ph.D.
C.F. Menninger Memorial Hospital, Topeka, Kansas

Mary Ann Dutton, Ph.D.
Department of Emergency Medicine,
George Washington University Medical Center, Washington, D.C.

Charles R. Figley, Ph.D.
Florida State University Psychosocial Stress Research Program and
Interdivisional Ph.D. Program in Marriage and Family,
Tallahassee, Florida

Lisa Fisher, Ph.D.
National Center for PTSD–Boston, Department of Veterans Affairs
Medical Center, and Tufts University School of Medicine,
Boston, Massachusetts

Chrys J. Harris, Ph.D.
Linder, Waddell & Harris, Greenville, South Carolina

Christine Makary, M.S.
National Center for PTSD–Boston, Department of Veterans Affairs
Medical Center, and Tufts University School of Medicine,
Boston, Massachusetts

Susan L. McCammon, Ph.D.
Department of Psychology, East Carolina University,
Greenville, North Carolina

James F. Munroe, Ed.D.
National Center for PTSD–Boston, Department of Veterans Affairs
Medical Center, and Tufts University School of Medicine, Boston,
Massachusetts

Shirley A. Murphy, Ph.D.
School of Nursing, University of Washington, Seattle, Washington

Laurie Anne Pearlman, Ph.D.
Traumatic Stress Institute, South Windsor, Connecticut

Kathryn Rapperport, M.D.
Private Practice, Lexington, Massachusetts

Francine L. Rubinstein
School of Psychology, Nova University, Ft. Lauderdale, Florida

Karen W. Saakvitne, Ph.D.
Traumatic Stress Institute, South Windsor, Connecticut

Jonathan Shay, M.D.
National Center for PTSD–Boston, Department of Veterans Affairs
Medical Center, and Tufts University School of Medicine,
Boston, Massachusetts

Paul Valent, M.B.B.S., D.P.M. (ENG), F.R.A.N.Z.C.P.
Monash Medical Centre, Melbourne, Australia

Janet Yassen, M.S.W., LICSW
Victims of Violence Program, Cambridge Hospital, OutPatient
Psychiatry Department (an affiliate of Harvard Medical School),
Cambridge, Massachusetts

Rose Zimering, Ph.D.
National Center for PTSD–Boston, Department of Veterans Affairs
Medical Center, and Tufts University School of Medicine,
Boston, Massachusetts

Introduction

Traumatology, or the field of traumatic stress studies, has become a dominant focus of interest in the mental health fields only in the past decade. Yet the origin of the study of human reactions to traumatic events can be traced to the earliest medical writings in Kunus Pyprus, published in 1900 B.C. in Egypt. Many factors account for the recent emergence of this field, including a growing awareness of the long-term consequences of shocking events. Among these consequences are violence toward others, extraordinary depression, dysfunctional behavior, and a plethora of medical maladies associated with emotional stress.

Many identify the publication of the American Psychiatric Association's third edition of the Diagnostic and Statistical Manual of Mental Disorders (DSM-III) in 1980 as a major milestone in the progress of this field of study. The publication provided credibility to various theories and research findings about psychological trauma emerging from the investigation of the long-term effects of war, hostage taking, rape, family abuse, natural disasters, accidents, and, most recently, the death of a loved one.

The DSM-III (APA, 1980) included the diagnosis of post-traumatic stress disorder (PTSD). For the first time the common symptoms experienced by a wide variety of traumatized persons were viewed as a psychiatric disorder, one that could be accurately diagnosed and treated. In the latest revision (APA, 1994), the symptom criteria were modified somewhat, and its popularity with professionals (including lawyers, therapists, emergency professionals, and researchers) working with traumatized people grew, as did the accumulation of empirical research that validated the disorder.

After nearly 12 years of usage, the rubric PTSD is commonly applied to people affected by one of many types of traumatic events. However, a review of the traumatology literature yields the following proposition: nearly all of the hundreds of reports focusing on traumatized people exclude those who were traumatized indirectly or secondarily and focus on those who were directly traumatized (i.e., the direct victims). But, descriptions of what constitutes a traumatic event (i.e., Category A in DSM-III, and DSM-III-R descriptions of PTSD) clearly suggest that simply the knowledge that a loved one has been exposed to a traumatic event can be traumatizing. If this is true, why are there so few reports of such traumatized people?

Perhaps even more important, the burnout and countertransference literature suggests that therapists are vulnerable to experiencing stress as a result of their jobs, yet few studies can identify the active ingredients that are most connected to this job/profession–related stress. It appears that secondary traumatic stress—or, as we prefer, compassion fatigue—is the syndrome that puts most therapists at risk.

OVERVIEW OF THE BOOK

As noted in the series editor's Editorial Note earlier in this volume, this is the latest in a series of books that have focused on the immediate and long-term consequences of highly stressful events. This series began with *Trauma and Its Wake* (Figley, 1985) and provided the initial historical, theoretical, and empirical grounding, and included several treatment chapters.

This is the latest in the series to concentrate on treating traumatic stress, and the third in the *Trauma and Its Wake* series. Here we focus on those who provide the therapy: therapists and crisis and trauma counselors. The purposes of the book, then, are (a) to introduce the concept of compassion fatigue as a natural and disruptive by-product of working with traumatized and troubled clients; (b) to provide a theoretical basis for the assessment and treatment of compassion stress and compassion fatigue: (c) to explain the difference between compassion fatigue and PTSD, burnout, and countertransference; (d) to identify innovative methods for treating compassion fatigue in therapists, and (e) to suggest methods for preventing compassion fatigue.

Here we define compassion stress as the natural behaviors and emotions that arise from knowing about a traumatizing event experienced by a significant other—the stress resulting from helping or wanting to help a traumatized person. In this volume the focus is exclusively on professional caregivers, especially therapists, but also Red Cross workers, nurses, doctors, and informed personnel who react in emergencies.

Compassion fatigue is identical to secondary traumatic stress disorder (STSD) and is the equivalent of PTSD. The following passage is taken from the PTSD description of what constitutes a sufficiently traumatic experience. The italicized sections emphasize that people can be traumatized without actually being physically harmed or threatened with harm.

> The person has experienced an event outside the range of usual human experience that would be markedly distressing to almost anyone: a serious threat to his or her life or physical integrity; serious threat or harm *to his children, spouse, or other close relatives or friends;* sudden destruction of his home or community; or *seeing another person seriously injured or killed in an accident or by physical violence* (APA, 1994).

Thus, there is a fundamental difference between the sequelae or pattern of response, during and following a traumatic event, for people exposed directly to harm (primary stressors) and for those exposed to those in harm's way (secondary stressors). Moreover, not only are therapists and other professionals vulnerable to compassion fatigue (secondary stress disorders), so too are the family and friends of people in harm's way (i.e., "victims") vulnerable to secondary traumatic stress (compassion stress) and stress disorder (compassion fatigue).

PURPOSE

The purpose of this groundbreaking book is fourfold: (a) to discuss the results of a systematic reevaluation of the field in general, and PTSD in particular, after more than a decade of use of the term; (b) to introduce a reconceptualization of trauma, traumatic events, traumatic stress, and traumatic stress disorders that appreciates the varying degrees of impact of traumatic events on individuals and interpersonal relationships or systems depending on the proximity to harm—primary, secondary, and tertiary traumatic stress reactions/disorders; (c) to review the scholarly and clinical literature vis-à-vis this new conceptualization; and (d) to propose new approaches to conceptualizing, researching, and treating traumatic stress built upon this new conceptualization.

ORGANIZATIONAL STRUCTURE AND CONTENT

Each chapter, written by a specialist in the field, follows a similar, basic outline. The primary questions addressed throughout the book are as follows:

1. What are compassion stress and compassion fatigue?
2. What are the unintended, and often unexpected, deleterious effects of providing help to traumatized people?
3. What are some examples of cases in which individuals were traumatized by helping, and how were they traumatized?
4. What are the characteristics of the traumatized helper (e.g., race, gender, ethnicity, age, interpersonal competence, experience with psychological trauma) that account for the development, sustenance, preventability, and treatability of secondary traumatization?
5. Is there a way, theoretically, to account for all these factors?
6. What are the characteristics of an effective program to prevent compassion stress and its unwanted consequences?
7. What are the characteristics of an effective treatment program to ameliorate compassion stress and its unwanted consequences?

Each chapter underwent peer review by the Series Editorial Board and other traumatologists knowledgeable about STSD/compassion fatigue.

CHAPTER CONTENT

In Chapter 1, "Compassion Fatigue as Secondary Traumatic Stress Disorder: An Overview," Charles R. Figley reviews the traumatology literature and suggests that what is missing is a conceptual accounting of how and why people not directly at risk in traumatic situations nevertheless can become traumatized—that knowing and especially treating someone who is traumatized is the systemic connector that links the traumatic feelings and emotions of the primary to the secondary "victims." The purpose of this chapter is fivefold: (a) to introduce the designation compassion fatigue to describe the result of working with traumatized people; (b) to provide a rationale for the stress-producing potential of these secondary traumatic stressors, which is equal to or greater than that of more conventional, direct traumatic stressors; (c) to discuss the advantages of separating out secondary stress reactions (compassion stress) and stress disorders (compassion fatigue) in the DSM from direct stress reactions and stress disorders; (d) to describe a theoretical model that accounts for and predicts the emergence of compassion stress and compassion fatigue among professionals working with traumatized people; and (e) to explicate the principles associated with accurate diagnosis, assessment, research, treatment, and prevention of compassion fatigue.

Chapter 2, "Survival Strategies: A Framework For Understanding Secondary Traumatic Stress and Coping in Helpers," by Paul Valent, a psychiatrist with extensive experience in emergency mental health services, presents a new framework. This model helps to categorize and conceptualize traumatic stress reactions as a *context* for understanding the nature and role of survival strategies. This view is helpful in understanding STSD, especially for psychotherapists and other professional helpers. He notes that whereas PTSD describes the reliving and avoidance of traumatic stress responses, there is a need for a framework for the great variety of such responses, some of which may even be contradictory (such as courage and fear). Valent suggests that the variety of traumatic stress responses corresponds to the variety of survival strategies that have evolved to deal with different traumatic situations. He presents eight survival strategies, which are described in their biological, psychological, and social aspects: rescue, attachment, assertiveness, adaptation, fight, flight, competition, and cooperation. According to Valent, survival strategies have other clinical applications, such as classifying emotions and tracing responses back to their original traumatic contexts. Secondary traumatic stress (STS) responses may be elicited in helpers through identifying with and complementing victim survivor strategies. Moreover, he suggests that STSD may develop if the identifications are too intense, the complementing survival strategies are inappropriate, or helpers cannot execute their own survival strategies adaptively.

Chapter 3, "Working with People in Crisis: Research Implications," by Randal D. Beaton and Shirley A. Murphy, includes as "crisis workers" the front-line, first responders such as firefighters, law enforcement personnel, and rescue workers, for whom exposure to occupational trauma is frequent and repetitive. Crisis workers also include persons with jobs in which they may be physically removed from the trauma incident scene, such as 911 dispatchers and emergency room nurses, but who are nonetheless exposed to traumatic stress and "absorb" it. Beaton and Murphy assert that crisis workers, by the nature of their duties and responsibilities, are at risk of experiencing secondary trauma stress (i.e., stress reactions that arise from being exposed to a traumatizing event or from assisting or wanting to assist a traumatized person). This important chapter reviews the unintended and deleterious effects on crisis workers that arise as a result of their providing help. These include negative consequences, relationship problems, and substance abuse. Various hypothetical and empirical similarities and differences between PTSD and compassion fatigue are enumerated and discussed. The contributions of individual, occupational, social, and community contextual variables to secondary traumatization are considered on the basis of the available research.

In Chapter 4, "Working with People with PTSD: Research Implications," Mary Ann Dutton and Francine L. Rubinstein review the relevant research literature to build a profile of the compassion fatigue of trauma workers' reactions. Of special concern are the professionals (mostly therapists) exposed to traumatic events through contact with survivors of trauma as well as with the perpetrators of traumatic events on others. Further, this chapter presents a theoretical framework that includes a discussion of traumatic events to which the trauma worker is exposed, the trauma worker's post-traumatic stress reaction, coping strategies for responding to the traumatic situation and to the psychological sequelae, and the personal and environmental mediators of trauma workers' secondary post-traumatic stress (PTS) reactions. Dutton and Rubinstein note several important implications for assessment, intervention, and prevention.

Most of the other chapters focus on methods of treatment and prevention with therapists and others working with traumatized people. All follow a common outline that first notes the importance of the focus of the chapter and estimates the number of persons affected (e.g., family members of people traumatized), then reviews the literature on effective ways in which these people have been helped, and then provides a detailed description of one or more suggested approaches to intervention (including assessment, establishment of a therapeutic alliance, agreement on goals and objectives, and a description of the treatment program/plan). The final section covers helpful suggestions to professionals working with similar clients.

Chapter 5, "Sensory-Based Therapy for Crisis Counselors," by Chrys J. Harris, identifies various assessment and treatment paradigms appropriate for helping crisis workers who suffer from STS/STSD. According to the author, crisis workers include immediate responders (firefighters and law enforcement personnel); later responders (medical, paramedic, and ambulance personnel); unexpected responders (passersby, others in the event); emergency room personnel; body recovery, identification, and burial personnel; crisis intervenors (clergy, medical, and mental health professionals); voluntary personnel (Red Cross, Salvation Army, and shelter/caregivers); remote responders (equipment maintenance personnel); and emergency support personnel (dispatchers). Harris presents a model for understanding the etiology of STS, followed by a brief discussion of ethnic and cultural issues. He introduces his "sensory-based therapy" as a promising approach. After a discussion of assessment characteristics, two treatment paradigms are presented: one preventative and the other ameliorative. Toward the end of the chapter, Harris argues for utilizing a sensory-based therapy in two ways: as a preventive intervention and in combination with more traditional PTS therapy to ameliorate compassion fatigue.

Chapter 6, "Debriefing and Treating Emergency Workers," by Susan L. McCammon and E. Jackson Allison, Jr., emphasizes the importance of promoting trauma resolution and healthy coping strategies in emergency workers. Strategies that can be implemented before, during, and after a traumatic event are summarized. Pretrauma interventions include the use of a stress audit, training regarding stress and its management, and policy development.

During a traumatic event, interventions include orientation to the trauma site, on-scene support, demobilization, and debriefing. Common elements among the several debriefing models described include the structuring of opportunities to review the events of the traumatic situation and to ventilate feelings, the learning of skills for integrating and mastering the event, and obtaining assistance in identifying, enlisting, and accepting help from one's support system. Post-trauma activities include individual follow-up sessions, the use of experimental procedures such as eye movement desensitization and reprocessing, and attention to anniversaries of traumatic events. A decade of anecdotal reports testifies to the effectiveness of debriefing and provides helpful insights into working with emergency responders. Currently, research efforts are under way to assess systematically the impact of debriefing. Future research should address the mediating effect of emergency workers' coping behaviors and cognitions.

Chapter 7, "Treating the 'Heroic Treaters,' " by Mary S. Cerney, focuses on treaters who work with psychologically and physically traumatized patients. Cerney notes that these therapists are especially vulnerable to STS and STSD, as the assault on their sense of personal integrity and belief in humanity can be so shattering that it places them in a special group of traumatized individuals who are similar in many ways to the individuals they treat, although each trauma victim, whether patient or therapist, is different. The author assesses the reactions of therapists who experience compassion stress and compassion fatigue, including issues of transference, countertransference, projective identification, and identification. She also describes factors that influence the experience and consequences of compassion stress/fatigue, preventive measures to minimize or prevent its occurrence, and ways to help the therapist who has suffered compassion fatigue.

Chapter 8, "Constructivist Self Development Approach to Treating Therapists with Secondary Traumatic Stress Disorders," by Laurie Anne Pearlman and Karen W. Saakvitne, like the previous chapter, focuses on

trauma therapists, with special emphasis on those who treat adult survivors of childhood sexual abuse. Pearlman and Saakvitne have
observed that these therapists find that their inner experiences of "self"
and "other" transform in ways that parallel the experience of the trauma
survivor. This transformation, which the authors deem "vicarious
traumatization," involves changes in the therapist's frame of reference.
This is a special manifestation of STSD that includes modifications in
one's identity and world view, self capacities, ego resources, psychological needs and cognitive schema, and sensory experiences that are part of
the authors' constructivist self development (CSD) theory. Based on
CSD theory, the authors suggest that treatment of STSD—especially vicarious traumatization in therapists—must focus on three realms: personal, professional, and organizational. They discuss specific strategies for
each realm to counteract the negative effects of trauma work on the therapists. The strategies emphasize the necessity for balance; the use of
external resources; self-atonement; connection; and the need to foster
one's sense of meaning, interdependence, and hope.

The final three chapters focus on prevention, and also follow a common outline. Unlike the treatment chapters, more emphasis is placed on
psychoeducation, preparedness, and planning. Moreover, unlike the previous chapter, in which mental health professionals exclusively design
and implement a treatment program, prevention is the business of many
more professionals. Policy makers, administrators, educators, emergency
workers, disaster preparedness workers, and community safety specialists are all responsible for some aspect of preventing compassion fatigue.

In Chapter 9, "Preventing Secondary Traumatic Stress Disorder,"
Janet Yassen offers a framework for prevention of compassion stress that
includes an appreciation of the primary, secondary, and tertiary dimensions of prevention. In the final section of the chapter, Yassen presents
practical guidelines for preventing STS, based on an ecological model.
This model assumes that prevention can be most successful if it incorporates both the individual and the environmental factors. Individual
strategies address the physical, social, and psychological aspects as of
STS, as well as its professional components. Environment interventions
include social, societal, and work-setting strategies.

Chapter 10, "Preventing Compassion Fatigue: A Team Treatment
Model," by James F. Munroe, Jonathan Shay, Lisa Fisher, Christine
Makary, Kathryn Rapperport, and Rose Zimering, suggests that isomor-
phic characteristics of compassion fatigue and PTSD, and the intensity
and duration of exposure by clients, is predictive of responses. The
authors assert that no therapists are immune to these effects. The chapter
deals with the thorny ethical questions in traumatology: the duty to

inform, educate, and act in connection with compassion fatigue among colleague therapists. This team of authors suggests that therapists working alone may be unable to identify their own responses. A team approach is described that prevents secondary trauma and enhances client treatment by actively modeling appropriate coping strategies. Recognizing the effects of secondary trauma, the authors argue, gives therapists not only a means of prevention for themselves, but also a window of understanding and an opportunity to intervene actively with their clients. They offer several examples of client patterns and team responses, and outline several specific practices for therapists.

In the final chapter, Chapter 11, "Preventing Institutional Traumatic Stress Disorder," by Don Catherall, institutions are the central point of interest, especially those that are vulnerable to acts of violence or other sources of traumatic stress. The author argues that well-prepared institutions establish ongoing mechanisms to deal with PTSD and compassion fatigue among their workers, including therapists. He maintains that the first step is to evaluate the degree of exposure and assign responsibility for prevention activities before incidents actually occur. The institution must then work to establish an atmosphere that acknowledges the normality of reactions to compassion stress and facilitates the processing of exposure to secondary stressors. This healthy atmosphere, according to Catherall, is similar to that in families that cope functionally with primary trauma (i.e., they identify the stressor as a problem for the entire group, and not just the affected individual) and that approach the problem in an open, supportive, nonblaming fashion. In addition, Catherall notes that institutions must attend to aspects of the institutional environment that affect the workers' abilities to function as a closely knit group. These elements include the hierarchical structure of most institutions, the impersonal and disempowering atmosphere of many bureaucracies, and the influence of the institutional mission. Finally, Catherall points out that institutions must attend to the dynamics of the group and ensure that affected workers are not viewed as having something wrong *with* them, but, rather, as having had something happen *to* them.

In the Epilogue we bring together the major axioms from the literature and recommendations noted throughout the book. We also provide models for understanding and predicting compassion stress and compassion fatigue. Last, the editor introduces the next volume in the series. That book will focus on the secondary effects of trauma on family members and friends struggling to recover from a traumatic event.

REFERENCES

American Psychiatric Association. (1980). *Diagnostic and statistical manual of mental disorders* (3rd ed. [draft]). Washington, D.C.: Author.
American Psychiatric Association. (1987). *Diagnostic and statistical manual of mental disorders* (3rd ed., rev.). Washington, D.C.: Author.
American Psychiatric Association. (1994). *Diagnostic and statistical manual of mental disorders* (4th ed.). Washington, D.C.: Author.
Figley, C. R. (Ed.). (1985). *Trauma and its wake: The study and treatment of post-traumatic stress disorder* (pp. 398–415) New York: Brunner/Mazel.
Figley, C. R. (1986). Traumatic stress: The role of the family and social support system. In C. R. Figley (Ed.), *Trauma and its wake: Vol. 2: Traumatic stress theory, research, and intervention* (pp. 39–54). New York: Brunner/Mazel.
Figley, C. R. (Ed.). (1989). *Treating stress in families.* New York: Brunner/Mazel.
Ochberg, F. M. (Ed.). (1988). *Post-traumatic therapy and victims of violence.* New York: Brunner/Mazel.
Veith, I. (1965). *Hysteria: The history of a disease.* Chicago: University of Chicago Press.
Wilson, J. P. (1989). *Trauma, transformation, and healing: An integrative approach to theory, research, and post-traumatic therapy.* New York: Brunner/Mazel.

1

Compassion Fatigue as Secondary Traumatic Stress Disorder: An Overview

CHARLES R. FIGLEY

There is a cost to caring. Professionals who listen to clients' stories of fear, pain, and suffering may feel similar fear, pain, and suffering because they care. Sometimes we feel we are losing our sense of self to the clients we serve. Therapists who work with rape victims, for example, often develop a general disgust for rapists that extends to all males. Those who have worked with victims of other types of crime often "feel paranoid" about their own safety and seek greater security. Ironically, as will be noted later, the most effective therapists are most vulnerable to this mirroring or contagion effect. Those who have enormous capacity for feeling and expressing empathy tend to be more at risk of compassion stress.

Mary Cerney (Chapter 7) notes that working with trauma victims can be especially challenging for therapists, since some may feel that they, in the words of English (1976), ". . . have taken over the pathology" of the clients (p. 191). Cerney suggests:

This affront to the sense of self experienced by therapists of trauma victims can be so overwhelming that despite their best efforts, therapists begin to exhibit the same characteristics as their patients— that is, they experience a change in their interaction with the

1

world, themselves, and their family. They may begin to have intrusive thoughts, nightmares, and generalized anxiety. They themselves need assistance in coping with their trauma.

The professional work centered on the relief of the emotional suffering of clients automatically includes absorbing information that is about
suffering. Often it includes absorbing that suffering itself as well.

Over the past 10 years, I have been studying this phenomenon.
Although I now refer to it as compassion fatigue, I first called it a form
of burnout, a kind of "secondary victimization" (Figley, 1983a). Since
that time, I have spoken with or received correspondence from hundreds of professionals, especially therapists, about their struggles with
this kind of stressor. They talk about episodes of sadness and depression, sleeplessness, general anxiety, and other forms of suffering that
they eventually link to trauma work.

This chapter and those that follow represent our best efforts to understand, treat, and prevent compassion fatigue. We begin with a discussion of the conceptual development of the concept of trauma and related
terms and ways of knowing about them.

Paul Valent (Chapter 2) presents a framework for the next century of
investigation of traumatic stress. "Survival strategies" are assigned to
each of the eight types of traumatic stressors, and each strategy is considered within the three reaction domains: biological, psychological, and
social. This synthesis of decades of research and theoretical work
appears to be a very useful framework for categorizing traumatic stress
reactions, including secondary traumatic stress (STS) and secondary
traumatic stress disorder (STSD) among therapists and others who care
for victims.

This chapter proposes a reconfiguration of post-traumatic stress disorder (PTSD) that is consistent with the current, scientifically based
views of the disorder, as specified in the revised third edition of the
DSM-III (American Psychiatric Association [APA], 1987) and of the new
version described in DSM-IV (APA, 1994) and ICD-10. As noted in the
introduction to this book, the criteria of a traumatic event in these diagnostic manuals take note of but do not discuss the implications of a person's being confronted with the pain and suffering of others. It will be
suggested later that PTS and PTSD retain the same set of symptoms, and
thus methods of assessment, but that parallel symptoms and methods of
assessment must be developed for STS and STSD. This chapter draws on
the research and theoretical literature, primarily presented in the chapters to follow, to support this new configuration.

What follows is an explication of STS and STSD, later called compassion stress/fatigue, because they have received the least attention from traumatology scholars and practitioners. This is followed by an illustrative review of the theoretical and research literature that supports the existence of STS. The last section of the chapter discusses the implications of the proposed reconfiguration for diagnostic nomenclature, research and clinical assessment, and theory development.

CONCEPTUAL CLARITY

The diagnosis of PTSD has been widely utilized in mental health research and practice, and its application has influenced case law and mental health compensation (Figley, 1986; Figley, 1992a, b). In a report of the review of trauma-related articles cited in *Psychological Abstracts*, Blake, Albano, and Keane (1992) identified 1,596 citations between 1970 and 1990. Their findings support the view that the trauma literature has been growing significantly since the advent of the concept of PTSD (APA, 1980). However, most of these papers lack conceptual clarity. They rarely consider contextual and circumstantial factors in the traumatizing experience or adopt the current PTSD nomenclature.

As noted in the introduction to this volume, although the psychotraumatology field has made particularly great progress in the past decade, the syndrome has an extremely long history. A field devoted exclusively to the study and treatment of traumatized people represents the culmination of many factors. One was the greatly increased awareness of the number and variety of traumatic events and their extraordinary impact on large numbers of people. As noted in the introduction, many identify the publication of the American Psychiatric Association's DSM-III in 1980 as a major milestone. It was the first to include the diagnosis of post-traumatic stress disorder.

With the publication of DSM-III, for the first time the common symptoms experienced by a wide variety of traumatized persons were viewed as a psychiatric disorder; one that could be accurately diagnosed and treated. Although a revision of DSM-III modified the symptom criteria somewhat (APA, 1987), the popularity of the concept among professionals working with traumatized people (including lawyers, therapists, emergency professionals, and researchers) grew, as did the accumulation of empirical research that validated the disorder.

After well over a decade of use, the term PTSD is more commonly applied to people traumatized by one of many types of traumatic events. Yet a review of the traumatology literature yields the following: Nearly all of the hundreds of reports focusing on traumatized people exclude those who were traumatized indirectly or secondarily and focus on those who were directly traumatized (i.e., the "victims"). But descriptions of what constitutes a traumatic event (i.e., Category [criterion] A in the DSM-III and DSM-III-R descriptions of PTSD) clearly indicate that mere knowledge of another's traumatic experiences can be traumatizing.

People are traumatized either directly or indirectly. The following excerpt is taken from the PTSD description in DSM-IV (APA, 1994) of what constitutes a sufficiently traumatic experience.

> The essential feature of posttraumatic stress disorder is the development of characteristic symptoms following exposure to an extreme traumatic stressor involving direct personal experience of an event that involves threatened death, actual or threatened serious injury, or other threat to one's physical integrity; or witnessing an event that involves death, injury, or a threat to the physical integrity of another person; or *learning about unexpected or violent death, serious harm, or threat of death or injury experienced by a family member or other close associates* (Criterion A1). Italics added; [p. 424]

The italicized phrases emphasize that people can be traumatized without actually being physically harmed or threatened with harm. That is, they can be traumatized simply by learning about the traumatic event. Later it is noted:

> Events experienced by others that are learned about include, but are not limited to, violent personal assault, serious accident, or serious injury experienced by a family member or a close friend; learning about the sudden, unexpected death of a family member or a close friend; or learning that one's child has a life-threatening disease. [p. 424]

This material has led to a conceptual conundrum in the field, although few have identified it. For example, I have pointed out (Figley, 1976; 1982; 1983a,b) that the number of "victims" of violent crime, accidents, and other traumatic events is grossly underestimated because only those directly in harm's way are counted, excluding family and friends of the victims. In a presentation (1982) and subsequent publications (1983b; 1985a,b; 1989), I noted a phenomenon I called "secondary catastrophic stress reactions," meaning that the empathic induction of a family member's experiences results in considerable emotional upset.

Parallel phenomena exist: fathers, especially in more primitive societies, appear to exhibit symptoms of pregnancy out of sympathy for those of their wives (i.e., *couvade*; see Hunter & Macalpine, 1963); a psychiatric illness can appear to be shared by the patient's spouse (folie à deux; Andur & Ginsberg, 1942; Gralnick, 1939). Other parallels have been reported in the medical and social science literatures, including copathy (Launglin, 1970); identification (Brill, 1920; Freud, 1959); sympathy (Veith, 1965); and hyperarousal, "mass hysteria," or psychogenic illness, which appears to sweep through groups of people, including children (see Colligan & Murphy, 1979). An emotional arousal appears to be associated with an empathic and sympathetic reaction. Also, in the process of dispensing this care, the support becomes exhausted. As noted elsewhere (Figley, 1983b):

> Sometimes . . . we become emotionally drained by [caring so much]; we are adversely affected by our efforts. Indeed, simply being a member of a family and caring deeply about its members makes us emotionally vulnerable to the catastrophes which impact them. We, too, become "victims," because of our emotional connection with the victimized family member. [p. 12]

In a later treatise (Figley, 1985), I commented that families and other interpersonal networks (e.g., friendships, work groups, clubs, and the client–therapist relationship) are powerful systems for promoting recovery following traumatic experiences. At the same time, these same systems and their members can be "traumatized by concern." We can classify this trauma as follows: (1) simultaneous trauma takes place when all members of the system are directly affected at the same time, such as by a natural disaster; (2) vicarious trauma happens when a single member is affected out of contact with the other members (e.g., in war, coal mine accidents, hostage situations, distant disasters); (3) intrafamilial trauma or abuse takes place when a member causes emotional injury to another member; and (4) chiasmal or secondary trauma strikes when the traumatic stress appears to "infect" the entire system after first appearing in only one member. This last phenomenon most closely parallels what we are now calling STS and STSD.

Richard Kishur, a master's student studying under the author's direction, reanalyzed a large data set of a study of New York City crime victims and their supporters (family members, neighbors, friends). Utilizing metaphorically the transmission of genetic material or "crossing over" that takes place between like pairs of chromosomes during meiotic cell division, Kishur (1984) coined the term "chiasmal effect." To him, this term best accounted for why there was such a strong correlation between the quality and quantity of the symptoms of crime victims and that of the supporters of these victims.

It is clear that a pattern of effects emerges in both victim and supporter. The crime victims as well as their supporters suffer from the crime episode long after the initial crisis has passed. Symptoms of depression, social isolation, disruptions of daily routine, and suspicion or feelings of persecution affect the lives of these persons. [p. 65]

Even in the absence of precise, conceptual tools, however, the literature is replete with implicit and explicit descriptions of this phenomenon. Some of the most cogent examples are reports by traumatized people who complain that family and friends discourage them from talking about their traumatic experiences after a few weeks because it is so distressing to the supporters (Figley, 1989).

I previously (Figley, 1989) expressed my dismay about seeing so many colleagues and friends abandon clinical work or research with traumatized people because of their inability to deal with the pain of others. "The same kind of psychosocial mechanisms within families that make trauma 'contagious,' that create a context for family members to infect one another with their traumatic material, operate between traumatized clients and the therapist" (p. 144). Those who are most vulnerable to this contagion are those who "begin to view themselves as saviors, or at least as rescuers" (pp. 144–145).

In summary, there has been widespread, although sporadic, attention in the medical, social science, family therapy, and psychological literature to the phenomenon we now refer to as compassion stress/fatigue or secondary traumatic stress/disorder. At the same time, in spite of the clear identification of this phenomenon as a form of traumatization in all three versions of the DSM, nearly all of the attention has been directed to people in harm's way, and little to those who care for and worry about them.

Why are there so few reports of these traumatized people? Perhaps it is because the psychotraumatology field is so young, although the focus of interest stretches back through the ages. Beaton and Murphy (Chapter 3) note that perhaps the field is in a "pre-paradigm state," as defined by Kuhn (1962, 1970). Kuhn, in his classic treatise on theory development, reasoned that paradigms follow the evolution of knowledge, and, in turn, influence the development of new knowledge. Knowledge about experiencing, reexperiencing, and reacting to traumatic material evolves in "fits and starts." Prevailing paradigms are viewed, suddenly, as anomalies when new information and paradigm shifts occur. This certainly applies to the prevailing, limiting view of PTSD and the need to recognize that the process of attending to the traumatic experiences and expressions may be traumatic itself.

The concept of PTSD, developed through both scholarly synthesis and the politics of mental health professions (see Scott, 1993), was introduced in DSM-III (APA, 1980) as the latest in a series of terms to describe the harmful biopsychosocial effects of emotionally traumatic events. This concept has brought order to a growing area of research that is now a field of study (Figley, 1988a, b, c; Figley, 1992a, b). After more than a decade of application of the concept and two revisions of the DSM, it is time to consider the least studied and least understood aspect of traumatic stress: secondary traumatic stress.

Why STSD?

It has been confirmed by a wide variety of sources (e.g., Ochberg, 1988; Wilson & Raphael, 1993) that the most important and frequently used remedies for people suffering from traumatic and post-traumatic stress are personal rather than clinical or medical. These personal remedies include the naturally occurring social support of family, friends, and acquaintances, and of professionals who care (see Figley, 1988a, b, c; Flannery, 1992; Solomon, 1989). Yet little has been written about the "cost of caring" (Figley, 1975, 1978, 1982, 1985b, 1986, 1989, 1993b, in press; Figley & Sprenkle). It is important to know how these supporters become upset or traumatized as a result of their exposure to victims. By understanding this process, we not only can prevent additional, subsequent traumatic stress among supporters, but we can also increase the quality of care for victims by helping their supporters.

Scholars and clinicians require a conceptualization that accurately describes the indices of traumatic stress for both those in harm's way and those who care for them and become impaired in the process. Alternate theoretical explanations for the transmission of trauma that results in this impairment are discussed in the latter part of this chapter.

Definition of Secondary Traumatic Stress and Stress Disorder

We can define STS as the natural consequent behaviors and emotions resulting from knowing about a traumatizing event experienced by a significant other—the stress resulting from helping or wanting to help a traumatized or suffering person (Figley, 1993a).

What is being asserted is that there is a fundamental difference between the sequelae or pattern of response during and following a traumatic event, for people exposed to primary stressors and for those exposed to secondary stressors. Therefore, STSD is a syndrome of symptoms nearly identical to PTSD, except that exposure to knowledge about a traumatizing event experienced by a significant other is associated with the set of STSD symptoms, and PTSD symptoms are directly connected to the sufferer, the person experiencing primary traumatic stress. Table 1 depicts and contrasts the symptoms of PTSD with those of STSD.

TABLE 1
Suggested Distinctions Between the Diagnostic Criteria for
Primary and Secondary Traumatic Stress Disorder

Primary	Secondary
A. Stressor:	**A. Stressor:**
Experienced an event outside the range of usual human experiences that would be markedly distressing to almost anyone; an event such as:	Experienced an event outside the range of usual human experiences that would be markedly distressing to almost anyone; an event such as:
1. Serious threat to self	1. Serious threat to traumatized person (TP)
2. Sudden destruction of one's environs	2. Sudden destruction of TP's environs
B. Reexperiencing Trauma Event	**B. Reexperiencing Trauma Event**
1. Recollections of event	1. Recollections of event/TP
2. Dreams of event	2. Dreams of event/TP
3. Sudden reexperiencing of event	3. Sudden reexperiencing of event/TP
4. Distress of reminders of event	4. Reminders of TP/event distressing
C. Avoidance/Numbing of Reminders	**C. Avoidance/Numbing of Reminders of Event**
1. Efforts to avoid thoughts/feelings	1. Efforts to avoid thoughts/feelings
2. Efforts to avoid activities/situations	2. Efforts to avoid activities/situations
3. Psychogenic amnesia	3. Psychogenic amnesia
4. Diminished interest in activities	4. Diminished interest in activities
5. Detachment/estrangements from others	5. Detachment/estrangements from others
6. Diminished affect	6. Diminished affect
7. Sense of foreshortened future	7. Sense of foreshortened future
D. Persistent Arousal	**D. Persistent Arousal**
Difficulty falling/staying asleep	Difficulty falling/staying asleep
2. Irritability or outbursts of anger	2. Irritability or outbursts of anger
3. Difficulty concentrating	3. Difficulty concentrating
4. Hypervigilance for self	4. Hypervigilance for TP
5. Exaggerated startle response	5. Exaggerated startle response
6. Physiologic reactivity to cues	6. Physiologic reactivity to cues

(Symptoms under one month duration are considered normal, acute, crisis-related reactions. Those not manifesting symptoms until six months or more following the event are delayed PTSD or STSD.)

At the same time, we suggest that PTSD should stand for primary traumatic stress disorder, rather than post-traumatic stress disorder, since every stress reactions is "post" by definition.

Contrasts Between STS and Other Concepts

The STS phenomenon has been called different names over the years. We suggest that compassion stress and compassion fatigue are appropriate substitutes. Most often these names are associated with the "cost of caring" (Figley, 1982) for others in emotional pain.

Among the few dozen references in this general area, this phenomenon is called secondary victimization (Figley, 1982, 1983b, 1985a, 1989), "co-victimization" (Hartsough & Myers, 1985), and secondary survivor (Remer & Elliot, 1988a, 1988b). McCann & Pearlman (1989) suggest that "vicarious traumatization" is an accumulation of memories of clients' traumatic material that affects and is affected by the therapist's perspective of the world. They propose a team-oriented approach to both preventing and treating this special kind of stress.

Miller, Stiff, and Ellis (1988) coined the term *emotional contagion* to describe an affective process in which "an individual observing another person experiences emotional responses parallel to that person's actual or anticipated emotions" (p. 254). Other terms that appear to overlap with STS or STSD include rape-related family crisis (Erickson, 1989; White & Rollins, 1981); "proximity" effects on female partners of war veterans (Verbosky & Ryan, 1988); generational effects of trauma (Danieli, 1985; McCubbin, Dahl, Lester, & Ross, 1977); the need for family "detoxification" from war-related traumatic stress (Rosenheck & Thomson, 1986); and the "savior syndrome" (NiCathy, Merriam, & Coffman, 1984). But "countertransference" and "burnout" are most frequently cited, and will be discussed separately in more detail in the following.

Countertransference and Secondary Stress

Countertransference is connected with psychodynamic therapy and often appears to be an emotional reaction to a client by the therapist. Although there are many definitions, countertransference in the context of psychotherapy is the distortion on the part of the therapist resulting from the therapist's life experiences and associated with her or his unconscious, neurotic reaction to the client's transference (Freud, 1959). Most recently, Corey (1991) defined countertransference as the process of seeing oneself in the client, of overidentifying with the client, or of meeting needs through the client.

Singer and Luborsky (1977), not bound by the limits of psychoanalysis, suggest that countertransference extends far beyond the context of psychotherapy. They include all of a therapist's conscious and unconscious feelings about or attitudes toward a client, and believe that these feelings and attitudes may be useful in treatment.

In the recent book *Beyond Transference: When the Therapist's Real Life Intrudes* (Gold & Nemiah, 1993), contributors recount how personal events in the lives of therapists affect the quality and characteristics of therapy. The most compelling part of the book, however, focuses on how clients, not the personal life experiences of the therapist, are stressful and difficult to handle. Countertransference was once viewed simply as the therapist's conscious and unconscious response to the patient's transference, especially if the transference connected with the therapist's past experiences. Johansen (1993) suggests that a more contemporary perception of countertransference views it as all of the emotional reactions of the therapist toward the patient—regardless of their sources. These sources include, for example, the life stressors—past or present—experienced by the therapist. But they also include the traumata expressed by the client and absorbed by the therapist. This, unfortunately, is rarely discussed in the literature, and is the major focus of this book.

A recent study (Hayes, Gelso, Van Wagoner, & Diemer, 1991) found that five therapist qualities appear to help therapists, in varying degrees, to manage countertransference effectively. These are anxiety management, conceptualization of skills, empathic ability, self-insight, and self-integration. The study surveyed 33 expert therapists regarding the importance of five factors, subdivided into 50 personal characteristics, which composed their five-item, Likert-response-type Countertransference Factors Inventory (CFI). Although all five were found to be important, expert therapists rated self-integration and self-insight as the most significant factors in managing countertransference.

In a follow-up study, Van Wagoner, Gelso, Hayes, and Diemer (1991) surveyed 93 experienced counseling professionals using the CFI to rate the factors for either therapists in general or excellent therapists in particular. Excellent therapists, in contrast to therapists generally, were viewed by the sample as (1) having more insight into and explanation for their feelings; (2) having greater capacity for empathy for and understanding of the client's emotional experience; (3) being more able to differentiate between the needs of self and client; (4) being less anxious with clients; and (5) being more adept at conceptualizing "client dynamics" in both the client's current and past contexts (p. 418).

One could argue, then, that STS includes, but is not limited to, what these researchers and other professionals view as countertransference. It is assumed that countertransference happens only within the context of psychotherapy, it is a reaction by the therapist to the transference actions on the part of the client, and it is a negative consequence of therapy and should be prevented or eliminated. However, STS, or event STSD, is a natural consequence of caring between two people, one of whom has been initially traumatized and the other of whom is affected by the first's traumatic experiences. These effects are not necessarily a problem but, more, a natural by-product of caring for traumatized people.

Burnout and Secondary Stress

Some view the problems faced by workers with job stress simply as burnout (Maslach & Jackson, 1984; cf. Pines, 1993). A 1993 literature search of *Psychological Abstracts* located more than 1,100 relevant articles and 100 books since the term was coined by Freudenberger (1974) and carefully explicated by Maslach (1976). According to Pines and Aronson (1988), burnout is "a state of physical, emotional and mental exhaustion caused by long term involvement in emotionally demanding situations" (p. 9). The most widely utilized measure of burnout is the Maslach Burnout Inventory (MBI), developed by Maslach and Jackson (1981). It measures three aspects: emotional exhaustion (e.g., "I feel emotionally drained by my work"); depersonalization (e.g., "I worry that the job is hardening me emotionally"); and reduced personal accomplishment (e.g., "I feel I'm positively influencing other people's lives through my work"). More recently, Pines and Aronson (1988) developed the Burnout Measure (BM), which measures physical exhaustion (e.g., feeling tired or rundown); emotional exhaustion (e.g., feeling depressed, hopeless); and mental exhaustion (e.g., feeling disillusionment, resentment toward people). Emotional exhaustion appears to be the key factor the two measures of burnout have in common. Burnout has been defined variously as a collection of symptoms associated with emotional exhaustion.

1. Burnout is a process (rather than a fixed condition) that begins gradually and becomes progressively worse (Cherniss, 1980; Maslach, 1976, 1982).
2. The process includes (a) gradual exposure to job strain (Courage & Williams, 1986), (b) erosion of idealism (Freudenberger, 1986; Pines, Aronson, & Kafry, 1981), and (c) a void of achievement (Pines & Maslach, 1980).

3. There is an accumulation of intensive contact with clients (Maslach & Jackson, 1981).

In a comprehensive review of the empirical research on the symptoms of burnout, Kahill (1988) identified five categories of symptoms.

1. Physical symptoms (fatigue and physical depletion/exhaustion, sleep difficulties, specific somatic problems such as headaches, gastrointestinal disturbances, colds, and flu).
2. Emotional symptoms (e.g., irritability, anxiety, depression, guilt, sense of helplessness).
3. Behavioral symptoms (e.g., aggression, callousness, pessimism, defensiveness, cynicism, substance abuse).
4. Work-related symptoms (e.g., quitting the job, poor work performance, absenteeism, tardiness, misuse of work breaks, thefts).
5. Interpersonal symptoms (e.g., perfunctory communication with, inability to concentrate/focus on, withdrawal from clients/co-workers, and then dehumanizing, intellectualizing clients).

In addition to depersonalization, burnout has been associated with a reduced sense of personal accomplishment and discouragement as an employee (see Maslach & Jackson, 1981). From a review of the research literature, it appears that the most salient factors associated with the symptoms of burnout include client problems—chronicity, acuity, complexity—that are perceived to be beyond the capacity of the service provider (Freudenberger, 1974, 1975; Maslach, 1976, 1982; Maslach & Jackson, 1981). Moreover, Karger (1981) and Barr (1984) note that service providers are caught in a struggle between promoting the well-being of their clients and trying to cope with the policies and structures in the human service delivery system that tend to stifle empowerment and well-being.

In contrast to burnout, which emerges gradually and is a result of emotional exhaustion, STS (compassion stress) can emerge suddenly with little warning. In addition to a more rapid onset of symptoms, with STS, in contrast to burnout, there is a sense of helplessness and confusion, and a sense of isolation from supporters; the symptoms are often disconnected from real causes, and yet there is a faster recovery rate. The Self Test for Psychotherapists was designed to help therapists differentiate between burnout and STS. This measure (see pp. 13–14) is discussed elsewhere (Figley, 1993a) in some detail.

Compassion Fatigue Self Test for Psychotherapists*

Name _____ Institution _____ Date _____
Please describe yourself: ___Male___Female; _____ years as practitioner. Consider each of the following characteristic about you and your current situation. Write in the number for the best response. Use one of the following answers:

1=Rarely/Never 2=At Times 3=Not Sure 4=Often 5=Very Often

Answer all items, even if not applicable. Then read the instructions to get your score.

Items About You:

1. __ *I force myself to avoid certain thoughts or feelings that remind me of a frightening experience.*
2. __ *I find myself avoiding certain activities or situations beause they remind me of a frightening experience.*
3. __ *I have gaps in my memory about frightening events.*
4. __ *I feel estranged from others.*
5. __ *I have difficulty falling or staying asleep.*
6. __ *I have outbursts of anger or irritability with little provocation.*
7. __ *I startle easily.*
8. __ *While working with a victim I thought about violence against the perpetrator.*
9. __ *I am a sensitive person.*
10. __ *I have had flashbacks connected to my clients.*
11. __ *I have had first-hand experience with traumatic events in my adult life.*
12. __ *I have had first-hand experience with traumatic evevts in my childhood.*
13. __ *I have thought that I need to "work through" a traumatic experience in my life.*
14. __ *I have thought that I need more close friends.*
15. __ *I have thought that there is no one to talk with about highly stressful experiences.*
16. __ *I have concluded that I work too hard for my own good.*
17. __ *I am frightened of things a client has said or done to me.*
18. __ *I experience troubling dreams similar to those of a client of mine.*
19. __ *I have experienced intrusive thoughts of sessions with especially difficult clients.*
20. __ *I have suddenly and involuntarily recalled a frightening experience while working with a client.*
21. __ *I am preoccupied with more than one client.*
22. __ *I am losing sleep over a client's traumatic experiences.*
23. __ *I have thought thatI might have been "infected" by the traumatic stress of my clients.*
24. __ *I remind myself to be less concerned about the well-being of my clients.*
25. __ *I have felt trapped by my work as a therapist.*
26. __ *I have felt a sense of hopelessness associated with working with clients.*
27. __ *I have felt "on edge" about various things and I attribute this to working with certain clients.*

Continued

28. __ I have wished that I could avoid working with some therapy clients.
29. __ I have been in danger working with therapy clients.
30. __ I have felt that my clients dislike me personally.

Items About Being a Psychotherapist and Your Work Environment:

31. __ I have felt weak, tired, rundown as a result of my work as a therapist.
32. __ I have felt depressed as a result of my work as a therapist.
33. __ I am unsuccessful at separating work from personal life.
34. __ I feel little compassion toward most of my co-workers.
35. __ I feel I am working more for the money than for personal fulfillment.
36. __ I find it difficult separating my personal life from my work life.
37. __ I have a sense of worthlessness/disillusionment/resentment associated with my work.
38. __ I have thoughts that I am a "failure" as a psychotherapist.
39. __ I have thoughts that I am not succeeding at achieving my life goals.
40. __ I have to deal with bureaucratic, unimportant tasks in my work life.

* Note, this instrument is under development. Please contact Dr. Charles R. Figley, Psychosocial Stress Research Program, Florida State University, MFT Center (F86E) (Phone: 904-644-1588; Fax, 904-644-4804) [11/93]

Scoring Instructions: (a) Be certain you responded to all items. (b) Circle the following 23 items: 1–8, 10–13, 17–26, and 29. (c) Add the numbers you wrote next to the items. (d) Note your risk of Compassion Fatigue: 26 or less = Extremely low risk; 27 to 30 = Low risk; 31 to 35 = Moderate risk; 36 to 40 = High risk; 41 or more = Extremely high risk.

Then, (e) Add the numbers you write next to the items not circled. (f) Note your risk of burnout: 17–36 or less = Extremely low risk; 37–50 = Moderate risk; 51–75 = High risk; 76–85 = Extremely high risk.

Scores for this instrument emerged using a sample of 142 pschotherapy practitioners attending workshops on the topic during 1992 and 1993. Psychometric properties of the scale are reported by Stamm and Vara (1993). Alpha reliability scores ranged from 94 to 86; structural analysis yielded at least one stable factor which is characterized by depressed mood in relationship to work accompanied by feelings of fatigue, disillusionment, and worthlessness. Structural Reliability (stability) of this factor, as indicated by Tucker's Coefficient of Congruence (cc), is .91.

Why Compassion Stress and Compassion Fatigue?

Thus although STS and STSD are the latest and most exact descriptions of what has been observed and labeled over hundreds of years, the most friendly term for this phenomenon, and one that will be used here, is compassion fatigue (Joinson, 1992). Webster's Encyclopedic Unabridged Dictionary of the English Language (1989) defines compassion as "a feeling of deep sympathy and sorrow for another who is stricken by suffering or misfortune, accompanied by a strong desire to alleviate the pain or remove its cause" (p. 299). Its antonyms include "mercilessness" and "indifference." My very informal research leads to the finding that the terms compassion stress and compassion fatigue are favored by nurses (Joinson first used the term in print, in 1992, in discussing burnout among nurses), emergency workers, and other professionals who experience STS and STSD in the line of duty. Therefore, the terms can be used interchangeably by those who feel uncomfortable with STS and STSD. Such discomfort might arise from a concern that such labels are derogatory. Feeling the stress, and even the fatigue, of compassion in the line of duty as a nurse or therapist better describes the causes and manifestations of their duty-related experiences.

Who Is Vulnerable to Compassion Fatigue?

In the epilogue to this book, two models are presented to account for how and why some people develop compassion fatigue while others do not. At the heart of the theory are the concepts of empathy and exposure. If we are not empathic or exposed to the traumatized, there should be little concern for compassion fatigue. Throughout this book, authors discuss the special vulnerabilities of professionals—especially therapists—who work with traumatized people on a regular basis. These "trauma workers" are more susceptible to compassion fatigue.

This special vulnerability is attributable to a number of reasons, most associated with the fact that trauma workers are always surrounded by the extreme intensity of trauma-inducing factors. As a result, no matter how hard they try to resist it, trauma workers are drawn into this intensity. Beyond this natural by-product of therapeutic engagement, there appear to be four additional reasons why trauma workers are especially vulnerable to compassion fatigue.

1. *Empathy is a major resource for trauma workers to help the traumatized.* Empathy is important in assessing the problem and formulating a treatment approach, because the perspectives of the clients—including the victim's family members—must be considered. Yet as noted earlier and throughout this volume (see Harris, Chapter 5) from research on STS and STSD we know that empathy is a key factor in the induction of traumatic material from the primary to the secondary victim. Thus the process of empathizing with a traumatized person helps us to understand the person's experience of being traumatized, but, in the process, we may be traumatized as well.

2. *Most trauma workers have experienced some traumatic event in their lives.* Because trauma specialists focus on the context of a wide variety of traumatic events, it is inevitable that they will work with traumatized people who experienced events that were similar to those experienced by the trauma worker. There is a danger of the trauma worker's overgeneralizing his or her experiences and methods of coping to the victim and overpromoting those methods. For example, a crime-related traumatization may be very different from that of the trauma worker, but the counselor may assume that they are similar and so listen less carefully. Also, the counselor may suggest what worked well for him or her but would be ineffective—or, at worst, inappropriate—for the victim.

3. Unresolved trauma of the worker will be activated by reports of similar trauma in clients. Trauma workers who are survivors of previous traumatic events may harbor unresolved traumatic conflicts. These issues may be provoked as a result of the traumatic experiences of a client. In this volume, the chapters by Cerney, by Yassen, and by others confirm the power of past traumatic experiences on current functioning.

4. Children's trauma is also provocative for therapists. Police officers, firefighters, emergency medical technicians, and other emergency workers report that they are most vulnerable to compassion fatigue when dealing with the pain of children (see Beaton & Murphy, Chapter 3). And because children so often are either the focus of trauma counseling or are important players, trauma workers are more likely than are other practitioners to be exposed to childhood trauma.

IMPLICATIONS FOR TRAINING AND EDUCATING THE NEXT GENERATION OF PROFESSIONALS

The chapters to follow more fully explicate the role of trauma in the lives of professionals. They review in detail the scholarly and practice literature to identify what we know and have known about compassion fatigue (i.e., STSD). Each of the contributors suggests his or her own theories, concepts, and methods of assessment and treatment. Few discuss the implications for trauma worker education, however.

As an educator, as well as a researcher and practitioner, this author is concerned about the next generation of trauma workers. Although we need to know a great deal more about compassion fatigue—who gets it when, and under what circumstances; how it can be treated and prevented—we know much already. We know enough to realize that compassion fatigue is an occupational hazard of caring service providers—be they family, friends, or family counselors.

Recognizing this, we as practicing professionals have a special obligation to our students and trainees to prepare them for these hazards. A place to start is to incorporate stress, burnout, and compassion fatigue into our curriculum, and especially our supervision in practica.

We can use the relatively protected environment of our educational centers and the clients who seek help there as a place for discussing these issues. Some fundamental principles for preventing compassion fatigue might be useful. In addition, training programs could (1) institute policies that require processing all clinical material that appears to be upsetting to either the individual worker or another team member (including a supervisor); and (2) recognize that upsetting clinical material is and should be discussed confidentially with confidants (spouse/partner), following prescribed ethical procedures, and that the confidant could, in turn, become upset; and (3) experiment with various methods for avoiding compassion fatigue while, at the same time, not sacrificing clinical effectiveness.

We must do all that we can to insure that trauma workers are prepared. As noted later in the book, we have a "duty to inform" them about the hazards of this work. But, at the same time, to emphasize that this work is most rewarding: to see people suffering from the shock of highly stressful events be transformed immediately from sadness, depression, and desperation to hope, joy, and a renewed sense of purpose and meaning of life. This transformation is equally possible for professionals who recognize that they themselves are suffering from compassion fatigue. We hope that the chapters to follow will help facilitate this transformation both in those in harm's way and in the professionals they go to for help.

REFERENCES

American Psychiatric Association. (1980). *Diagnostic and statistical manual of mental disorders* (3rd ed.). Washington, D.C.: Author.
American Psychiatric Association. (1987). *Diagnostic and statistical manual of mental disorders* (3rd ed., rev.). Washington, D.C.: Author.
American Psychiatric Association. (1994). *Diagnostic and statistical manual of mental disorders* (4th ed.). Washington, D.C.: Author.

Andur, M., & Ginsberg, T. (1942). Folie à deux. Medical bulletin of the Veterans Administration, 14, 230–263.

Barr, D. (1984). Burnout as a political issue. Catalyst, 4(4), 68–75.

Blake, D. D., Albano, A. M., & Keane, T. M. (1992). Twenty years of trauma: Psychological abstracts 1970 through 1989. Journal of Traumatic Stress, 5(3), 477–484.

Brill, A. (1920). The empathy index and personality. Medical Record, 97, 131–134.

Cherniss, C. (1980). Staff burnout: Job stress in the human services. Beverly Hills, Calif.: Sage.

Colligan, M. J., & Murphy, L. R. (1979). Mass psychogenic illness in organizations: An overview. Journal of Occupational Psychology, 52, 77–90.

Corey, G. F. (1991). Theory and practice of counseling psychotherapy. Belmont, Calif.: Brooks Cole.

Courage, M. M., & Williams, D. M. (1986). An approach to the study of burnout in professional care providers in human service organizations. Journal of Social Service Research, 10(1), 7–22.

Danieli, Y. (1985). The treatment and prevention of long-term effects and intergenerational transmission of victimization: A lesson from holocaust survivors and their children. In C. Figley (Ed.), Trauma and its wake: Study and treatment of PTSD (pp. 295–313). New York: Brunner/Mazel.

English, O. S. (1976). The emotional stress of psychotherapeutic practice. Journal of the American Academy of Psychoanalysis, 4, 191–201.

Figley, C. R. (1975, February 19). Interpersonal adjustment and family life among Vietnam veterans: A general bibliography. Congressional Record.

Figley, C. R. (1978). Psychosocial adjustment among Vietnam veterans: An overview of the research. In C. R. Figley (Ed.), Stress disorders among Vietnam veterans: Theory, research, and treatment (pp. 57–70). New York: Brunner/Mazel.

Figley, C. R. (1982, February). Traumatization and comfort: Close relationships may be hazardous to your health. Keynote presentation, Families and close relationships: Individuals in social interaction. Conference held at Texas Tech University, Lubbock.

Figley, C. R. (1983a). Catastrophe: An overview of famiy reactions. In C. R. Figley & H. I. McCubbin (Eds.), Stress and the family: Vol. 2. Coping with catastrophe (pp. 3–20). New York: Brunner/Mazel.

Figley, C. R. (1983b). The family as victim: Mental health implications. In P. Berner (Ed.), Proceedings of the VIIth World Congress of Psychiatry (pp. 377–383). London: Plenum.

Figley, C. R. (1985a). From victim to survivor: Social responsibility in the wake of catastrophe. In C. R. Figley (Ed.), Trauma and its wake: The study and treatment of post-traumatic stress disorder (pp. 398–415). New York: Brunner/Mazel.

Figley, C. R. (1985b). The role of the family: Both haven and headache. In M. Lystad (Ed.), Role stressors and supports for emergency workers (pp. 84–94). Washington, D.C.: U.S. Government Printing Office (DHHS Publication No. ADM 85-1408).

Figley, C. R. (1986). Traumatic stress: The role of the family and social support system. In C. R. Figley (Ed.), Trauma and its wake: Vol. 2. Traumatic stress theory, research, and intervention (pp. 39–54). New York: Brunner/Mazel.

Figley, C. R. (1988a). A five-phase treatment of PTSD in families. Journal of Traumatic Stress, 1(1), 127–139.

Figley, C. R. (1988b). Toward a field of traumatic stress. Journal of Traumatic Stress, 1(1), 3–16.

Figley, C. R. (1988c). Victimization, trauma, and traumatic stress. Counseling Psychologist, 16(4), 635–641.

Figley, C. R. (1989). Helping traumatized families. San Francisco: Jossey-Bass.

Figley, C. R. (1992a). Posttraumatic stress disorder, Part I: Empirically based conceptualization and symptom profile. Violence Update, 2(7), 1, 8–11.

Figley, C. R. (1992b). Posttraumatic stress disorder, Part IV: Generic treatment and prevention approaches. Violence Update, 3(3).

Figley, C. R. (1993a, February). Compassion stress and the family therapist. Family Therapy News, pp. 1–8.

Figley, C. R. (1993b). Coping with stressors on the home front. Journal of Social Issues, 49(4), 51–72.

Figley, C. R. (in press,). The family and PTSD. In G. Everly & J. Lating (Eds.), Post-traumatic stress: Key papers and core concepts. New York: Plenum.

Figley, C. R., & Sprenkle, D. H. (1978). Delayed stress response syndrome: Family therapy indications. *Journal of Marriage and Family Counseling, 4,* 53–59.
Flannery, R.B., Jr. (1992). *Post-traumatic stress disorder: The victim's guide to healing and recovery.* New York: Crossroads.
Freud, S. (1959). Future prospects of psychoanalytic psychotherapy. In J. Strachey (Ed., Trans.), *The standard edition of the complete psychological works of Sigmund Freud* (Vol. 2, pp. 139–151). London: Hogarth Press. (Original work published 1910.)
Freudenberger, H. J. (1974). Staff burnout. *Journal of Social Issues, 30*(1), 159–165.
Freudenberger, H. J. (1975). Staff burnout syndrome in alternative institutions. *Psychotherapy, 12*(1),73–82.
Freudenberger, H. J. (1986). The issues of staff burnout in therapeutic communities. *Journal of Psychoactive Drugs, 18*(2), 247–251.
Gold, J. H., & Nemiah, J. C. (1993). *Beyond transference: When the therapist's real life intrudes.* Washington, D.C.: American Psychiatric Press.
Gralnick, A. (1939). Folie à deux—the psychosis of association. *Psychiatric Quarterly, 15,* 277–279.
Hartsough, D., & Myers, D. (1985). *Disaster work and mental health: Prevention and control of stress among workers.* Washington, D.C.: NIMH, Center for Mental Health Studies of Emergencies.
Hayes, J. A., Gelso, C. J., Van Wagoner, S. L., & Diemer, R. A. (1991). Managing counter-transference: What the experts think. *Psychological Reports, 69,* 138–148.
Hunter, R., & Macalpine, I. (1963). *Three hundred years of psychiatry, 1535–1860.* London: Oxford University Press.
Johansen, K. H. (1993). Countertransference and divorce of the therapist. In J. H. Gold & J. C. Nemiah (Eds.), *Beyond transference: When the therapist's real life intrudes* (pp. 87–108). Washington, D.C.: American Psychiatric Press.
Joinson, C. (1992). Coping with compassion fatigue. *Nursing, 22*(4), 116–122.
Kahill, S. (1988). Interventions for burnout in the helping professions: A review of the empirical evidence. *Canadian Journal of Counselling Review, 22*(3), 310–342.
Karger, H. (1981). Burnout as alienation. *Social Service Review, 55*(2),268–283.
Kishur, R. (1984). *Chiasmal effects of traumatic stressors: The emotional costs of support.* Unpublished master's thesis, Purdue University, West Lafayette, Ind.
Kuhn, T. (1962). *The structure of scientific revolutions.* Chicago: University of Chicago Press.
Kuhn, T. (1970). *The structure of scientific revolutions* (2nd ed.). Chicago: University of Chicago Press.
Laughlin, H. P. (1970). *The ego and its defenses.* New York: Appleton-Century-Crofts.
Maslach, C. (1976). Burn-out. *Human Behavior, 5*(9), 16–22.
Maslach, C. (1982). *The burnout: The cost of caring.* Englewood Cliffs, N.J.: Prentice-Hall.
Maslach, C., & Jackson, S. E. (1981). The measurement of experienced burnout. *Journal of Occupational Behavior, 2*(2), 99–113.
Maslach, C., & Jackson, S. E. (1984). Patterns of burnout among a national sample of public contact workers. *Journal of Health and Human Resources Administration, 7*(2), 189–212.
McCann, L., & Pearlman, L. A. (1989). Vicarious traumatization: A framework for under-standing the psychological effects of working with victims. *Journal of Traumatic Stress, 3*(1), 131–149.
McCubbin, H. I., Dahl, B. B., Lester, G. R., & Ross, B. (1977). The POW and his children: Evidence for the origin of second generational effects of captivity. *International Journal of Sociology of the Family, 7,* 25–36.
Miller, K. I., Stiff, J. B., & Ellis, B. H. (1988). Communication and empathy as precursors to burnout among human service workers. *Communication Monographs, 55*(9), 336–341.
NiCathy, G., Merriam, K., & Coffman, S. (1984). *Talking it out: A guide to groups for abused women.* Seattle: Seal Press.
Ochberg, F. M. (1988). *Post-traumatic therapy and victims of violence.* New York: Brunner/Mazel.
Pines, A. M. (1993). Burnout. In L. Goldberger & S. Breznitz (Eds.), *Handbook of stress: Theoretical and clinical aspects* (2nd ed., pp. 386–402). New York: Free Press.
Pines, A. M., & Aronson, E. (1981). *Burnout.* Schiller Park, Ill.: M.T.I. Teleprograms.

Pines, A. M., & Aronson, E. (1988). *Career burnout: Causes and cures.* New York: Free Press.

Pines, A., Aronson, E., & Kafry, D. (1981). *Burnout: From tedium to personal growth.* New York: Free Press.

Pines, A., & Maslach, C. (1980). Combatting staff burnout in child care centers: A case study. *Child Care Quarterly, 9,* 5–16.

Remer, R., & Elliot, J. (1988a). Characteristics of secondary victims of sexual assault. *International Journal of Family Psychiatry, 9*(4), 373–387.

Remer, R., & Elliot, J. (1988b). Management of secondary victims of sexual assault. *International Journal of Family Psychiatry, 9*(4), 389–401.

Rosenheck, R., & Thomson, J. (1986). "Detoxification" of Vietnam War trauma: A combined family–individual approach. *Family Process, 25,* 559–570.

Scott, W. J. (1993). *The politics of readjustment: Vietnam veterans since the war.* New York: Aldine De Gruyter. Singer & Luborsky (1977).

Solomon, Z. (1989). A three year prospective study of PTSD in Israeli combat veterans. *Journal of Traumatic Stress, 2*(1), 59–73.

Stamm, B. H., & Varra, M. E. (Eds.). *Instrumentation in the field of traumatic stress,* Chicago: Research and Methodology Interest Group, International Society for Traumatic Stress Studies.

Stanton, M. D., & Figley, C. R. (1978). Treating the Vietnam veteran within the family system. In C. R. Figley (Ed.), *Stress disorders among Vietnam veterans: Theory, research, and treatment* (pp. 281–290). New York: Brunner/Mazel.

Van Wagoner, S. L., Gelso, C. J., Hayes, J. A., & Diemer, R. A. (1991). Countertransference and the reputedly excellent therapist. *Psychotherapy: Theory, Research and Practice, 28,* 411–421.

Veith, I. (1965). *Hysteria: The history of a disease.* Chicago: University of Chicago Press.

Verbosky, S. J., & Ryan, D. A. (1988). Female partners of Vietnam veterans: Stress by proximity. *Issues in Mental Health Nursing, 9,* 95–104.

Webster's Encyclopedic Unabridged Dictionary of the English Language. (1989). New York: Gramercy.

White, P. N., & Rollins, J. C. (1981). Rape: A family crisis. *Family Relations, 30*(1), 103–109.

Wilson, J. P., & Raphael, B. (1993). *International handbook of traumatic stress syndromes.* New York: Plenum.

2

Survival Strategies: A Framework for Understanding Secondary Traumatic Stress and Coping in Helpers

PAUL VALENT

In order to understand the secondary traumatic stress (STS) reactions of those who deal with traumatized people, it is necessary to understand the responses of the primary victims, because it is the primary victims' responses that evoke the secondary responses. This chapter explores which specific responses arise in which situations, as well as their secondary effects and their means of transmission.

Whereas one line of traumatic stress literature deals with the reliving and avoidance responses in post-traumatic stress disorder (PTSD) (APA, 1987), another describes a very wide variety of often contradictory responses in traumatic stress situations. For instance, among other impact phase responses, Raphael (1986) notes numbness and apathy as well as arousal and resoluteness; effectiveness as well as helplessness; fight as well as flight.

Editor's Note: In this chapter, Valent proposes a solution to an important problem in the psychotraumatology field: the need for a framework that can accommodate the great variety of sources of stress and methods of coping with these stressors from a psychological, social, and biological perspective. Valent's model, presented in Table 1, is organized around eight survival strategies: rescuing, attaching, asserting, adapting, fighting, fleeing, competing, and cooperating. Valent suggests that the secondary traumatic stress responses may be elicited in helpers through identification with, and/or complementing victim survivor strategies. Secondary traumatic stress disorders may develop if the identifications are too intense, the complementing survival strategies are inappropriate, or helpers cannot execute their own survival strategies adaptively.

21

In a previous paper (Valent, 1984), I suggested that contradictory and fluctuating responses in disasters depend on changing survival responses to rapidly fluctuating circumstances. In this chapter, I explore further these different survival responses, which I call survival strategies (SSs). I suggest that while PTSD draws attention to the reliving and avoidance of traumatic stress responses, SSs provide a framework for the variety of physiological, emotional, and behavioral responses that are relived and avoided. I postulate that there are eight basic SSs that have evolved to deal with severe threats: rescue, attachment, assertiveness, acceptance, fight, flight, competition, and cooperation. I draw on evidence for the SSs from the fields of anatomy, physiology, ethology, anthropology, sociology, psychology, and traumatic stress.

BACKGROUND

Hippocrates wrote: "It is changes that are chiefly responsible for diseases, especially the greatest changes, the violent alterations. . ." (Dubos, 1968). Since his time, this principle has undergone a continuous cycle of being forgotten and then rediscovered and described under different labels. Trimble (1985) has noted this phenomenon for modern times. For instance, "shell-shock" and Kardiner's (1941) "[post]traumatic neurosis" came from World War I, and "combat exhaustion" (Bartemeier, Kubie & Menninger, 1946), "A-bomb disease" (Lifton, 1967), and "survivor syndrome" (Krystal, 1968) came from World War II. PTSD is a legacy of the Vietnam War. In the same period, many labels stemmed from specific disasters, such as "railway spine" (Clevenger, 1889) and "Buffalo Creek syndrome" (Titchener & Kapp, 1976).

Each of these syndromes included biological, psychological, and social manifestations. This is important to note because another series of developments in the understanding of traumatic stress arose separately in biological, psychological, and social streams of stress research, representing three perspectives with little cross-fertilization. However, they meet again in SSs. Let us now look at the three historically separate streams.

Biological Perspective

Early research was statistical/epidemiological and physiological. Statistically, a variety of traumatic situations, such as concentration camps (Eitinger, 1973), prisoner of war camps (Beebe, 1975), natural disasters (Bennet, 1970; Raphael, 1986; Trichopolous, Katsouyanni, & Zavitsanos, 1983), and bereavement (Raphael, 1984) were seen to lead to

the increased incidence of physical morbidity and mortality, as compared with control populations. However, even in more ordinary situations, the more intense the stresses, the more serious were a wide variety
of consequent illnesses (Holmes & Rahe, 1967). This was part of a gener-
ality approach: stress gave rise to illness.

In contrast, specificity theories held that certain types of stresses in
certain people were associated with certain specific illnesses. According
to Alexander's (1950) basic premise, specific emotions must have specific
physiological correlates, which in a conflict (stressful) situation, and
with particular physical vulnerabilities, lead to specific symptoms and
illnesses. He examined seven such "psychosomatic" illnesses, including
hypertension, duodenal ulcer, and asthma. Weiner (1977) updated the
theory in the light of much more complex physiological data. However,
and this is the situation till today, although prediction is easier in individuals in whom certain stresses reevoke the same illnesses, stresses add
little statistical (even if significant) weight in predicting specific illnesses
over large populations. Although some used this fact to discredit the
importance of stresses in illnesses as artifacts (e.g., Andrews & Tennant,
1978), it may be that greater sophistication is needed to gather stress
data (which may, in fact, be underreported [Monroe, 1982]) to identify
core phenomena in stresses that are significant, and to identify interven-
ing variables that need to be controlled. Thus, even though the paradigm of stress leading to specific illness has been very promising, its
clinical use has been compromised by conceptual difficulties.

Physiological research involving the autonomic nervous system
(Gellhorn, 1970), hormones (Mason, 1968), the immune system (Ader,
1981), and a variety of neurotransmitters and neuromodulators (Smith,
1991) indicated a close association of all these systems with, and their
high responsivity to, a wide range of stresses. New techniques made this
area a fertile field for study. Yet the situation has remained basically the
same as in 1968, when Mason called for a taxonomy that could make
sense of the great variety of physiological responses evoked in different
stress experiments. Again, clinical use has been hampered by conceptual
difficulties.

Psychological Perspective

Epidemiological studies have long suggested that major stresses are
followed by a variety of psychological dysfunctions. Kinston and Rosser
(1974) have suggested a 400% increase in nonpsychotic disorders following disasters. In reviewing the literature, Raphael (1986) found that
between 20% and 70% of populations suffered significant psychological
morbidity after disasters.

Nature of the morbidity
Epidemiological studies show that about one third of the populations suffer from PTSD. The others suffer a wide variety of anxiety, depressive, and somatoform disorders. A range of disorders that is similar, but includes depressive and paranoid disorders, has been described in wartime civilian (Murphy, 1975) and combat (Brill, 1966; Lindy, 1988) populations. There has been little suggestion of specific stresses leading to specific disorders, though Paykel (1979) noted that exit losses were predictive of depression. Clinically, stresses are usually allowed at least a contributory role in psychiatric disorders generally, as noted in Axis IV in DSM-III-R (APA, 1987) and DSM IV (APA, 1994).

Also, there has been a stream of research associating cognitions and emotions with stresses and psychological illnesses.

Cognitions

Breuer and Freud (1893/1975) and Janet (1920) described both the "printing" of traumatic experiences on the mind and the mind's simultaneous "splitting of consciousness" (Freud) and "dissociation" (Janet) from these experiences. Both the reliving of the traumatic experiences and their suppression (Freud, 1920/1975), with the addition of later psychological defenses, constituted the core of neuroses. More recently, Horowitz (1976) described similar features of what he called stress response syndromes, although he explored further the importance of meaning and its processing in resolving these syndromes. Finally, the reliving and avoidance of traumatic experiences constitute the core of PTSD. However, as Weiner (1985) pointed out, it may also be a feature of other DSM diagnoses. Perhaps the content and the manner of reliving and avoidance determine these diagnoses.

Whenever traumatic situations leave room for ambiguity and choice, appraisals, as well as the passive searing of events that leaves no room for thought, become incorporated in traumatic stress responses. Appraisals of whether, and which, events were dangerous were called primary appraisals by Lazarus and Folkman (1984). These were vector results of sensory perceptions of reality and subjective meanings. A variety of factors, such as past experience, role, desire and perceived authority of those giving information, could feed into the subjective aspects of primary appraisals. According to Lazarus and Folkman, secondary appraisals then determined what strategies could be applied to deal with the stresses. Reappraisal involved processing the progress of the strategies. All these appraisals are subject to avoidance and reliving.

Emotions

Anxiety and depression have been noted commonly as stress responses. Pathological grief was considered as possibly associated with depression and physical illnesses (Raphael, 1984). Anger was noted in disaster
and combat literature, and guilt was found in survivors of concentration
camps (Krystal, 1968). Schmale (1972) described the "given-in/given-
up" syndrome, which included hopelessness and helplessness. This syndrome was said to predispose to a variety of illnesses, such as cancer.

On the whole, however, it is striking that until the innovative efforts
of Plutchik (1980), there were no attempts to classify emotions or to find
a theoretical framework for them. This applied not only to the commonly described emotions such as anxiety, depression, anger, and guilt, but
even more so to a great variety of emotions such as insecurity, contentment, power, and revenge. Panksepp (1989b) noted that the study of
emotions has been assiduously avoided as unscientific, leaving a com-
pulsory central lacuna in our understanding of the physiological and
behavioral responses to stress.

Social Perspective

Perhaps because sociologists do not use an illness model, they have
drawn special attention to people's capacities to cope through adaptive
responses to stress. Further, they emphasize the positive aspects of family and community support (Quarantelli & Dynes, 1977).

Figley (1986) analyzed the factors in this support that acted as antidotes
to stress disorders. They were emotional care, comfort, love and affection,
encouragement, advice, companionship, and tangible aid. He also noted
that the family and other helpers became vulnerable through their empathy,
and could develop secondary traumatic stress disorders. It is now widely
acknowledged that helpers are frequent secondary victims (e.g., Berah,
Jones, & Valent, 1984). Mileti, Drabek, and Haas (1975) drew attention to the
various system levels (individual, family, group, and community) that
operate in disasters. Figley (1989) examined the family system in disasters.

The divisions among the biological, psychological, and social perspectives have been wide; for instance, each perspective has separate journals and institutional attachments. There has been some cross-fertilization—for instance, in biopsychosocial medicine (Engel, 1977). Another
field has been that of strategies of survival.

Precursors to the Concept of Survival Strategies

Charles Darwin (1890/1965) noted that in order to deal with a variety
of dangers, animals and humans evolved a variety of specific emotions

and behaviors. Cannon (1939), drawing on Darwin's observations, described fight and flight responses associated with the sympathetic nervous system.

Selye (1946) described a different physiological response to stress, which he called the general adaptation syndrome (GAS). This included secretion of the hormone cortisol, and suppression of the immune response. This physiological response does indeed facilitate adaptation (rather than fighting or fleeing stressors), but it cannot be considered a general stress response. In fact, the GAS is evoked in conditions of surrender (Blanchard & Blanchard, 1988; Henry, 1986b), and of the need for acceptance, as in bereavement (Irwin, Daniels, & Weiner, 1987).

Attachment, although not previously designated as a strategy of survival, is nevertheless a very important means of survival for the weak. As a biobehavior, it was first described by the Harlows (1965) in monkeys, and by Bowlby (1971) in humans. It has been described recently in many other species, as has its stressful opposite, separation (Panksepp, Siviy, & Normansell, 1985).

A number of recent developments has facilitated a more comprehensive approach to strategies of survival and their use as unifying concepts. First, evolutionary theory replaced the previous survival unit of the fittest individuals, by the breeding genes in a population (Wilson, 1982). This removed the apparent paradox of altruism, whereby the fittest often sacrificed themselves for weaker members. However, if through their actions greater numbers of group genes would survive, such altruism made evolutionary sense. Similarly, giving and taking (reciprocal altruism) could enhance group survival. This new evolutionary view allowed care of the weak and mutual cooperation to be potential SSs.

Second, advances in the study of animal behavior teased apart different survival behaviors that were previously under the single rubric of agonistic, or socially aggressive, behavior. Thus it was noted that postures of attack and sites of bites are quite different in predation (hunting), antipredator defense (self-defense, fight), and hierarchical struggles (competition). This finding meant that hunting, fighting predators, and competition could be three separate survival behaviors (Blanchard & Blanchard, 1988), each with its own type of aggression, anger, and physiology (Blanchard & Blanchard, 1988; Moyer, 1986; Olivier, Moss, & Brain, 1987; Shaikh, Brutus, & Siegel, 1985).

Third, emotions became a respectable field of scientific study (Panksepp, 1989b), because the use of complex new techniques such as computer digitization allowed them to be correlated for the first time with specific neurophysiological events and biobehaviors. The subjective self could now be correlated with objective data.

All these developments allowed propositions of relatively complex schemata of survival behavior, expanding the simple dyads such as fight and flight. Plutchik (1980) postulated eight specific survival behaviors, while Panksepp (1989a) postulated five survival "biobehavioral circuits." Although their approaches and semantics varied, these authors added four further potential survival biobehaviors to fight and flight: foraging (for food and water), attachment, grief, and sharing. Both authors emphasized the integral biopsychosocial nature of these survival behaviors.

Summary

Since Hippocrates' initial observations, it has been confirmed again and again that "the greatest changes, the violent alterations" may be "responsible for diseases." It is still difficult to conceptualize how this happens, and to know which disturbances may lead to which disorders. However, it seems possible that certain survival behaviors elicited in the circumstances of greatest changes and violent alterations (situations of traumatic stress) may provide vital clues that may make some sense of the variety of traumatic stress responses.

A number of leading workers have called for a theory that would connect and organize the vast array of available data. As noted, Mason (1968) almost 30 years ago asked for a taxonomy to organize his voluminous physiological data. Lazarus and Folkman (1984) said that even the most sophisticated (physiological) research might be sterile without a theory that included appraisals and emotions. Weiner (1989) concluded that there was a need to conceptualize the human response to particular stressors, and to link the highly complex neurochemical responses with tasks of survival. Panksepp (1986b) similarly called for a psychobiological theory that would demonstrate stress response patterns to be, in a deep sense, simple and logical.

It is suggested that SSs are important building blocks that help distill the volume of biological, psychological, and social data into meaningful, "simple and logical" patterns of biopsychosocial responses that serve survival. Survival strategies will be shown to be central concepts in delineating successful, adaptive, coping responses and unsuccessful, maladaptive, traumatically stressed responses. These strategies provide a framework for the variety of these responses, which is then applicable to both primary and secondary victims.

THE PLACE OF SURVIVAL STRATEGIES IN A CONCEPTUAL FRAMEWORK

Definitions

For the purposes of this chapter, a *stress* (Figure 1) is an event that disturbs the equilibrium of a person in such a way as actually or potentially to shorten the person's lifespan. *Appraisals* of the means of survival are cognitive processes that include sensory perceptions, past learning, and views of oneself, such as one's role and capacities. The appraisals evoke stress responses, which counter the noxious effects of stresses. They may be relatively simple instinctual responses, such as retrieval of balance or removal of body parts from painful stimuli. Survival strategies are stress responses of a higher level of complexity, including ideas, emotions, and social interactions. They will be defined further below.

Stress responses may be *adaptive* or *maladaptive* (Figure 2). Adaptive stress responses deal with stresses in such a way that life is not actually or potentially compromised. Maladaptive responses are either insufficient or the wrong ones to prevent actual or potential compromise of the lifespan. In such a case, other stress responses may be evoked. If these are not adaptive, strain, trauma, illnesses, or death occur. Both adaptive and maladaptive stress responses express themselves in a unified manner in *biological, psychological,* and *social* arenas. In fact, all the components being defined have such biological, psychological, and social aspects.

Strain is an unresolved tension between stresses and stress responses. *Trauma* occurs when stress responses fail to reestablish prestress life-enhancing equilibria. It is an amalgam of all the previous components. The situation in which trauma occurs is a traumatic situation. The stress that leads to trauma is *traumatic stress*. *Defenses* minimize the damage of trauma or its repetition. In the psychological arena, numbing and fragmentation in the early phase, and repression, phobias, displacement,

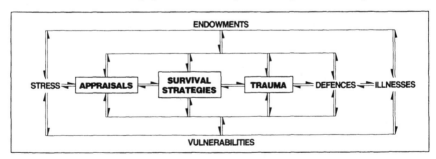

Figure 1. The place of survival strategies in traumatic stress

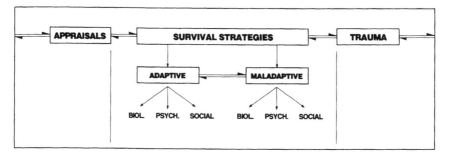

Figure 2. Survival strategies

and so on in the later phases, are examples of defenses. *Illnesses* may be defined as compromise equilibria following trauma. They include both the trauma, aspects of which are still relived, and the defenses against it. Symptoms are individual indicators of such compromise equilibria. It is suggested that illness seriousness is determined by the difference between pre- and post-stress equilibria, and that illness nature depends on the components of trauma, including survival strategies. Benefits occur when responses are adaptive and poststress equilibria are more life enhancing than prestress ones.

Throughout the whole process, *endowments* resist, while *vulnerabilities* facilitate, the noxious effects of stresses. For example, family may be a social strength, whereas isolation may be a social vulnerability.

Secondary traumatic stress (STS) responses occur when a person is secondarily influenced by the stress responses of another person. Components of stress leading to illness similar to those in Figure 1 become important in the secondarily affected person.

Let us now look at descriptions of SSs in more detail.

CHARACTERISTICS OF SURVIVAL STRATEGIES

The following features are suggested to characterize SSs.

1. *Evolutionary adaptedness.* The SSs are hereditary models present in humans and animals that have evolved to enhance the survival and perpetuation of evolutionary social units in the face of stressful situations.
2. *Level of operation.* Anatomically, SSs are intimately involved with MacLean's (1973) "old mammalian" brain—that is, the midbrain, limbic system, and primitive cortex—areas whose

role is to elaborate "emotional feelings that guide behavior with respect to the two basic life principles of self-preservation and preservation of the species." This area has rich, two-way connections with areas concerned with more primitive reflexes and instincts and with higher cortical levels.

3. *Biopsychosocial* (BPS).   Each SS has integrated biological, psychological, and social aspects that act as functional units.

4. *Finite number with a multitude of combinations.* There is a small number of discrete SSs. However, they may occur in a wide range of combinations and proportions. For instance, a soldier whose buddy is killed may grieve, kill to exact revenge, or seek death in order to be reattached to his friend.

5. *Adaptiveness and maladaptiveness.* Survival strategies may be adaptive or maladaptive, and this may change according to circumstances. For instance, to choose continuation of combat in the face of massive enemy reinforcements may become maladaptive. Similarly, the previously mentioned soldier's combat skills may be affected adversely by his need to kill or be killed. When SSs are not adaptive, their subsequent continued intense replay and/or suppression may become components of trauma and lead to symptoms, disorders, and illnesses.

6. *Interpersonal effects.* Survival strategies may evoke identificatory or complementary SSs in others. For instance, another soldier's helplessness may evoke a complementary SS of rescue. In contrast, his surrender (to enemies, death) may elicit a similar SS in other soldiers through identification.

7. *Modulation of SSs.* In addition to physiological feedback, internal and external judgments of the appropriateness of SSs (reappraisals) modulate their actions. For instance, using the above example, the surviving buddy may reappraise his impulse to homicide or suicide through fear or internal admonitions, or other soldiers may put strong restrictions on his impulses. Often the reappraisals are in the form of severe moral judgments, such as, "You are going to get us all killed!" Without such monitorings, survival of self and others may be compromised.

8. *Higher-level symbolizations.* Survival strategies contribute to higher-level symbolizations, which include meaning, human values, and existential purpose. Thus the surviving buddy (and, later, his clinician) may have to struggle with the meaning of the buddy's death, the use of revenge, the point of human sacrifice, the morality of surviving, and the overall purpose of war and life and death. Not only sensory reminders of the original

event, but cues relating to these dilemmas as well, may evoke SS responses from the original situation.

Evidence for the SSs that follow are derived from literature in the fields of anatomy, physiology, ethology, human development, psychology, sociology, and traumatic stress. Although of necessity biological, psychological, and social aspects of SSs are described sequentially, one must not lose sight of their integral functioning. In this chapter, the processes leading to appraisals are not detailed, nor are the many feedback systems and illnesses, important as they are.

The eight SSs are presented in Table 1. They may be considered as four complementary pairs of survival possibilities. The first line in each psychological and social cell deals with feelings and responses relating to one's own and others' physical selves. The second line deals with feelings and responses relating to distribution of resources. The third line (in italics) is a combination of the other two. In fight and flight, physical selves and resources merge.

Rescuers, helpers, and professionals may consider the responses listed in the table and the accompanying text as applying both to their patients or clients and to themselves. Thus both groups enjoy the satisfactions and fulfilments (even if initially at the cost of some pain) inherent in successful SSs. However, strained and maladaptive responses also apply to both victims and helpers, and ultimately so do trauma responses. Maladaptive responses in helpers may be seen as STS responses; the trauma responses noted in Table 1 provide a variety of primary and secondary traumatic stress disorder (STSD) symptoms. Helpers need to be wary when they experience STS responses, and they may well need actual help when they exhibit STSD manifestations.

What follows is a brief summary of SSs. A fuller review of their functions and ramifications will be set out in another work (Valent, in press). This will include ramifications of survival and fulfilment ranging from judgments and morals to human meanings, religion, ideology, and purpose.

Let us now look at each SS in turn.

THE SURVIVAL STRATEGIES

Rescuing–Care–Altruism

This SS is commonly evoked in disaster workers, and in medical and mental health professionals as they care for their charges. However, it is also evoked more widely, whenever it is clear that one needs to rescue, protect, or provide in order to enable others to survive. The paradigm

TABLE 1
Survival Strategy Components

Appraisal of Means of Survival	Survival Strategies	Successful/Adaptive Responses			Unsuccessful/Maladaptive Responses			Trauma Responses
		Biological	Psychological	Social	Biological	Psychological	Social	
Must save others	**Rescuing** Protect Provide	↑Estrogen ↑Oxytocin ↑Opioids	Care Empathy *Devotion*	Responsibility Nurture *Altruism*	Sympathetic & Parasymp Arousal	Resentment Depletion *Self-Concern*	Burden Neglect *Rejection*	Anguished Survivor guilt Caused death
Must be saved by others	**Attaching** Protected Provided	?↑Opioids	Yearning Need *Contentment*	Reaching out Crying out *Union*	↓Opioids	Abandonment Deprivation *Aloneness*	Clinging Demanding *Separation*	Dread Cast out Left to die
Must achieve goal	**Asserting** Combat Work	↑E, NE ↓Cortisol ↑Immunocomp	Strength High morale *Potency*	Will Success *Control*	↑↑E, NE Depletion E, NE ↑BP, ?CHD	Frustration Low morale *Powerlessness*	Willfulness Failure *Lost control*	"Burn-out" "Learned helplessness"
Must surrender goal	**Adapting** Accept Grieve	Parasymp Arousal ↑Cortisol	Acceptance Mourning *Hope*	Yielding Loss *Turn to new*	↑Cortisol ↓Immunocomp ↑Infection,↑CA	Helplessness Depression *Despair*	Overwhelmed Withdrawal *Given in*	Vulnerability Given up Succumbing
Must remove danger	**Fighting** Defend Rid	Symp Arousal ⊙↑NE, E ↑BP	Threat Revenge *Frighten*	Deterrence Wounding *Riddance*	↑↑Symp Arousal ↓Cortisol	Hatred Persecution *Killing*	Attack Eradication *Destruction*	Horror Evil Murder
Must remove oneself from danger	**Fleeing** Retreat Save oneself	Sympathetic & Parasymp Arousal	Fear Terror *Deliverance*	Hiding Flight *Escape*	NE Depletion ↑E & Cortisol	Phobia Paranoia *Engulfment*	Aviodance Panic *Annihilation*	"Inescapable shock," being hunted, killed
Must obtain scarce essentials	**Competing** Struggle Acquire	↑Testosterone Symp arousal	Winning Possession *Power*	Dominance Privilege *Take*	↓Testosterone Female horms ↑Cortisol	Defeat Greed, envy *Crushed*	Submission Plundered *Emptied*	Terrorization Marginalization Elimination
Must create more essentials	**Cooperating** Trust Mutual gain	↑Opiates ↓BP, E, NE	Mutuality Generosity *Creativity*	Reciprocity Sharing *Synthesis*	↓Opiates ?↑Parasymp Arousal	Ident w aggr Exploited *Stagnation*	Appeasement Robbed *Disintegration*	Alienation Fragmentation Decay

for such a one-way investment is maternal or parental care, an evolutionary survival milestone (Wilson, 1982) and one that differentiates later species from reptiles (MacLean, 1985). The SS subsumes nursing, nesting, protecting, retrieving and staying close (Rosenblatt, 1989), and maternal aggression (Troisi, D'Amato, & Carnera, 1988). The provision of parental care is characteristic of all mammals, and of humans from all cultures. A biogram for this SS already seems to be present in young children who play at parenting, and who in dire circumstances may assume parental roles. Its evolutionary survival value lies in the preservation of the next generation and, thereby, the species. It also preserves the currently weak, who nevertheless may be useful in the future.

Hormonal studies on male parental behavior are not available (Capitano, Weissberg, & Reite, 1985), but dominant primate males do show almost maternal solicitude to infants, and they protect the young in their troops (Wilson, 1982).

Parental behavior may be exercised with regard to nonprogeny (such as through adoption) in higher vertebrates (Goodall, 1988; Wilson, 1985). In primitive societies, uncles often care for their sisters' children. Parental-type care may be offered even more widely (MacLean, 1985; Zahn-Waxler, Cummings, & Ianotti, 1986), even to needy adult strangers. This is commonly noted in disasters.

The SS is served by specific parts of the limbic system, with connections to the higher centers (MacLean, 1985). These areas are activated by female sex hormones such as estrogen and progesterone (Rosenblatt, 1989).

The adaptive mode of the SS is associated with feelings of care, empathy, devotion, and responsibility. When the responsibility is too great, and carers cannot cope, there is a sense of resentment toward the needy, a sense of depletion of one's own strained resources, and consequently neglect, and even rejection, of the unwanted burdens. Altruism turns to self-concern.

The failed SS in the traumatic state includes anguish and guilt for not saving life, or perhaps even contributing to death. This anguish is relived and avoided in traumatic stress symptoms.

Attaching

This SS is evoked when it is perceived that others are needed to effect one's survival by providing protection and satisfaction of needs. The paradigmatic situation is an infant attached to its mother. MacLean

(1985) considers the evolution of attachment concomitant with maternal care, with which it is reciprocal, and which it evokes.

Attachment promotes psychobiological synchrony (the mother's capacity to modulate the infant's physiological and psychological responses). Thus attachment preserves vulnerable progeny and gives a solid base for future life. Failure in this area may compromise short- and long-term integrated physiological and psychosocial function (Coe, Lubach, & Ershler, 1989; Reiter & Capitano, 1985).

The biological concomitants of secure, contented attachment are not known. However, the emotions of separation and abandonment may be processed by parts of the hypothalamus and the cingulate gyrus (Panksepp et al., 1985), and may be associated with low levels of internal opiates. The administration of opiates reliably suppresses the crying out (distress vocalizations) of separation in all tested species (Panksepp, Meeker, & Bean, 1980).

In adaptive attaching, crying and reaching out lead to appeasement of yearning and satisfaction of needs. Union with an attachment figure gives a sense of security and contentment. Maladaptive attachment is experienced as abandonment, deprivation, and utter aloneness. Yearning, clinging, and demanding may become desperate, with a high level of separation anxiety. In the traumatic state, separation is associated with a dread of having been cast out to die. Van der Kolk (1987) suggests that the loss of the secure base that attachment provides leads to some of the well-known manifestations of the trauma response.

Attachment also may be directed toward fathers and other members of the group, and may be active in all adults who feel vulnerable. Society provides attachment figures in government and in religion. Attachment ideation, in which an important figure is imagined to be present, may help survival in dire circumstances.

Rescuers and helpers do not use this SS as a matter of choice. However, when their own superiors do not support them, or when through their own needs they attach themselves to their clients, maladaptive attachment responses may become evident. For instance, carers may feel anxious without their clients and may cling to them to an extent beyond that beneficial to the clients.

Assertiveness (Goal Achievement)

This SS is evoked by the appraisal that one must achieve certain goals to survive. The paradigm for this SS is hunting, though forces of nature may symbolize wild animals. We may forget that hunting has been a major feature of the human species for the first 99% of its evolutionary existence (Washburn & Lancaster, 1977). Laughlin (1977) notes that hunting has been the master behavior pattern of the human species, directing the evolution of the human body, technology, and society. Hunting's derivatives in the modern world are work and combat. They serve the need to obtain food and shelter (essential goals), and to control the environment in order to do so. The force used in this SS is often confused with violence in fight. However, "aggression" in this SS is called "instrumental" (Olivier et al., 1987), that is, "without affect," as when a cat kills a mouse quietly and efficiently.

The SS is served by specific parts of the midbrain and limbic system (Shaikh et al., 1985), and it is associated with arousal of the sympathetic nervous system, with secretion of epinephrine (E) and norepinephrine (NE) (Dienstbier, 1989; Ursin, Baade, & Levine, 1978). Immunocompetence, the capacity of the immune system (the cells and antibodies that deal with bacteria, viruses, and cancer cells), is enhanced, whereas cortisol secretion is suppressed (Dienstbier, 1989; Henry, 1986b). These physiological responses are the opposite of those described by Selye (1946) for the GAS, and those found in the next SS. The depletion of E and NE is cushioned by a sense of control and confidence in success (Dienstbier, 1989), whereas NE depletion (a hallmark of traumatic stress in flight as well) occurs in animals that have learned that they cannot control pain (Weiss, Stone, & Harrell, 1970).

Goal achievement is associated with feelings of strength and of one's will prevailing, high morale, potency, and control. Failure is associated with frustration, demoralization, powerlessness, a sense of loss of control, and exhaustion resulting from continued effort. Extremes of these responses have been described in the traumatic state of "combat exhaustion" (Bartemeier et al., 1946), and may be part of the syndrome of "burnout." The responses also resemble those in "learned helplessness" (Abramson, Garber, & Seligman, 1980), where there is repeated failure to achieve goals. Van der Kolk and Greenberg (1987) have speculated that this also may be part of the trauma response.

Combat exhaustion and compassion fatigue may overlap to some extent in the different contexts of the army and the helping professions. Certainly, burnout occurs in both, and is characterized by the fatigue, frustration, and powerlessness associated with the inability to achieve goals. Learned helplessness may be the long-term outcome of trauma involving this SS. Degrees of burnout are common in rescue teams (Berah, Jones, & Valent, 1984) and in helping teams such as those dealing with very ill patients in hospitals.

Sustained maladaptive assertiveness may contribute to the Type A personality, and to hypertension and coronary heart disease (CHD) (Appels & Mulder, 1989; Henry, 1986b; Van Doornen & van Blokland, 1989).

Adapting (Goal Surrender—Rolling with the Punches)

This SS is evoked with the appraisal that old goals must be surrendered to new ones. The paradigmatic situation is having to accept a major loss, and to grieve it. The grieving process may be a relatively new evolutionary adaptation; its precursors are present only in several species, such as birds (Lorenz, 1968) and primates (Goodall, 1988), and weeping is characteristic only of humans. Nevertheless, mourning rituals are found in all cultures. We may speculate that this SS provides a buffer zone for recuperation and readjustment to new circumstances.

The anatomical substrate for this SS probably includes the hippocampus and septum, and it is mediated by the parasympathetic, rather than the sympathetic, nervous system (Henry, 1986b).

As Selye (1946) noted, there is increased activity of the pituitary–adrenocortical axis, with increased cortisol secretion. In humans, this response is already present in infants, for example, just prior to delivery and after circumcision (Joffe, Vaughn, & Barglow, 1985). In bereaved adults many studies show increased corticosteroid activity (Irwin et al., 1987; Wolff, Hofer, & Mason, 1964), and diminished immunocompetence (Bartrop, Luckhurst, & Lazarus, 1977; Calabrese, Kling, & Gold, 1987). Both arise in proportion to the lack of denial and presence of distress and depression in the bereaved subjects (Irwin et al., 1987). Diminished immunocompetence may lead in turn to diminished resistance to inflammation and tumors in monkeys (Coe et al., 1989) and humans (Calabrese et al., 1987).

The psychosocial readjustment in adaptation is yielding, accepting and mourning loss, and then turning in hope to a new future. In the maladaptive situation, people feel overwhelmed and helpless, withdraw into depression and give in to despair. In the traumatic state, they have given up, their vulnerability is fully exposed, and they succumb. Succumbing to overwhelming stress has been a common view of trauma.

Helpers may themselves be overwhelmed and despair of being able to help. This is frequently seen when devastation is great, traumatic bereavements have occurred, or patients have been diagnosed with an incurable disease or are dying. Helpers need to accept death and destruction, and their own limits and vulnerabilities. Inability to accept loss often leads to inappropriate exhortations to "cope," to "not cry." At worst it can lead to denigration of victims and callousness in helpers. Helpers will ultimately also need to grieve the loss of their charges as they become self-sufficient.

Fighting–Defending

This SS is evoked by the appraisal that one is being attacked, and so must defend oneself and be freed of the threat at any cost. The paradigmatic situation is that of being attacked by a predator—animal or human—and the evolutionary function of the SS is to deter or eliminate such attacks.

Deterrent threat postures described by Darwin (1890/1965) are similar in all vertebrates (Blanchard & Blanchard, 1988) and all cultures. They are naturally present in children, including the deaf and the blind (Henry, 1986b). The amygdala and the hypothalamus seem to be associated with fight (Blanchard & Blanchard, 1988). As Cannon (1939) pointed out, there is arousal of the sympathetic nervous system. NE secretions are increased, especially that of NE, when the response is especially directed and aggressive. Clinically, the heart rate and blood pressure are elevated (Henry, 1986b). Cortisol secretion may increase, but only in the short term (Leshner, 1983). Although often reported as raised in male aggression, testosterone is raised mainly in competitive aggression (Blanchard & Blanchard, 1988). In fact, castrated animals can fight well against external danger, although they compete poorly against their own kind (discussed later). The physiological responses of this SS are sometimes seen as the markers of PTSD (Friedman, 1991).

If threatening postures and vocalizations are not sufficient deterrents, inflicting damage on the enemy in proportion to one's own actual or potential (as yet small) wound is used to signal to the enemy that it is "a tooth for a tooth, an eye for an eye, a life for a life." This talionic principle is accompanied by a feeling of seeking revenge and may deter attack or a further attack. If these defensive maneuvers of adaptive fighting fail to frighten off the enemy, defense becomes attack and is associated with "affective aggression" (Kling, 1986)—that is, hatred and a desire to kill. Maladaptive fighting includes persecution, eradication, destruction, and killing on a large scale. The traumatic reaches of this SS involve violence, murder, and atrocities, with later horror at the evil of the killing.

The traumatic reliving of this SS among Vietnam veterans has recently drawn much attention. It is uncommon in helpers, although it is advisable to be aware of hatred and the desire to be rid of patients and clients who have come to be perceived as threats.

Fleeing

This SS is evoked by the appraisal that it is essential to escape from danger—paradigmatically, predators, but also natural disasters. When distancing is impossible, the animal may hide or make itself small (Henry, 1986b) and "freezes,"—emitting low-aggression-releasing cues to others. Animals and humans in such situations may also "cut off"— avert their heads from the source of attack, and close their eyes and ears (Dixon & Kaesermann, 1987), as well as their minds. Flight is a ubiquitous SS in animals and humans of all ages and all cultures. It is common during disasters and wars.

Flight is served by parts of the hypothalamus, amygdala, and midbrain (Henry, 1986b). It is also associated with activity of the sympathetic nervous system, though E, NE, and cortisol ratios vary from those with other arousal SSs, and the parasympathetic nervous system may be active as well. This demonstrates that it is not only the physiological markers that may distinguish different SSs, but also their different combinations and ratios.

Adaptive flight is associated with feelings of fear and terror, which turn to relief and a sense of deliverance with escape. When escape is blocked, panic may set in, with a sense of persecution and incipient engulfment and annihilation. Alcohol and benzodiazepines (e.g., Valium) may diminish engulfment anxieties (Dixon & Kaesermann, 1987).

In the traumatic state, the organism senses that it is being hunted and is about to be caught and killed. Van der Kolk and Greenberg (1987) suggest that the inability to escape aversive events ("inescapable shock") may be relevant to the trauma response. It is associated with NE depletion in the chronic state (see also "Assertiveness"). Panksepp (1986a) draws attention to the fact that flight symptoms are common components of startle responses, nightmares, and phobias (as also noted in PTSD). Phobias and paranoia may be symptoms of reliving prior terrors of being "hunted" and engulfed.

Helpers may themselves feel the need to escape the stressors that affect their charges. They may also become fearful of their clients and their own responsibilities for them. In either case, helpers may find rationalizations for escaping their involvements. Premature withdrawal of services is common, the usual excuse being lack of funds.

Competing

This SS is evoked when one appraises that one must obtain scarce resources before others do. The paradigm is a contest for food. In early evolutionary theory, the fittest were seen to win such struggles more frequently, leading to their "natural selection" and differential survival (Scott, 1989).

It is now clear that it is more adaptive, safe, and economical for animal communities to establish hierarchies, which then determine the distribution of scarce resources, than for all to struggle against all others each time. Status in hierarchies is determined by prior (nonlethal) ritualized contests (Wilson, 1982). Hierarchical competition (pecking order) is ubiquitous among social animals and in primitive cultures (Lienhardt, 1966). It is present in toddlers by the age of two (Cummings, Hollenbeck, & Iannotti, 1986).

Competition for status among males, or "social aggression," has been studied the most physiologically. High status is reflected very sensitively in high levels of sex hormone levels, especially of testosterone, and this is constant across species (Knol & Egberink-Alink, 1989; Mazur, 1983). In humans, even winning or losing a tennis match is reflected in testosterone levels (Booth, Shelley, & Mazur, 1990). Defeat is associated with low levels of testosterone, as well as of female sex hormones, and increased levels of the "adaptation" hormone cortisol (Henry, 1986b; Leshner, 1983).

Interfemale competition may be facilitated by testosterone, as well as by female sex hormones (Henry, 1986b). The medial hypothalamic sites that selectively take up testosterone seem to be involved in competition.

In a situation of scarce resources, winning a dominant position is adaptive because it confers privileged access to and possession of food, sex, shelter, and comfort. Power also gives the privilege of taking the largest share and then distributing the rest down the hierarchy.

When competing is maladaptive, defeat and submission may become self-perpetuating, with new challenges being met with increased levels of corticosterones and compromised immunocompetence (Fleshner, Laudenslager, & Simons, 1989). The confident efforts in high-status individuals, in contrast, are facilitated by high testosterone, E, and NE levels (Henry, 1986b).

When hierarchies break down, a struggle for resources ensues. Ordered distribution fails, greed and envy take over, and the strong plunder the weak. The defeated may be crushed and emptied, and in traumatic situations the weak may be terrorized, marginalized, and finally eliminated. This is where the classical evolutionary notion of all struggling against all, and survival of the fittest is most appropriate.

Those who continue power struggles without winning may be vulnerable to hypertension and infections (Jemmott, 1987), while defeated and dejected Type A personalities (those constantly struggling against deadlines and other people) may be predisposed to CHD (Appels & Mulder, 1989).

Helpers may become agents and advocates in the competitive struggles of victims, and may use their status and influence to effect better distribution of resources. However, helpers may also compete among themselves for status and leadership within their own groups, or access to clients, funds, and research greater than those of other helping groups. At worst, victims themselves become a resource to compete for and use, rather than help.

Cooperation–Affiliation

This SS is evoked when it appears necessary to become a trusting partner with others to create mutual essentials. The biological paradigm is procreation. Cooperation has been present in evolution since protozoa (Scott, 1989), and its function is to preserve and increase the community's gene pool.

When reciprocity is not immediate, the initial giving may be seen as altruistic. Trivers (1971) called this "reciprocal altruism," because in a community such giving is reciprocated over time. Reciprocal altruism is found in animals and humans. All cultures have customs of giving and taking, and mutual obligation. Even babies share—they take and hand back (Eibl-Eibesfeldt, 1980). Such activity establishes bonding or a "social glue" (Youniss, 1986).

Social bonding is associated with parasympathetic responses such as decreases in blood pressure, pulse, and E and NE secretion (Henry, 1986b). Sexual activity and social bonding involve the amygdala and temporal and orbital cortices (Steklis & Kling, 1985)—the precise areas highest in mu-like opiate receptors. We may speculate that opiates attach to these sites, enhancing a sense of social comfort, while their withdrawal intensifies a sense of social need. We may further speculate that external opiate drugs may be used to attempt to simulate the calm of social bonds.

In nature, adaptive cooperating—as seen, for instance, in postdisaster euphoria—is associated with the emotions of trust, mutuality, generosity, reciprocity, sharing, and love. Its outcome is creativity and synthesis. When the SS is maladaptive, there is initially identification with, and appeasement of, the noncooperating partner. This is akin to identification with the aggressor (i.e., paradoxical gratitude, pathological transference, the Stockholm Syndrome as noted by Ochberg [1988]). However, feelings of being betrayed, exploited, and robbed emerge. There is a sense of stagnation and disintegration in place of synthesis and creativity. In the traumatic state, there is a final sense of alienation, decay, and falling apart.

Cooperation, generosity, and cohesiveness are commonly noted in traumatic situations (Turner, 1967). Social support is recognized as ameliorating traumatic stress (Figley, 1986). Maladaptive cooperation, however, exacerbates traumatic stress. Jemmott (1987) found that affiliative personalities were relatively protected from high blood pressure and had better immunocompetence than did controls.

Helpers themselves may become imbued with a surge of generosity and giving, which is reciprocated with gratitude by those helped. Cooperation between victims and helpers may lead to creative solutions. If the expected generosity or gratitude is not forthcoming, there may be disappointment and a sense of being exploited or betrayed. The previously creative mutual helping process may stagnate or disintegrate.

Judgments as an Example of the Applications of SSs

We can see that different SSs evoke qualitatively different stress responses. However, as mentioned above, they are also associated with the foundations of higher-level ramifications, of which judgments are one example. Judgments may be conceptualized as one form of psychosocial feedback (reappraisal) on the functioning of SSs. One type of judgment, let us presume, is "right and wrong." Communication of right and wrong includes anger and guilt, both of which are commonly noted in association with traumatic stress. We may say that anger is a feedback judgment on the maladaptive nature of others' SSs, while guilt is a judgment on the maladaptive nature of one's own SSs. The two interact and may fluctuate. Anger and guilt may themselves be adaptive or maladaptive. Let us see how SSs may allow us to refine and understand the various angers and guilts associated with different SSs.

- *Rescuing.* Helpers may feel wrath toward victims who do not accept help, or who may even put helpers into hazardous situations by their actions, such as people who refuse to evacuate burning houses. Alternately, rescuers feel survivor guilt for not doing enough to save others.
- *Attaching.* Those who feel abandoned protest angrily or assume guilt for having displeased their attachment figures. ("Why?!" and "Why me?!" are expressions of anger relating to another judgment—justice—and express the injustice of being "punished" even if one has been good.)
- *Asserting.* The anger here stems from frustration when thwarted, and the guilt is that of failure.
- *Adapting.* Anger is at others' lack of support; guilt is for not missing the lost person.
- *Fighting.* Fury is felt toward a threatening object, but guilt for mur-

der facilitates adaptive fighting.

- *Fleeing*. The anger is felt toward hindrances to escape, while the guilt is for endangering the self and others by being stuck.
- *Competing*. There is outrage at the threat to one's status, which may be balanced by priority guilt for improper precedence over others. These responses facilitate the establishment of an adaptive hierarchy.
- *Cooperating*. There is anger with a straying partner and the guilt of betrayal.

A fuller exploration of judgments is presented elsewhere (Valent, in press).

DISCUSSION

It seems that SSs could help to provide a meaningful psychobiological framework for the variety of contradictory biological, psychological, and social responses in traumatic situations. Their biopsychosocial nature, their fluctuations according to circumstances, combinations of SSs in different permutations and proportions, together with the "culture" and phases of specific traumatic situations and the people in them, account for the richness of traumatic stress responses. Understanding SSs can help to understand the nature, reason, and manner of production of traumatic stress responses.

It is also suggested that SSs provide an important part of a framework for understanding the components and connections between stresses and illnesses. They help to establish a framework for appraisals and stress responses, whether adaptive or maladaptive, biological, psychological, or social. They set up a framework for the multitude of stress responses and help to give them sense and purpose in terms of the survival of one's self and others. They help to explain the beneficial effects of stress. Survival strategies are also trauma and illness components, and as such they help us to understand the nature of trauma and some of the reasons for particular illness symptoms. Thus SSs are useful to a theory that tries to meet the stress-leads-to-illness paradigm.

With regard to a theoretical view of traumatic stress, it is suggested that PTSD may be seen as the umbrella concept that indicates how traumatic stress responses are reexperienced and avoided. On the other hand, SSs describe what is reexperienced in disorders and why. Therefore, SSs supplement the wealth of the concept of PTSD. They also suggest that what have been variously designated as core aspects of trauma may be the traumatic states of different SSs.

Objections may be raised against delineations of certain SSs. On the whole, however, SSs correspond well to the survival behaviors described by Plutchik (1980) and Panksepp (1989a). Certainly, opinion is consistent about the existence of a relatively small number of discrete basic survival behaviors. Some differences are semantic, and the ultimate honing and naming of SSs may depend on further research in various disciplines.

What was said about the SSs is even more applicable to their components. There are a variety of physiological, and emotional and social, nuances that are difficult to capture in one or two words, and indeed need to be altered for slightly different situations. This area requires further exploration.

The specificity of SSs may be questioned. For instance, in the physiological area, some chemicals (E, NE, cortisol, opioids) are present in more than one SS. However, as Panksepp (1986b) tells us, it is likely that nature performs its usual economies by using the same chemicals for different purposes. As noted above, physiological profiles and proportions may matter at least as much as the actual chemicals. It is here that the study of appraisals and emotions is particularly useful, since subjective explanations of feeling and intention may crystallize meaning to a myriad of measurements.

Applications of the SS Framework

Clinical Application

The conceptualization of SSs is ". . . in a deep sense, simple and logical . . ." (Panksepp, 1986a) in promoting an understanding of traumatic stress responses. The responses make sense in terms of PTSD symptoms too, as SSs from the traumatic situation still being relived and avoided. Therapeutically it may provide great relief to victims to define the source and function of a variety of their responses that may initially seem irrational to them.

Further, the responses and symptoms themselves may give clues to the specific SSs evoked in the original traumatic stress situations, and help recover them and their contexts if they have been unprocessed or forgotten. Even judgments, moral conflicts, and struggles with existential meanings may give clues to the nature and context of SSs in the original context.

Last, the concurrent biological, psychological, and social natures of SSs draw attention to concurrent biological, psychological, and social dysfunctions. This enhances more comprehensive treatment.

As an example, the soldier whose friend was killed may present years later as a Vietnam veteran who evidences periods of depression, suicidal behavior, and outbursts of aggression for no apparent reason. He may also be deeply cynical about society and his own worth, and physically may suffer violent headaches and be hypertensive. Each of these end symptoms can be traced back to the original traumatic stress(es). Then each can be explained and treated in a meaningful way, not only as a symptom, but in the context of the original trauma.

Research

Survival strategies have opened a new window of opportunity to investigate the meaning of physiological, psychological, and social responses to stress. They make it possible to validate more clearly the intuitive understanding that separation distress, grief, arousal to fight, and so on have different physiological and psychosocial associations. On the one hand, one can study more clearly the associations of a "pure" SS. On the other hand, one can clarify the significance of responses by knowing which SSs are being evoked at the time. This may be determined by knowing the subjective state of the person's appraisals and emotions (Panksepp, 1989a). This knowledge may be quite important even in simple experiments such as an examination, because the stress may evoke a number of SSs, such as assertiveness, competition, flight, and acceptance.

Toward a Framework for Emotions and Social Actions

It may be said that Table 1, which lists emotions and social responses according to SSs, provides a framework for those responses and denotes their significance and function. For instance, depression is associated with maladaptive (impacted, unresolved) grief. We may speculate that the illness depression may contain this emotion, as well as other maladaptive and traumatic features relating to adaptation (mitigated by defenses). Depression (and defenses) may obscure the initial traumatic situation.

Note that anxiety does not appear in Table 1. It is a less specific emotion, applicable to each SS, but with different overtones in each, akin to anger and guilt as described earlier. Thus I suggest intuitively that the anxiety of, say, being caught and killed (flight) is different from the anxiety of killing someone. If this were not so, global anxiety would prevent the choice of any specific SSs. Also the traumas associated with each SS are associated with the ultimate dreads of humankind, and each feels somewhat different.

Further, while anxieties that arise during SSs are functioning as negative feedback signals and may be called ego anxieties, the anxieties that arise in response to negative judgments may be called superego anxieties. The anxieties of using the wrong SS may be called id anxieties. Each of these anxieties is a little different. In researching anxiety, it is important to know which anxiety is being considered.

Secondary Traumatic Stress Responses

People's SSs influence not only those with whom they share a current traumatic situation, but also those who try to ameliorate its later effects. This group includes family, emergency workers, and helping professionals. The interactive nature of emotions and actions in SSs may help to explain the ubiquitousness of STS responses. The mechanisms of STS may be described in the following.

Identifying with and Experiencing Victims' SSs
Empathizing with and being devoted to victims opens the helper to feeling all the maladaptive SSs and traumatic responses of victims. Hence the initially adaptive identification and understanding of victims may lapse into the helper's becoming a fellow victim.

Responding to Victims' SSs with Own SSs
The emotions and actions of victims may evoke a complementary (or another) SS in helpers. For instance, conveying a sense of a helpless dread of death or of anger at being abandoned (attachment cues) may evoke care and responsibility, or potential guilt for causing harm, in a helper, and elicit a rescuing SS. Ideally the appropriate adaptive SSs are elicited—that is, those that help rectify victims' maladaptive ones.

However, the SSs evoked in helpers may be maladaptive too. This may happen if the helpers themselves are overburdened or are inadequate to the task. Another difficulty may lie in helpers' misinterpreting victims' responses as belonging to the present, instead of understanding that the victims are reenacting their traumatic situations (transference). In either case, helpers may respond with inappropriate SSs. For instance, they may retreat (flight) in the face of victim anger, or they may care too much because of their own guilt.

Survival strategies enable helpers to define their own responses and understand them in the context of their involvements with victims. This could be considered as using countertransference.

Secondary Traumatic Stress Disorder

From this perspective, when helpers cannot execute their own SSs adaptively, their unsuccessful maladaptive SSs (that is, their traumatic stress reactions) may deteriorate into STSD. For helpers, rescuing and asserting are commonly used SSs. So when not coping, helpers may come to feel, respectively, burdened, resentful, rejecting, and guilty; and frustrated, demoralized, not in control, exhausted, and "burned out."

Associated with STSD, they may feel judgments of guilt such as survivor guilt and guilt for failure and incompetence. They may also suffer the different angers and anxieties of these SSs.

STSD, like STS responses, can also develop through intense identification with victims' maladaptive and traumatic responses, and intense inappropriate eliciting of a variety of inappropriate helper SSs.

Helpers need to identify the variety of STS responses and STSD symptoms they experience, and integrate them into debriefing meetings or into counseling and therapy. And those involved with helpers may themselves be affected in the same way as the helpers and become tertiary victims.

Wider Applications

Because trauma is situated between life and death, health and illness, normality and abnormality, it occupies a crucial place for humans. It may not be death, as much as it is trauma, that provides the feared counterpoint to life. As such, it ramifies all aspects of life. We already noted trauma's presence in the biological, psychological, and social fabric; in various moral judgments; and in different social groupings. We noted that trauma is symbolized in morality, justice, values, meaning, and purpose. To examine these aspects in any depth requires much future exploration. However, such research is necessary to fully understand the extraordinary scope of trauma in human existence.

REFERENCES

Abramson, L.Y., Garber, J., & Seligman, M. (1980). *Learned helplessness in humans.* New York: Academic Press.

Ader, R. (Ed.) (1981). *Psychoneuroimmunology.* New York: Academic Press.

Alexander, F. (1950). *Psychosomatic medicine.* New York: Norton.

American Psychiatric Association. (1987). *Diagnostic and statistical manual of mental disorders* (3rd ed., rev.). Washington, D.C.: Author.

American Psychiatric Association. (1994). *Diagnostic and statistical manual of mental disorders* (4th ed.). Washington, D.C.: Author.

Andrews, G., & Tennant, C. (1978). Being upset and becoming ill: An appraisal of the relation between life events and physical illness. *Medical Journal of Australia, 1,* 324–327.

Appels, A., & Mulder, P. (1989). Fatigue and heart disease: The association between "vital exhaustion" and past, present and future coronary heart disease. *Journal of Psychosomatic Research, 33,* 727–738.

Bartemeier, L.H., Kubie, L. S., & Menninger K. (1946). Combat exhaustion. *Journal of Nervous and Mental Disease, 146,* 358–389.

Bartrop, R.W., Luckhurst, E., & Lazarus, L. (1977). Depressed lymphocyte function after bereavement. *Lancet, 1,* 834–836.

Beebe, G.W. (1975). Follow-up studies of World War II and Korean prisoners. *American Journal of Epidemiology, 101,* 400–422.

Bennet, G. (1970). Bristol floods 1968: Controlled survey of effects on health of local community disaster. *British Medical Journal, 3,* 454–458.
Berah, E. F., Jones, H. J., & Valent, P. (1984). The experiences of a mental health team involved in the early phase of a disaster. *Australian and New Zealand Journal of Psychiatry, 18,* 354–358.
Blanchard, D. C., & Blanchard, R. J. (1988). Ethoexperimental approaches to the biology of emotion. *Annual Review of Psychology, 39,* 43–68.
Booth, A., Shelley, G., & Mazur, A. (1990). Testosterone, and winning and losing in human competition. *Journal of Cell Biology, 110,* 43–52.
Breuer, J., & Freud, S. (1975). On the psychical mechanism of hysterical phenomena: Preliminary communication. *The standard edition of the complete psychological works of Sigmund Freud* (Vol. 2, pp. 3–251). London: Hogarth Press. (Original work published 1893.)
Bowlby, J. (1971). *Attachment.* Harmondsworth, England: Penguin.
Brill, N. Q. (1966). Hospitalization and disposition. In R. Anderson (Ed.), *Neuropsychiatry in World War II.* Washington, D.C.: Office of the Surgeon General, Department of the Army.
Calabrese, J. R., Kling, M. A., & Gold, P. W. (1987). Alterations in immunocompetence during stress, bereavement, and depression: Focus on neuroendocrine regulation. *American Journal of Psychiatry, 144,* 1123–1134.
Cannon, W. B. (1939). *The wisdom of the body.* New York: Norton.
Capitano, J. P., Weissberg, M., & Reite, M. (1985). Biology of maternal behavior: Recent findings and implications. In M. Reite & T. Field (Eds.), *The psychobiology of attachment and separation.* New York: Academic Press.
Clevenger, S. V. (1889). *Spinal concussion.* London: Davies.
Coe, C. L., Lubach, G., & Ershler, W. B. (1989). Immunological consequences of maternal separation in infant primates. *New Directions in Child Development, 45,* 65–91.
Cummings, E. M., Hollenbeck, B., and Iannotti, R. (1986). Early organization of altruism and aggression: Developmental patterns and individual differences. In C. Zahn-Waxler, E. M. Cummings, & R. Iannotti (Eds.), *Altruism and aggression (biological and social origins).* Cambridge, England: Cambridge University Press.
Darwin, C. (1965) *The expressions of emotions in man and animals.* Chicago: University of Chicago Press. (Original work published 1890.)
Dienstbier, R. A. (1989). Arousal and physiological toughness: Implications for mental and physical health. *Psychological Review, 96,* 84–100.
Dixon, A. K., & Kaesermann, H. P. (1987). Ethopharmacology of flight behavior. In B. Olivier, J. Mos, & P. F. Brain (Eds.), *Ethopharmacology of agonistic behavior in animals and humans.* Dordrecht, Netherlands: Nijhoff.
Dubos, R. (1968). *Man, medicine and environment* (p. 67). London: Pall Mall Press.
Eibl-Eibesfeldt, I. (1980). Strategies of social interaction. In R. Plutchik & H. Kellerman (Eds.), *Emotion: Theory, research, and experience.* New York: Academic Press.
Eitinger, L. (1973). A follow-up study of the Norwegian concentration camp survivors' mortality and morbidity. *Israeli Journal of Psychiatry and Related Sciences, 11,* 199–209.
Engel, G. L. (1977). The need for a new medical model: A challenge for biomedicine. *Science, 196,* 129–135.
Figley, C. R. (1986). Traumatic stress: The role of the family and social support system. In C. R. Figley (Ed.), *Trauma and its wake: Vol. 2 Traumatic stress theory, research, and intervention.* New York: Brunner/Mazel.
Figley, C. R. (1989). *Treating stress in families.* New York: Brunner/Mazel.
Fleshner, M., Laudenslager, M. L., Simons L., & Maiers, S. F. (1988). Reduced serum antibodies associated with social defeat in rats. *Physiology and Behavior, 45,* 1183–1187.
Freud, S. (1975). Beyond the pleasure principle. In J. Strachey (Ed. and Trans.), *The standard edition of the complete psychological works of Sigmund Freud* (Vol. 18, pp. 1–64). London: Hogarth Press. (Original work published 1920.)
Friedman, M. J. (1991). Biological approaches to the diagnosis and treatment of post-traumatic stress disorder. *Journal of Traumatic Stress, 4,* 67–91.
Gellhorn, E. (1970). The emotions and the ergotropic and trophotropic systems. *Psychologische Forschungen, 34,* 48–94.

48   Compassion Fatigue

Goodall, J. (1988). *In the shadow of man*. London: Weidenfeld & Nicholson.
Halliday, T. R. (1981). Sexual behavior and group cohesion. In H. Kellerman (Ed.), *Group cohesion: Theoretical and clinical perspectives*. New York: Grune & Stratton.
Harlow, H. F., & Harlow, M. K. (1965). The affectional systems. In A. M. Schreier, H. F. Harlow, & M. Stollnitz (Eds.), *Behaviour of nonhuman primates* (Vol. 2). New York: Academic Press.
Henry, J. P. (1986a). Mechanisms by which stress can lead to coronary heart disease. *Postgraduate Medical Journal, 62,* 687–693.
Henry, J. P. (1986b). Neuroendocrine patterns of emotional response. In R. Plutchik & H. Kellerman (Eds.), *Emotion: Theory, research and experience* (Vol. 3). New York: Academic Press.
Holmes, T. H., & Rahe, R. (1967). The social readjustment scale. *Journal of Psychosomatic Research, 11,* 213–218.
Horowitz, M. J. (1976). *Stress response syndromes*. New York: Jason Aronson.
Irwin, M., Daniels, M., & Weiner, H. (1987). Immune and neuroendocrine changes during bereavement. *Psychiatric Clinics of North America, 10,* 449–465.
Janet, P. (1920). *The major symptoms of hysteria*. New York: Macmillan.
Jemmott, J. B. (1987). Social motives and susceptibility to disease: Stalking individual differences in health risks. *Journal of Personality, 55,* 267–298.
Joffe, L. S., Vaughn, B. E., & Barglow, P. (1985). Biobehavioral antecedents in the development of infant–mother attachment. In M. Reite & T. Field (Eds.), *The psychobiology of attachment and separation*. New York: Academic Press.
Kardiner, A. (1941). *The traumatic neuroses of war*. New York: Paul B. Hoeber.
Kinston, W., & Rosser, R. (1974). Disaster: Effects on mental and physical state. *Journal of Psychosomatic Research, 18,* 437–456.
Kling, A. S. (1986). The anatomy of aggression and affiliation. In R. Plutchik & H. Kellerman (Eds.), *Emotion: Theory, research and experience* (Vol. 3). New York: Academic Press.
Knol, B. W., & Egberink-Alink, S. T. (1989). Androgens, progestagens and agonistic behavior: A review. *Veterinary Quarterly, 11,* 94–101.
Krystal, H. (Ed.) (1968). *Massive psychic trauma*. New York: International Universities Press.
Laughlin, W. S. (1977). Hunting: An integrating biobehavior system and its evolutionary importance. In R. B. Lee & I. DeVore (Eds.), *Man the hunter*. Chicago: Aldine.
Lazarus, R. S., & Folkman, S. (1984). *Stress, appraisal and coping*. New York: Springer.
Leshner, A. I. (1983). Pituitary-adrenocortical effects on inter-male agonistic behavior. In B. B. Svare (Ed.), *Hormones and aggressive behavior*. New York: Plenum Press.
Lienhardt, G. (1966). *Social anthropology*. Oxford: Oxford University Press.
Lifton, R. J. (1967). *Death in life: Survivors of Hiroshima*. New York: Simon & Schuster.
Lindy, J. D. (1988). *Vietnam: A casebook*. New York: Brunner/Mazel.
Lorenz, K. (1968). *On aggression* (p. 18). London: Methuen.
MacLean, P. D. (1973). *A triune concept of the brain and behavior* (p. 12). Toronto: Toronto University Press.
MacLean, P.D. (1985). Brain evolution relating to family, play, and the separation call. *Archives of General Psychiatry, 42,* 405–416.
Mason, J. (1968). The scope of psychoendocrine research. *Psychosomatic Medicine, 30,* 565–574.
Mazur, A. (1983). Hormones, aggression, and dominance in humans. In B. B. Svare (Ed.), *Hormones and aggressive behavior*. New York: Plenum Press.
Mileti, D., Drabek, T. E., & Haas, J. E. (1975). *Human systems in extreme environments*. Boulder: University of Colorado, Institute of Behavioral Science.
Monroe, S. M. (1982). Assessment of life events. *Archives of General Psychiatry, 39,* 606–610.
Moyer, K. E. (1986). Biological bases of aggressive behavior. In R. Plutchik & H. Kellerman (Eds.), *Emotion: Theory, research and experience* (Vol. 3). New York: Academic Press.
Murphy, J. M. (1975). Psychological responses to war stress. *Acta Psychiatrica Scandinavica [Suppl], 263,* 16–21.
Ochberg, F. M. (1988). Post-traumatic therapy and victms of violence. In F. M. Ochberg (Ed.), *Post-traumatic therapy and victims of violence* (pp. 3–20). New York: Brunner/Mazel.

Olivier, B., Mos, J., & Brain, P. F. (Eds.). (1987). *Ethopharmacology of agonistic behavior in animals and humans*. Dordrecht, Netherlands: Nijhoff.

Panksepp, J. (1986a). Brain emotion circuits and psychopathologies. In M. Clynes & J. Panksepp (Eds.), *Emotions and psychopathology*. New York: Plenum Press.

Panksepp, J. (1986b). The neurochemistry of behavior. *Annual Review of Psychology, 37*, 77–107.

Panksepp, J. (1989a). The neurobiology of emotions: Of animal brains and human feelings. In H. Wagner & A. Manstead (Eds.), *Handbook of social pychophysiology*. New York: Wiley.

Panksepp, J. (1989b). The psychobiology of emotions: The animal side of human feelings. *Experimental Brain Research, 18*, 31–55.

Panksepp, J., Meeker, R., & Bean, N. (1980). The neurochemical control of crying. *Pharmacology, Biochemistry, & Behavior, 12*, 437–443.

Panksepp, J., Siviy, S. M., & Normansell, L. A. (1985). Brain opioids and social emotions. In M. Reite & T. Field (Eds.), *The psychobiology of attachment and separation*. New York: Academic Press.

Paykel, E. S. (1979). Recent life events in the development of depressive disorders. In R. A. Depue (Ed.), *The psychobiology of the depressive disorders: Implications for the effects of stress*. New York: Academic Press.

Plutchik, R. (1980). A general psychoevolutionary theory of emotion. In R. Plutchik & H. Kellerman (Eds.), *Emotion: Theory, research, and experience* (Vol. 1). New York: Academic Press.

Quarantelli, E. L., & Dynes, R. R. (1977). Response to social crisis and disaster. *Annual Review of Sociology, 3*, 23–49.

Raphael, B. (1984). *The anatomy of bereavement* (pp. 55–67). London: Hutchinson.

Raphael, B. (1986). *When disaster strikes*. London: Hutchinson.

Reiter, M., & Capitano, J. P. (1985). On the nature of social separation and social attachment. In M. Reite & T. Field (Eds.), *The psychobiology of attachment and separation*. New York: Academic Press.

Rosenblatt, J. S. (1989). The physiological and evolutionary background of maternal responsiveness. *New Directions in Child Development, 26*, 15–30.

Schmale, A. H. (1972). Giving up as a final common pathway to changes in health. *Advances in Psychosomatic Medicine, 8*, 20–40.

Scott, J. P. (1989). *The evolution of social systems: Monographs in psychobiology* (Vol 3, pp. 53, 174). New York: Gordon & Breach.

Selye, H. (1946). The general adaptation syndrome and the diseases of adaptation. *Journal of Clinical Endocrinology, 6*, 117–196.

Shaikh, M. B., Brutus, M., & Siegel, H. E. (1985). Topographically organized midbrain modulation of predatory and defensive aggression in the cat. *Brain Research, 336*, 308–312.

Smith, G. C. (1991). The brain and higher mental function. *Australian and New Zealand Journal of Psychiatry, 25*, 215–230.

Steklis, H. D., & Kling, A. (1985). Neurobiology of affiliative behavior in nonhuman primates. In M. Reite & T. Field (Eds.), *The psychobiology of attachment and separation*. New York: Academic Press.

Titchener, J. L., & Kapp, F. T. (1976). Family and character change at Buffalo Creek. *American Journal of Psychiatry, 133*, 295–299.

Trichopolous, D., Katsouyanni, K., & Zavitsanos, X. (1983). Psychological stress and fatal heart attack: The Athens earthquake natural experiment. *Lancet, 1*, 441–443.

Trimble, M. R. (1985). Post-traumatic stress disorder: History of a concept. In C. R. Figley (Ed.), *Trauma and its wake*. New York: Brunner/Mazel.

Trivers, R. L. (1971). The evolution of reciprocal altruism. *Quarterly Review in Biology, 46*, 35–57.

Troisi, A., D'Amato, F. R., & Carnera, A. (1988). Maternal aggression by lactating group-living Japanese macaque females. *Hormones and Behavior, 22*, 444–452.

Turner, R. H. (1967). Types of solidarity in the reconstituting of groups. *Pacific Sociological Review, 10*, 60–68.

Ursin, H., Baade, E., & Levine, S. (Eds.). (1978). *Psychobiology of stress: A study of coping men.* New York: Academic Press.

Valent, P. (1984). The Ash Wednesday bushfires in Victoria. *Medical Journal of Australia, 141,* 291–300.

Valent, P. (in press). *From survival to fulfillment.* New York: Brunner/Mazel.

Van der Kolk, B. A. (1987). The separation cry and the trauma response: Developmental issues in the psychobiology of attachment and separation. In B. A. van der Kolk (Ed.), *Psychological trauma.* Washington, D.C.: American Psychiatric Press.

Van der Kolk, B. A., & Greenberg, M. S. (1987). The psychobiology of the trauma response: Hyperarousal, constriction, and addiction to traumatic reexposure. In B. A. van der Kolk (Ed.), *Psychological trauma.* Washington, D.C.: American Psychiatric Press.

Van Doornen, L. J., & van Blokland, R. W. (1989). The relation of Type A behavior and vital exhaustion with physiological reactions to real life stress. *Journal of Psychosomatic Research, 33,* 715–725.

Washburn, S. L., & Lancaster, C. S. (1977). The evolution of hunting. In R. B. Lee & I. DeVore (Eds.), *Man the hunter.* Chicago: Aldine.

Weiner, H. (1977). *Psychobiology and human disease.* New York: Elsevier North-Holland.

Weiner, H. (1985). The concept of stress in the light of studies on disasters, unemployment, and loss: A critical analysis. In M. R. Zales (Ed.), *Stress in health and disease.* New York: Brunner/Mazel.

Weiner, H. (1989). The dynamics of the organism: Implications of recent biological thought for psychosomatic theory and research. *Psychosomatic Medicine, 51,* 608–635.

Weiss, J. M., Stone, E. A., & Harrell, N. (1970). Coping behavior and brain norepinephrine levels in rats. *Journal of Comparative Physiology and Psychology, 72,* 153–160.

Wilson, E. O. (1982). *Sociobiology: A new synthesis.* (pp. 279, 349, 351, 415). Cambridge, Mass.: Harvard University Press.

Wolff, C. T., Hofer, M. A., & Mason, J. W. (1964). Relationship between psychological defenses and mean urinary 17 OHCS excretion rates: II. Methodological and theoretical consideration. *Psychosomatic Medicine, 26,* 592–609.

Youniss, J. (1986). Development in reciprocity through friendship. In C. Zahn-Waxler, E. M. Cummings, & R. Iannotti (Eds.), *Altruism and aggression (biological and social origins).* Cambridge, England: Cambridge University Press.

Zahn-Waxler, C., Cummings, E. M., & Iannotti, R. (Eds.), (1986). Introduction. In C. Zahn-Waxler, E. M. Cummings, & R. Iannotti (Eds.), *Altruism and aggression (biological and social origins).* Cambridge, England: Cambridge University Press.

3

Working with People in Crisis: Research Implications

RANDAL D. BEATON and SHIRLEY A. MURPHY

All crisis workers are at risk of experiencing secondary traumatic stress (STS). In this chapter, evidence is presented suggesting that crisis worker exposure to trauma is repetitive, potentially cumulative, and threatening to personal safety, health, and well-being. Professional crisis workers include firefighters, paramedics, emergency medical technicians, ambulance drivers, law enforcement personnel, rescue workers, and disaster response teams. (We have also included research findings for some volunteer groups, such as firefighters, who are exposed to trauma even though they are not professional crisis workers.) Crisis workers are front-line first responders for whom potential exposure to occupational trauma is a fact of daily life (Hartsough & Myers, 1985; Hurrell, Pate, & Kheisnnet, 1984; Mitchell & Bray, 1990; Robinson, 1986; Stratton, Parker, & Snabble, 1984).

Editor's Note: This chapter reviews the empirical literature that includes implications for professionals working with people in crisis. There are very few studies of therapists, but Beaton and Murphy are able to cite and synthesize what is known about other professionals who work with such people. Their axioms emerging from this review, along with the theoretical models that account for them, have major implications for therapists who work with people in crisis. As you read this chapter, consider how the observations can be applied to therapists.

Somewhat less vulnerable are hospital trauma and emergency room staff and 911 dispatchers. Persons in these jobs are physically removed from the trauma scene and victim, but are present emotionally and "absorb" stress (Burno, Kirilloff & Close, 1983; Keller & Koenig, 1989; Solomon, 1992).

Table 1 summarizes some key differences in trauma exposure between the two groups. These distinctions are important since there is some evidence that disaster-scene workers and paramedics are more likely to report post-traumatic and other stress symptoms than are at-hospital workers (Hammer, Mathews, Lyons, & Johnson, 1986 McCammon, Durham, Allison, & Williamson, 1988).

The costs of not attending to the problems of STS in crisis workers include short-term and long-term emotional and physical disorders, strains on interpersonal relationships, substance abuse, burnout, and shortened careers. Few crisis workers are adequately trained to respond to personal emotional turmoil in the aftermath of traumatic incidents (Mitchell, 1985a). Role conflict arises between self-imposed demands to function effectively as a professional and personal needs to take care of one's own mental and emotional reactions to trauma. The result of role conflict may be STS reactions. Finally, occupational and organizational

TABLE 1
Differences and Similarities Between Crisis Worker
Populations in Terms of Exposure to Trauma

	Personal Direct Exposure to Life-Threatening Trauma	Incident Site and Body Handling[1]	Direct, Indirect, or Secondary Exposure: Average Frequency/Shift
Firefighters	Yes	Yes	Weekly–daily
Paramedics	Yes	Yes	Daily
EMTs	Yes	Yes	Varies
Ambulance drivers	Yes	Yes	Varies
Urban trauma and emergency room physicians and staff	Rarely	No[2]	Daily
Rescue workers[3]	Yes	Yes	Varies
Law enforcement officers[4]	Yes	Yes	Daily
911 dispatcher	No	No	Daily
Pararescue personnel	Yes	Yes	Varies

[1] McCammon and colleagues (1988) reported that in the wake of a series of tornados, disaster workers who encountered a dead victim reported more post-trauma symptoms.
[2] While in-hospital workers do not encounter and handle dead victims at the rescue scene, they are obviously exposed to dead and dying victims.
[3] Rescue workers include Red Cross and disaster workers, as well as National Guard personnel mobilized for a nonmilitary emergency.
[4] Includes police, highway patrol, sheriff, and other law enforcement personnel.

barriers prevent the recognition and treatment of such STS reactions. The effects of repeated exposure among workers, the lack of recognition, and the failure to treat secondary stress contribute to burnout (Herbison, Rando, & Plante, 1984; Maslach, 1978).

SECONDARY TRAUMATIC STRESS OF CRISIS WORKERS: A DEFINITION

In Chapter 1, Figley defines STS as the natural consequent behaviors and emotions resulting from knowledge about a traumatizing event experienced by a significant other or from helping or wanting to help a traumatized person. In addition to this working theoretical definition, STS has three operational components: (1) having witnessed or been confronted by actual or threatened death or injury, or by a threat to the physical integrity of oneself or others; (2) provocation by the stressor of responses of fear, horror, and helplessness; and (3) direct or indirect exposure to an exceptional mental or physical stressor, either brief or prolonged (Figley, Chapter 1 this book). There is a growing body of evidence that supports these operational definitions of STS.

Witness of Actual or Threatened Death or Serious Injury to Others or Self

Multiple studies have documented that exposure to the injured and dying is highly stressful and has significant negative effects on mental health. For example, Taylor and Fraser (1982) collected four waves of data from 180 crisis workers who witnessed massive death and mutilation as a result of a DC-10 airplane crash. Administration of the SCL-90 showed that 80% of the body handlers experienced changes in sleep and appetite, 53% had moderately severe scores on the Global Severity Index (GSI) of the SCL-90, and 40% showed changes in social interaction. Similar results were obtained by Green, Grace, Lindy, Titchener, and Lindy (1983) following a supper club fire. Raphael, Singh, Bradbury, and Lambert (1983–1984) found that deaths of young people, multiple deaths, and the sights and smells of dead persons were significant sources of strain among 70% of disaster workers.

Some crisis workers are exposed to events that threaten personal survival. Beaton and Murphy (1993) surveyed 2,000 Washington State firefighters and paramedics. Nearly 80% of the respondents reported some apprehension regarding their personal safety because of the dangerous job conditions. Similarly, during the 1989 San Francisco earthquake, Red Cross and other disaster personnel were involved in dangerous relief efforts such as searching for survivors in collapsed sections of the I-880 freeway while aftershocks were still occurring (Armstrong, O'Callahan, & Marmar, 1991; Stuhlmiller, 1991).

Law enforcement officers are often put into dangerous situations in which they or colleagues may be shot, and possibly killed (Solomon & Horn, 1986). It is not surprising that these same investigators found that a significant proportion (40–50%) of a sample of police officers involved in a line-of-duty shooting subjectively reported a "heightened sense of danger" and "fear and anxiety" about future shooting situations.

Responses of Fear, Horror, Helplessness as a Result of Stressors

In addition to intense emotional responses to exposure to trauma, some crisis workers identify with victims whom they attempt to assist, particularly if the victims have characteristics similar to those of a worker's "significant other." For example, role relationships and the ages of victims evoke overidentification with them, and even a form of attachment (Martin, McKean, & Veltkamp, 1986). Thus victims are seen as similar in some important way to the crisis worker or to a close friend or relative, which results in vicarious victimization or "covictimization" (Hartsough & Myers, 1985).

Direct or Indirect Exposure to an Expected Mental or Physical Stressor, Either Brief or Prolonged

Crisis worker exposure is repetitive and possibly cumulative. Based on an analysis of survey self-reports of nearly 2,000 professional firefighters and paramedics conducted in 1989, Beaton and Murphy (1990) concluded that 80–90% of these firefighter/paramedic crisis worker survey respondents had actually experienced at least one critical incident in the line of duty within the past year. Little is known about the density, severity, or nature of the critical incidents, but, based on the theory of life change (Holmes & Masuda, 1973; Holmes & Rahe, 1967; Rahe, 1977; Sarason, Levine, & Sarason, 1982), the effects of multiple traumatic events may accumulate and thus parallel the effects of various degrees of combat exposure seen in Vietnam veterans (Fischer, 1991).

Furthermore, life change research has frequently documented a delayed onset of illness similar to that of the post-traumatic stress disorder (PTSD) (Holmes & Masuda, 1973). Exposure of crisis workers to trauma is much more than just "knowledge of" the trauma. Like secondhand cigarette smoke, its effects are real, but difficult to measure precisely.

The conceptual framework of this chapter is based on an organizational systems model adapted from Matteson and Ivancevich (1987), in which seven domains or sets of factors are considered. The model was selected for two reasons. First, it facilitates discussion of multiple contexts—individual, organizational, and community—all of which are germane to crisis worker secondary stress reactions. Second, the model allows for a broad spectrum of literature to be reported, ranging from clinical anecdotes to longitudinal research studies (see Figure 1).

UNINTENDED AND DELETERIOUS EFFECTS ON CRISIS WORKERS AS A RESULT OF PROVIDING HELP

This section presents evidence for three major types of deleterious effects or negative consequences: on health (which includes secondary post-traumatic stress and other health consequences), relationship disturbances, and substance use/abuse. Next, similarities and differences between primary and secondary post-traumatic stress are discussed. Finally, a critique of the negative-consequences research is presented.

Health Consequences

Evidence of Secondary Post-taumatic Stress Symptoms
A wide range of post-trauma symptoms have been documented in crisis workers, which may be due to their psychodological diversity rather than magnitude of outcome. The literature exemplifies diverse occupational samples, differences in measurement, differing traumatic event factors, and degrees of proximity to harm, as well as mediating contextual variables and worker characteristics as described below.

Immediate Post-exposure Effects
During a critical incident or traumatic event, the major stressors for crisis workers include the handling of dead bodies, being exposed to dangerous situations, witnessing property and environmental loss, working under suboptimal conditions, physical strain, and the necessity of conveying the tragic news to the family or friends of victims (Raphael, 1986). Because of time pressures and the grotesqueness of the scene, crisis workers often report perceptual and time distortions. For instance, Solomon and Horn (1986) point out that during a shooting incident, police officers may not even recall hearing their firearm discharge or will say that it sounded like a "pop gun." (Police officers are exposed to a wide variety of potential secondary traumata, including high-speed chases and "drug busts." Moreover, according to one knowledgeable source, they actually provide assistance to victims in 80% of their work

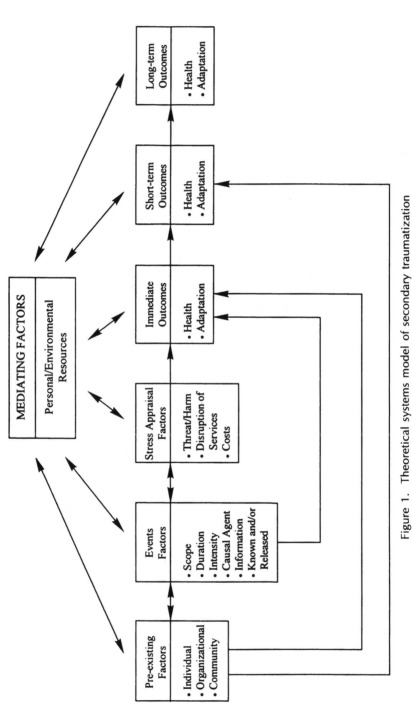

Figure 1. Theoretical systems model of secondary traumatization
(Reprinted from Murphy, 1991, "Human Response to Catastrophe," *Annual Review of Nursing Research, 9,* p. xx.)

[Bard, 1976].) Usually, crisis workers overestimate the amount of time involved in an incident or rescue (Mitchell & Bray, 1990). However, Jurkovich and others found that paramedics tended to overestimate the time elapsed during short runs and to underestimate time on long runs (Jurkovich, Campbell, Padrta, & Luterman, 1987).

Another immediate trauma symptom frequently reported by crisis workers is that of depersonalization. They may feel a sense of unreality during a catastrophe, but continue to function. In fact, if any conclusion can be drawn regarding the immediate effects of trauma, it is that the vast majority of crisis workers continue to function in spite of the crisis. Role identification and training may be important antecedents (Raphael, 1986; Stuhlmiller, 1991). In one of the few studies of volunteer firefighters' reactions to traumatic stress, only 10% of a "nonprofessional" firefighter sample (n = 58) reported that personal stress reactions interfered with the ability to act effectively during a hotel-fire rescue operation (Hytten & Hasle, 1989). Overwhelming emotions are usually suppressed during the incident so that aid can be rendered effectively.

Nevertheless, Sanner (1983) reported that health care workers faced with mass casualties very often experience grief reactions, loss of confidence, and "triage stress." Presumably, crisis workers more removed from the disaster scene (e.g., 911 operators) are less likely to have these immediate cognitive and emotional trauma reactions, but there seems to be no definitive research demonstrating such differential effects.

Short-Term Post-exposure Effects

Horowitz (1974) suggested that crisis workers report the same panoply of post-trauma reactions, albeit usually milder, as those reported by Vietnam veterans (Figley, 1978) and rape victims (Burge, 1988). Acute or short-term post-trauma reactions include reexperiencing the traumatic event (e.g., nightmares) and numbing of responsiveness (Durham, McCammon, & Allison, 1985; Horowitz, 1976; Horowitz, Wilner & Alvarez, 1979). (In the immediate aftermath of an incident, the acute phase begins and presumably lasts for several months. It is not unusual for both traumatized victims and crisis workers initially to experience shock/numbing and to deny any intense emotions for hours, days, or even longer following a critical incident [Solomon & Horn, 1986].)

Durham and colleagues reported that 80% of rescue personnel (which included fire, rescue, police, and in-hospital personnel) had at least one post-traumatic symptom following an apartment building explosion. The most common symptom, intrusive thoughts about the disaster, was seen in 74% of disaster-site rescue personnel. Likewise, Myles, Levine,

Ramsden, and Swanson (1990) reported that many volunteer emergency medical technicians/ambulance attendants experienced vivid, involuntary and uncontrollable thoughts, feelings, and images following a cardiopulmonary resuscitation (CPR) attempt. The findings of Myles and colleagues are important since they suggest that even "routine" CPR has the potential to cause post-traumatic symptoms in crisis workers.

McFarlane (1988a, 1988b, 1988d) examined post-traumatic reactions of a sample of 469 firefighters exposed to an Australian bushfire. Using a longitudinal follow-up design, he found that 30% of the firefighter sample had some acute psychiatric symptoms four months after the fire. Furthermore, only 9.2% of the sample that displayed post-traumatic morbidity (based on General Health Questionnaire replies) four months after the fire were asymptomatic 11 months following the disaster. Average Impact of Event Scale (IES) scores at four months after the disaster in McFarlane's firefighter sample ranged from 20.0 to 33.4, reflecting a mild-to-moderate level of intrusive images and post-trauma avoidance symptoms. In another Australian study of rescue personnel, 70% showed signs of passing stress reactions after a train disaster (Raphael et al., 1983–1984).

On the other hand, one of the few available rigorous clinical research studies that collected predisaster baseline data and used a matched control group failed to document significant post-traumatic distress or psychiatric morbidity in a group of police officers who were involved in disaster-related body-handling duties (Alexander & Wells, 1991). These findings are in stark contrast to most of the available research findings and conclusions regarding crisis worker trauma (Raphael et al., 1986). In fact, McCafferty, Domingo, and McCafferty (1990) feel that police officers in particular are predisposed to PTSD similar to that seen in Vietnam veterans, and that such exposure leads to "demoralization and brutalization" (p. 546).

Markowitz, Gutterman, Link, and Rivera (1987) found that firefighter subjects (n = 80) exposed to a toxic chemical fire experienced significantly more demoralization, as well as emotional distress specifically related to the fire and perceived threats to their physical health, relative to a nonrandom comparison group of 15 firefighters not exposed to the chemical fire. However, the duration of symptoms and their resolution were not assessed because data were collected only once approximately one to two months after the incident.

Hytten and Hasle (1989) collected data concerning acute stress reactions from 58 nonprofessional firefighters within seven to 21 days following a hotel fire rescue operation. They found that 43% felt anxious and irritable to a "moderate or strong degree" and 57% experienced restlessness during this time (mean = 14 days). Loo (1986) writes that most police officers experience "stress reactions" within three days of a shooting, with the average "return to normality time" reported by the 66 officer participants as 20 weeks.

Long-Term Post-exposure Effects

McFarlane concluded that nearly 20% of firefighters exposed to the Australian bushfire could be classified as undergoing a "delayed onset" of post-trauma symptoms (onset was more than 11 months following the bushfire). Three chronic disorder patterns emerged in more than 20% of the sample. Thus the acute patterns of morbidity were less common than delayed-onset or chronic forms in McFarlane's study sample of firefighters (McFarlane, 1988a, 1988b).

The present authors examined the prevalence and magnitude of postincident stress symptoms in 2,000 Washington State firefighters and paramedics. Using a modification of the IES (Horowitz et al., 1979), firefighter and paramedic respondents were asked to recall their most stressful line of duty experience within the past year. With that incident in mind, they were to report the frequency of various post-trauma symptoms of intrusion and avoidance during the past week. Information about the specific nature of the incident(s) was not collected, nor was the date of the incident(s) within the past year (Beaton & Murphy, 1990).

Eighty-seven percent of the sample reportedly experienced at least one post-trauma symptom following an unspecified line of duty incident within the past year, that is, they endorsed at least one post-trauma symptom within the past week as having occurred, if rarely (total IES score more than 1). The total average IES score for the sample represented a mild-to-moderate level of post-trauma symptomatology and was approximately of the same magnitude as those of the treated catastrophe survivors in the initial validation study and approximately a standard deviation below that of the untreated male standardization sample (Horowitz et al., 1979).

The robust correlation between these two subscales (Pearson's $r = .78$) showed that avoidance and intrusive symptoms coexisted in this firefighter/paramedic sample. The IES survey results are comparable to those reported by McFarlane (1988a, 1988b) for firefighters and those of Ersland, Weisaeth, and Sund (1989) regarding rescue workers involved in an oil rig disaster. However, the IES data did not support Horowitz's (1976) conceptualization or Gersons's (1989) two-dimensional model of PTSD based on analyses of police officer data following shooting incidents. In the present authors' sample, a denial symptom pattern occurred along with the "reexperiencing" symptom pattern. Contrary to the theoretical formulations cited above, denial and reexperiencing "states of mind" were not mutually exclusive.

As part of the firefighter and paramedic survey conducted by the authors, the Symptoms of Stress (SOS) inventory was also administered (Beaton, Egan, Nakagawa-Kogan, & Morrison, 1991). The SOS inventory is a 94-item checklist that prior research had shown correlated significantly ($r = .75$) with the GSI of the SCL-90R (Derogatis, 1977). The SOS data obtained from Washington State firefighters and paramedics clearly documented widespread somatic, emotional, and behavioral complaints of these crisis workers (Beaton, Murphy, & Pike, 1992a, 1992b). Mortality data from crisis workers further support subjective complaints. More than half of on-the-job firefighter fatalities in the United States are attributable to cardiovascular causes (National Fire Protection Agency, 1988). This finding is all the more dramatic when one considers how healthy firefighters are at the outset of their careers.

Other mortality statistics also bear out the long-term health consequences of crisis work. In Washington State from 1950 to 1979, firefighter deaths as a result of duodenal ulcers were 2.6 times greater than expected. During this same period, also in Washington State, police officer deaths resultin from pulmonary embolism and infarction were more than twice the expected levels. Cirrhosis of the liver also showed elevated proportional mortality rates (Milham, 1983).

Some crisis workers, especially emergency first responders, are directly exposed to dangerous situations and circumstances. The following example, based on an interview conducted by the first author, graphically demonstrates direct exposure.

Case Study 1. The emergency worker was a 35-year-old male urban paramedic with more than 10 years of experience. As he discussed various stressful aspects of his job and prior incidents, certain peripheral psychophysiologic indicators, such as his skin conductance and skin temperature, were simultaneously monitored. During the interview, he recalled a critical incident that had taken place more than eight years earlier. In that incident, he and his paramedic partner had been dispatched to the scene of a shooting. They arrived on the scene within just a few minutes of the call, and, as the worker entered the building with his gear, the perpetrator, brandishing a firearm, literally bumped into him. He vividly recalled his feelings of terror during this incident, and as he did so during the interview, his peripheral finger skin temperature dropped 10 degrees Fahrenheit within 30 seconds. The vasoconstriction was a psychophysiological indication of a "fight or flight" autonomic nervous system sympathetic activation caused by an eight-year-old memory. He recalled that he had suppressed his immediate feelings of terror and then provided emergency medical aid for the victim at the scene. He felt he probably had saved the victim's life. He received no debriefing or therapy regarding this incident. He also reported that he had not consciously thought about the incident for some time.

Such physiological reactivity to "reminders," as well as recollected imagery of an incident, as in this case, is one of the DSM's diagnostic signs of a PTSD (American Psychiatric Association, 1987). A published series of case studies documented similar physiological reactivity. In these cases, victims of motor vehicle accidents evinced cardiac acceleration in response to recollected images of their accidents (Blanchard, Hickling, & Taylor, 1991). A well-controlled study demonstrated similar autonomic activation (i.e., increased heart rate) in Vietnam veterans exposed to combat images and sounds (Pitman, Orr, Forgue, de Jong, & Claiborn, 1987).

There is a body of research focusing on physiological indices of acute stress reactivity obtained primarily from firefighters and paramedics. For example, reactions to the klaxon (fire alarm) has been a stimulus for study. In general, the klaxon causes cardiac acceleration and catecholamine excretion in firefighters (Kalimo, Lehtonen, Daleva, & Kourinka, 1980; Kuorinka & Korkonen, 1981). It is not known how or if the repeated elicitation of the fight-or-flight emergency response affects the long-term health of crisis workers, but, for affected personnel, the klaxon alarm (or any emergency call) is probably a potent and frequent reminder of prior traumatic incidents. Apparently, no research studies have investigated this association of the alarm with previous traumatization.

Another common emotion/symptom reported by police officers in the aftermath of a shooting is anger, which may be directed at a variety of sources, including administrative superiors. As Horowitz (1974) has noted, trauma victims often express rage at those whom they blame for their emotional distress. Cross (1990) referred to this phenomenon in Vietnam veterans as the PTSD-resentment continuum. Like Vietnam veterans, crisis workers often feel angry and helpless. And, as with Vietnam veterans, these feelings are often directed at the administration in charge which may have to bear the brunt of the anger.

Thus there is considerable evidence that most crisis workers experience both acute and chronic post-trauma symptoms during their careers. Trauma symptoms are manifest in intrusion, avoidance, hypervigilance, disturbed sleep, demoralization, anger, fear, or physiological reactivity. Other chronic and long-term post-trauma symptoms that have been reported in crisis workers include a sense of alienation, isolation/withdrawal, delayed loss of confidence, guilt, feelings of insanity and loss of control, and even suicidal thoughts (Dunning & Silva, 1980; Solomon & Horn, 1986). There is also epidemiological evidence to support crisis workers' high levels of stress-related mortality (Milham, 1983).

To summarize the section on health consequences, it is important to emphasize the number of studies that have been conducted, as well as the range of outcomes studied. Although design and sampling have not reached the desired sophistication, study results show important trends: (1) The range of health outcome effects suggests that crisis worker exposure is very important. Workers who have body-handling duties appear to be the most severely affected. (2) The findings support the premise that some responses are normal reactions to extreme situations and are not psychiatric disorders.

Relationship Problems and Marital Discord in Crisis Workers

Rescue personnel may experience marital discord at rates higher than those in the general population (Dunning & Silva, 1980). Data from law enforcement, and especially from Vietnam veterans' families, if they can be generalized, also suggest that deleterious effects of crisis work on the family are common (Besner & Robinson, 1982; Figley, 1985). As Figley has noted, families of crisis workers are indirectly exposed via "spillover" to the same sources of stress as the worker. Symptoms of traumatic stress are manifest as personality changes, including withdrawal, alienation, and even an inability to show affection (Besner & Robinson, 1982). Police officers' spouses may feel "shut out" because of the confidential nature of police work and the officers' reluctance to share feelings.

In contrast, findings from the authors' firefighter/paramedic survey did not support an adverse effect on families (Beaton & Murphy, 1991). The firefighter and paramedic respondents reported divorce rates of less than 10%, about average for U.S. males. Approximately 80% of firefighter/paramedic survey respondents were currently married, and, on the whole, reported relatively high levels of social satisfaction with their off-job family and marital social support (Beaton & Murphy, 1991).

Substance Use/Abuse

Substance use refers to the ingestion of alcohol and other drugs (AOD). Alcoholic beverages are consistently the preferred drug of choice in the United States (DHHS, 1990). Problem drinking can be of two types: abuse and dependence. DSM-III-R diagnostic criteria are established for both patterns and consequences of use (APA, 1987).

Although there are "reports" that crisis workers are likely to take drugs, especially alcohol (Raphael et al., 1983–1984), only one study was found that explored this topic. Murphy and Beaton (1991) studied leisure patterns in 165 urban firefighters as a "study within a study" of sources of stress among the 2,000 firefighter/paramedic respondents described above. Male firefighter respondents (*n* = 155) reported that alcohol use was involved in five (19%) of all leisure activities engaged in weekly or daily. These activities included: entertaining, eating out, playing tavern games, going to bars or clubs, and watching sports on television.

Some studies suggest that substances may be used to escape or avoid PTSD symptoms of intrusive thoughts and nightmares (Elder & Clipp, 1988). However, substance use was not measured by standardized quantity and frequency scales nor was it assessed over time. It is imperative that studies of crisis worker responses begin to include an assessment of substance use and its potential abuse. As Raphael (1986) so poignantly stated, "The sense of protest about the extent and reality of death, feelings of helplessness and fatigue, denial and disbelief, anger and rage, and a sense of giving in to the traumatic overload of death and loss" (p. 238) place workers at risk for substance abuse.

Since crisis workers are vulnerable to post-trauma symptoms of intrusive thoughts and nightmares, they are at risk to use substances known to dull sensation and perception. Clinical populations of Vietnam veterans report using substances to avoid or to escape from troubling symptoms. Moreover, a thesis of this chapter is that repeated exposure to trauma is one factor that differentiates crisis workers from most trauma victims. Thus both the quality and quantity of emergency work place crisis workers at risk.

Two aspects of AOD assessment are important: (1) the documentation of the amount and frequency of use of multiple substances, such as alcohol, tobacco products, and prescribed medications such as sleeping pills, and illegal drugs; and (2) the change over time in the amount and frequency of substance use related to a specific event, or by crisis workers who undergo repeated exposures to traumatic events.

In summary, as a result of frequent, repetitive, and cumulative exposures to trauma, many crisis workers experience various post-trauma symptoms and have increased levels of stress-related morbidity and mortality. As a result, they also can experience spillover that theoretically can affect their relationships with family and friends, and perhaps even "drive them to drink." However, with regard to the latter health consequences, the data are somewhat equivocal.

Similarities and Differences Between Primary and Secondary PTSD

Similarities

In massive death situations, there may be few differences between the stress reactions of victims and of crisis workers (Lifton, 1967; McCafferty et al., 1990; Wilkinson, 1983). Intrusive reexperiencing and avoidance symptoms seen in crisis workers assigned to an incident are similar to those reported by survivors of the catastrophe (Horowitz et al., 1979; McFarlane, 1988a, 1988d). In the aftermath of a traumatic incident, virtually all of the DSM III-R PTSD symptoms/outcomes have been documented as occurring to some degree in a significant percentage of crisis workers (McFarlane, 1988c; Raphael et al., 1983, 1984; Wilkinson, 1983). In most cases, post-trauma symptoms in both primary and secondary victims are mild to moderate, that is, subclinical. Except for rare and novel events, neither all crisis workers nor all primary victims experience post-traumatic symptoms. This finding strongly suggests that pre-existing stress appraisal and other mediating factors affect outcomes (Murphy, 1991).

The available literature suggests that the nature and magnitude of certain overwhelming disasters elicit post-trauma symptoms in virtually all victims and emergency crisis workers. For example, based on interview data, Wilkinson (1983) reported that in the aftermath of the collapse of the Hyatt Regency skywalk in Kansas City, Missouri, rescue workers, uninjured hotel guest observers, and injured victims all had psychiatric symptoms. Furthermore, only slight differences among rescue workers, observers, and victims five months after the disaster were reported. Wilkinson's findings support research conclusions pertaining to Vietnam veterans suggesting that the amount and severity of combat exposure is the single most important factor in determining the presence of post-traumatic symptomatology (Boulanger, 1985; Fischer, 1991). In the theoretical model elaborated in this chapter, event factors are predominant (see Figure 1).

Differences

In general, two factors seem to differentiate crisis-worker PTSD effects from those of primary victim PTSD. First, crisis workers view trauma as part of their work, as a "fact of everyday life"; therefore, stress reactions are likely to be less severe. Most crisis workers are a self-selected group, though this is probably an oversimplification. They chose, perhaps due in part to personality variables, employment as crisis workers (Mitchell & Bray, 1990). They invariably are dedicated and committed to saving lives, an essential feature of their occupational role identity. In contrast, many PTSD victims experience trauma that intrudes in an unexpected manner on their personal safety and well-being, such as rape, assault, and natural disasters.

Second, although crisis workers in various occupations are exposed to different kinds of trauma, they all accept exposure to trauma as "part of the job." The concern is that for the vast majority of crisis workers exposure to trauma is repetitive. Based on the life change literature, an argument can be made that such trauma exposures have cumulative effects (Holmes & Masuda, 1973; Holmes & Rahe, 1967; Shealy, 1984). A recent report by a Canadian investigator documented cumulative effects of the number of duty-related trauma exposures in a large sample of urban firefighters (Corneil, 1992). However, the present authors' research with firefighters and paramedics did not document any effect of "years of service" (and presumably cumulative traumatization) on any of the measures of stress employed. Furthermore, the research findings of Hytten and Hasle (1989) suggest that experienced volunteer firefighters seemed to "digest" a hotel fire rescue disaster more easily than inexperienced volunteers, that is, the experienced or seasoned firefighters had significantly lower IES scores. The effects of experience may be curvilinear; longitudinal studies are needed.

Most crisis workers are invariably and constantly exposed to reminders of past critical incidents as long as they continue in an active-duty status. Every alarm or call carries with it the potential for an event similar to that which triggered their original post-trauma reaction. A crisis worker cannot avoid constant reminders or triggers unless he or she: (1) quits the profession, (2) takes a leave of absence, or (3) transfers to a nonemergency position.

Crisis workers are exposed to a variety of job-related stressors in addition to workplace trauma that may compound or interact with traumatic stressors. For example, based on a factor analysis of the 1989 survey replies of firefighters and paramedics (n = 2,000), evidence was found for 14 statistically distinct occupational stressor factors, of which "past critical incidents" is just one (Beaton & Murphy, 1993). Crisis workers are invariably exposed to uncertainty, lack of predictability, and ambiguity on every shift, which probably potentiates their traumatic symptomatology.

Some crisis workers, especially firefighters, also have little job latitude due to a heavy reliance on teamwork and paramilitary organizational structures (Karasek & Theorell, 1990). Many crisis workers are also shift workers. Sleep disturbances, one of the major post-trauma symptoms, are ubiquitous in shift workers (Tasto, Colligan, Skjei, & Polly, 1978). Finally, another potentially traumatic role stressor identified as distressing for firefighters and paramedic crisis workers is that of "conveying news of a tragedy" to the next of kin or friends (Beaton & Murphy, 1993). It is unclear how other occupational stressors might interact with traumatic/critical incident stressors and associated secondary post-trauma stress symptoms in crisis workers.

Finally, in contrast to most trauma victims, crisis workers' post-trauma reactions are generally mild to moderate. Only a small percentage of crisis workers develop "full-blown" PTSD (Mitchell & Bray, 1990), whereas 25% to 30% of Vietnam veterans have been estimated to do so (Kulka, Schlenger, Fairbank, Hough, Jordan, Marmar, & Weiss, 1990), and according to Frederick (1986), 89%–96% of victims of violent acts showed some symptoms of PTSD. Of physical assault victims studied by Frederick (1986), 36% showed evidence of severe to very severe PTSD. Approximately one half of prisoner-of-war victims were similarly categorized (Frederick, 1986).

Summary/Critique of Negative-Consequences Research

Study Methods

Most of the published accounts of crisis worker studies are descriptive. Some of the studies reviewed here are important first steps, but need to be followed up rapidly by quasi-experimental, longitudinal designs with experimental and comparison groups of sufficient size and representation to allow statistical analyses beyond the descriptive statistics reported thus far. Most studies reviewed were single group static designs, which poses numerous threats to their internal and external validity (Campbell & Stanley, 1963).

Sampling was based primarily on volunteers. We did not find any studies that randomly selected subjects. A few studies stratified samples by job categories or levels of impairment. It was impossible to make comparisons across studies, since only a few used the same or even similar measures. For example, mental distress was measured by the SCL-90 in only two studies (Taylor & Fraser, 1982; Wilkinson, 1983). Therefore, no firm conclusions can be drawn.

However, some trends did emerge; specifically, varying degrees of mental distress, including PTSD, were apparent in both short- and long-term outcome studies (Markowitz et al., 1987; McFarlane, 1988a, 1988d; Solomon & Horn, 1986).

Population Groups Studied

The most commonly studied crisis workers were police officers and firefighters. The majority of studies viewed the individual as the unit of analysis and described the deleterious effects of crisis work on personnel. Of primary interest appeared to be whether PTSD (i.e., psychiatric disability) or temporary functional impairment was commonplace. Also of interest was whether crisis workers experienced primary or secondary PTSD. Few studies examined contextual variables.

Critique

Several reasons likely account for the overrepresentation of descriptive studies: the state of the science pertaining to secondary stress, the difficulties inherent in studying crisis phenomena (i.e., less research planning time), and the limited amount of funding available on a "quick turnaround" basis. Nonrandom sampling is problematic due to threats to both internal and external validity. Finally, there is a need to extend research to a variety of crisis worker populations beyond police officers and firefighters.

FACTORS CONTRIBUTING TO SECONDARY TRAUMATIZATION

Individual, organizational, social, community, and traumatic event factors potentially may either increase or decrease one's vulnerability to STS. Factors supported by the literature are reviewed in this section.

Individual Context/Personality Traits

Several individual factors have been shown directly to affect outcome variables or to produce significant outcome differences. In this section, we review the effects of demographic variables, the history of psychiatric symptoms, personality traits, and postexposure symptom trajectories. McFarlane's (1988a–d) longitudinal studies with firefighters exposed to an Australian bushfire are among the few studies that have identified individual vulnerability factors that may be predictive of posttrauma reactions. For example, neuroticism, measured by the Eysenck Personality Inventory (EPI), was a predictor of persistent chronic PTSD. However, the EPI was administered 29 months following the disaster, and even though subjects were instructed to answer the EPI "according to the way they saw themselves before the disaster," such retrospective accounts are not entirely reliable. Firefighters with chronic PTSD were more likely to have experienced intense post-trauma imagery during the acute period. Thus one of the best predictors of the development of chronic PTSD symptomatology in the sample was the presence of acute symptomatology (McFarlane, 1988d).

History of Psychiatric Symptoms

In a follow-up study of a subsample (*n* = 27), McFarlane (1988c) found that some firefighters were still experiencing PTSD 42 months after the event, and that the only post-trauma symptom that differentiated the PTSD subjects from the "no PTSD subjects" was a difficulty concentrating eight months following the disaster. A history of treatment for a psychological disorder before the disaster was reported by all of the firefighters categorized by McFarlane (1988d) as suffering from chronic PTSD. Although the findings cannot be generalized due to the retrospective design and sampling techniques, the results suggest that a history of a diagnosed psychological disorder and acute symptoms are associated with the development of long-term PTSD in crisis workers. These findings have been confirmed in other studies that examined responses to traumatic events (Burgess & Holstrom, 1974; Murphy, 1986; Vachon, 1976). Furthermore, certain emerging post-trauma symptoms (e.g., difficulties in concentrating) seem to be associated with more protracted post-trauma symptoms.

Demographic Characteristics: Age, Ethnicity

Jones (1985) conducted a survey of nearly 600 U.S. Air Force personnel who recovered and transported the bodily remains of the some 1,000 victims of the Jonestown, Guyana, mass suicide. He found that those respondents who were less than 25 years old, were of African-American ethnicity, and were enlisted personnel (versus officers) reported more short-term "dysphoria." It should be noted that these Air Force personnel were not trained as crisis workers. Also, research with ethnically diverse Vietnam combat veterans suggests that African Americans and Hispanic minorities experienced higher prevalence rates of PTSD (Kulka et al., 1990). (See Penk and Allen [1991] for methodological and clinical considerations in assessing trauma in minority combat veterans.) However, the present authors' research with ethnically diverse firefighters and paramedics in Washington State did not identify any significant relationships between ethnicity and post-trauma symptoms (Murphy & Beaton, 1990). Currently, most crisis workers are white males; ethnically diverse groups and women are underrepresented in these occupations. It is possible that, in time, cohort effects may emerge.

Stress Appraisal

An important appraisal factor in the development of secondary post-traumatic reactions is identification with the victim. Martin and colleagues (1986) studied post-trauma stress in a sample of 53 police officers. One quarter of the respondents met the DSM-III criteria for PTSD.

The data suggested that police officers' responses to stress were related to their degree of identification with the victim.

The following case study illustrates the importance of appraisal and identification with the victim in the development of secondary post-traumatic stress.

> *Case Study 2.* Mr. S., a 32-year-old paramedic with nearly 10 years of emergency medical service experience, was referred to the first author for an individualized debriefing after a relatively "routine" highway fatality incident. The fatality, explained the paramedic, was a freak mishap involving a construction vehicle and a bicyclist. The male bicyclist, who was approximately the same age and build as the paramedic, had been lawfully cycling alongside a roadway when a heavy piece of construction equipment flew off of the construction vehicle involved and struck the cyclist on his back without warning. The paramedic, who had been referred for the debriefing because his commanding officer had observed him to be quite moody and sullen, was the first emergency worker to arrive on the scene. He immediately noted that the cyclist/victim was dead, because, as he put it, "his entire chest area was blown out." During the debriefing, the paramedic repeated many times, "It could have been me, it could have been me." The paramedic in question, an avid cyclist, cycled on that roadway almost every day. After a few days of leave, he returned to work without any apparent long-term ill effects and declined to participate in any further therapy. This was the first time during his career that this paramedic had had any therapy or had taken part in a debriefing.

McCammon and co-workers (1988) reported that emergency workers frequently coped with such disastrous events by using cognitive strategies akin to "searching for meaning," "attempting to achieve mastery of the situation," and "seeking emotional support." Perhaps unrealistic cognitive self-expectations foster adverse reactions. For example, the superhuman notion that one should be able to "save everyone" can be a "perceptual burden" (Hartsough, 1985). In the extreme, most emergency workers recognize this attitude as the "God syndrome," which may lead to burnout and paralysis. Some literature hints that a sense of humor might well be an important coping strategy for crisis workers (Corneil, 1989).

Among preexisting individual and personal mediating factors that could contribute to duty trauma are (1) preexisting life events stress (Dutton, Smolensky, Lorimor & Leach, 1978); (2) role conflict, as between one's professional and personal roles (Murphy, 1991); (3) method of assimilating (finding meaning) in the trauma (Gersons, 1989; Raphael, 1986), and (4) the "rescue personality" (Mitchell & Bray, 1990). However, to date none of these individual factors has been shown to predict the onset, severity, or duration of post-trauma symptoms.

Organizational/Occupational Context

Organizational influences on the recognition of and recovery from on-the-job trauma include (1) authority and chain of command, (2) size of the crisis worker organization, (3) role conflicts and ambiguities, and (4) rank of the crisis worker (Hartsough & Myers, 1985). The development of group norms arises from these factors.

The cultural norms present in crisis worker occupations dictate, in part, how a given individual should (and will) respond to a line of duty trauma (Stuhlmiller, 1991). The fire service culture, for example, encourages group cohesiveness and the image of self-control. Fears, anxieties, or personal vulnerabilities are rarely discussed (Hartsough, 1985). This "conspiracy of silence" norm is generally functional and protective because, without a certain amount of self-deception, firefighters might be overwhelmed by their fears. The "no talk rule" itself, however, is a cultural impediment to reducing stress in the aftermath of a trauma.

The vast majority of police officers, firefighters, and other crisis workers are male (emergency and trauma room nurses are exceptions), which may account, in part, for the widespread macho attitudes that pervade the crisis worker culture. The crisis workers' occupational culture is important not only in terms of the admission and recognition of a post-trauma reaction, but also in terms of recovery and the acceptance of restorative treatment.

Experience, training, role orientation, and second-job stress may contribute to secondary stress reactions. For example, Hytten and Hasle (1989) found that volunteers and crisis workers with little prior trauma experience were more susceptible to its effects. Professional role orientation and training can reduce the impact of a traumatic incident (Hytten & Hasle, 1989; Raphael, 1986). Although little researched, there is the possibility that second-job stress might spill over and affect trauma response. Beaton & Murphy (1993) found that between a third and 40% of firefighters and paramedics worked (usually part time) at second jobs while not on duty. Finally, the preexisting and post-trauma use of alcohol and other drugs needs to be investigated. Such use may be widespread, but systematic data have not been obtained.

Social Context

Social context refers to the interpersonal milieu that gives meaning to the work roles and responses of crisis workers. Social network studies (i.e., the size and density of workers' interpersonal relationships) have been replicated and have shown that individuals need both principal attachment figures and friends and colleagues to help in managing stressful events (Burke & Weir, 1977). House (1981) defined social support as "an interpersonal transaction involving one or more of the following: emotional concern, instrumental aid, information, and appraisal" (i.e., quality of perceived help) (p. 39). More recently, Jacobsen (1986) suggested that both the types of support (i.e., information focused and emotion focused) and their timing (i.e., during both crisis and transition) are important considerations in the relationship between stressors and outcomes. The bidirectional effects of "spillover" (Eckenrode & Gore, 1990) involving work and family roles among crisis workers provide an important concept for study.

Research to date has been conducted primarily at the descriptive level. There evidently have been few explorations of conflicted relationships, the type and timing of support, reciprocity, or spillover. Among firefighters, Markowitz and colleagues (1987) included social support as a study variable, but did not state how it was measured. Similarly, McFarlane (1988a, 1988d) did not provide information regarding the measurement of co-worker support. Beaton and Murphy (1991) measured social support and network conflict at home and at work in a large firefighter sample ($n = 1750$). Satisfaction with social support at work and at home correlated negatively with ratings of how "bothered" they had been within the past 10 shifts by duty-related critical incidents, sleep disturbance, personal vulnerability, and the need to convey news of a tragedy. Significant positive correlations were also found between the network conflict measure and appraisal of trauma-related occupational stressors; that is, social conflict was associated with more bothersome post-trauma symptoms. Finally, although Raphael (1986) suggested that both family members and co-workers provide social support to disaster workers as a general group, no empirical findings were presented.

Community Context

According to Wilkinson and Vera (1985), communities are composed of subsystems with interrelated functions that include economic, religious, educational, and political activities. Following a crisis, communities must assess the harm and loss associated with seven basic processes:

preservation of life; restoration of essential services, including water, gas, electricity, communication, and information; social control; maintenance of morale; return of economic activity; emergency social and personal services; and maintenance of leisure and recreation (Mileti, Drabek, & Haas, 1975).

Because communities are sometimes extremely disrupted, they have been the subject of inquiry in numerous previous studies. However, we address communities as contexts in which crisis workers live, work, and find meaning in their experiences and so reviewed only relevant studies. Communities play an important role in sanctioning loss and grief. See, for example, Erikson's (1976) account of the Buffalo Creek disaster and the sense of loss of community among the residents who survived and remained in the area.

A variable that has received limited attention is predisaster mobilization status and preparation time. For many first responders, the time between a call (or alarm) and arrival on the scene may be a short ride in an emergency vehicle. First responders, to be successful, must provide aid during an "optimal time window." Other crisis workers, such as Red Cross rescue personnel, may not be mobilized for hours or even days following a disaster. By the time they reach the scene, the later arrivals usually have more information regarding the nature of the disaster.

Laube (1973) conducted a unique study of crisis workers' potential family and community role conflicts following a tornado. Family–community conflict referred to perceived forced role choices made by workers when asked to provide community assistance. Fifty percent of the female subsample ($n = 81$) and 41% of the male subsample ($n = 20$) had family responsibilities and chose family roles; that is, they decided to remain with their families during the event. The remaining workers chose community roles. Emotional distress, measured by the Psychiatric Status Schedule, was higher for health care providers who chose community over family roles, but all scores were in the normal range (Laube, 1973).

Characteristics of Traumatic Events

Traumatic events vary according to the predictability, suddenness, and duration of impact; controllability; and the extent of damage/destruction. The type and magnitude of events interact with antecedent, mediating, and outcome factors.

Potential for Personal Loss, Injury, and Death
Apparently, no studies have documented the personal losses of crisis

workers; however, the extent of worker concern for personal injury has been documented (Armstrong et al., 1991; Beaton & Murphy, 1993; Solomon, & Horn, 1986). Raphael (1986) discussed the threat of actual and potential injury in the context of multiple role stressors.

"Mission" Failure

The impact of some events is so profound that those who are first on the scene experience major role stress because of their inability to carry out the tasks that they were trained for and are prepared to do (Raphael et al., 1983, 1984; Wilkinson & Vera, 1985). Thus firefighters and paramedics may experience feelings of impotence and helplessness more frequently than do other crisis workers.

> *Case Study 3*. The third game of the 1989 World Series was about to be played in San Francisco on October 17, and many people were traveling home early to watch it on television. At 5:00 p.m., an earthquake struck along the San Andreas fault. More that 100 people were killed immediately, most as a result of the collapse of the I-880 freeway. A large number of rescue workers were at the collapse site, and were the focus of a study conducted by Stuhlmiller (1991).

The purpose of the study was to make sense of the situation and to describe the experiences of rescue workers in an effort to narrow two gaps in the literature: the incorporation of context frequently omitted in studies based on positivist science, and the avoidance of premature conclusions that worker outcomes are primarily pathological. Tape-recorded interviews were conducted with 42 informants: 15 firefighters, 15 California Department of Transportation (Caltrans) workers, six military pararescue personnel, and six coroners. Informants were involved in securing the area, removing bodies, and freeing those who were trapped in the rubble, thus meeting the direct-exposure inclusion criterion.

According to Stuhlmiller (1991), "The most striking thread throughout this story is the reservoir of shared cultural meanings related to personal commitment, dedication to saving human lives, avoiding suffering, facing death, and comforting families from which these people drew to help their fellow human beings" (p. 91). Two themes from the data are incorporated here: role identity with a particular occupational group and patterns of involvement and concerns congruent with roles and responsibilities and short-term outcomes.

Firefighter identity and involvement were based on what firefighters do. Suppression of a fire is much less frequently called for than is a response to an emergency. Teamwork is critical and stress arises in situations that threaten the team. Caltrans workers (engineers and maintenance workers) expressed pride in their building and maintaining of structures. Their involvement in the rescue was based on obligation to the public. The role identity and involvement of the pararescuers were based on their pride in being uniquely trained as medics for both military and civilian service. Coroner involvement was based on an obligation to do a job that no one else likes to do—"We retrieve bodies so life can go on."

Study informants were survivor/rescuers, and thus met more than one criterion for secondary stress trauma. However, exposure to personal danger and to the threat of death was perceived as an empowering survival experience. The role of rescuer raised numerous concerns reported in the literature, such as obtaining legitimacy; wondering who is in charge; dismissing feelings of being threatened and focusing on the job; dealing with gruesome details; and coping with suffering, smells, and the handling of dead bodies. Contrary to past reports of coping as distancing of self, making crude jokes, and referring to persons as objects, one informant said, "It is that capacity to feel that makes us alive and life meaningful" (p. 223).

The most frequently reported aftereffect in these crisis workers six months following the event was anxiety about being near freeway structures, such as overpasses and bridges. Verbatim accounts are suggestive of symptoms of acute PTSD. Entering parking garages and crossing bridges produced sights and sounds that evoked disturbing stimuli. Other effects concerned intimate relationships, which had both positive and negative outcomes; beliefs that the rescue experience had changed their lives forever; awareness of their own mortality; and a sense of time's standing still ("When I returned to work, I kept wondering why everything was going so slowly").

In summary, factors contributing to STS have not been studied as extensively as have the consequences of exposure. However, clinical data support the importance of contributing phenomena. Research conducted with other populations can guide replication studies with crisis workers. For example, Pennebaker's (1990) research on self-disclosure and college students' experiences with stressful events demonstrates the potential value of such disclosure with crisis workers. A study of organizational contents shows the potential for much needed policy development. Finally, there is the opportunity to study the "natural history" of STS in professional groups whose daily job demands interact with all the contexts reviewed in this section.

Implications for Assessment and Diagnosis

Three assumptions related to assessment and diagnosis are that classification systems, as well as trained personnel, are available, and that those with symptoms can report them, and will do so. However, this is not the case. The first two assumptions are discussed elsewhere in this volume.

Undoubtedly, a major, if not the primary, barrier to identifying secondary stress in crisis workers is the "John Wayne syndrome" (Mitchell, 1985b). The macho, male cultural characteristic of most crisis workers does not permit them easily to assume "patient roles." Professional crisis workers perceive role conflict when they themselves must seek help. They feel out of control by admitting weakness and vulnerability and fear that their "manhood" may be questioned. Furthermore, most crisis workers consciously and unconsciously use psychic protective mechanisms such as denial, repression, and suppression, thereby deceiving themselves, as well as others.

A second barrier is that co-workers, and even family members, may not be able to detect secondary post-trauma symptoms as most post-trauma symptoms are subjective in nature. Family and friends may find the trauma symptoms difficult to understand since "they (the crisis workers) must have known what they were getting into." Traumatized crisis workers often engage in self-blame, second-guess their own decisions (what if?), and may become depressed (Mitchell & Bray, 1990).

Research with firefighters and other rescue workers (e.g., Hytten & Hasle, 1989) has shown that most crisis workers do have mild to moderate post-trauma symptoms, but, in most cases, their reactions do not strictly meet the DSM-III-R criteria for PTSD; that is, they do not have a diagnosable mental disorder. Available research with firefighters and paramedics suggests there may be a variety of relatively independent post-trauma stress "pathways," including fears about their personal safety, somatizing, depression, denial/numbing, and reexperiencing. These secondary post-trauma pathways may or may not coexist in the same crisis worker further complicating diagnoses (Beaton et al., 1992a, 1992b).

Finally, traumatized crisis workers are subjected to more stigma than are most victims. Their traumatization is troubling to their supervisors and co-workers since it reminds them that it could also happen to them (Janoff-Bulman, 1992). If there is a heavy reliance upon teamwork, identified co-worker trauma victims are watched carefully and with some suspicion, because crisis workers need to operate effectively and efficiently under suboptimal, and even chaotic, conditions. PTSD is known to interfere with communication, interpersonal functioning, and information processing (Van der Kolk, 1988). An ultimate threat to traumatized crisis workers and co-workers is "stress disability," which reportedly is on the increase (Mitchell & Bray, 1990).

Implications for Prevention and Treatment

The REAPER model proposed by Mitchell and Bray (1990) provides a comprehensive framework for preventive and treatment responses to crisis worker stress, including traumatic stress: *recognition* of the existence of stress and the reactions to it; *education* of line workers, administrators, family, and CISD team members as part of crisis worker training and continuing education; *acceptance*—a key to the acceptance process is the provision of empathy; *permission* to deal openly with feelings and to provide whatever level of psychological support is needed; *exploration*—identification of resources after debriefing short of counseling; *referral* for crisis workers who need more intensive psychological support .

The REAPER levels of prevention and treatment should all be codified via specific written work-site policies regarding trauma and trauma symptoms. One of the implications of a review of the crisis worker clinical literature is that cultural and organizational similarities and differences among crisis worker occupations need to be considered in developing preventive and post-traumatic interventions. Another implication of the literature review for crisis worker treatment programs is that nearly all crisis workers experience at least some post-trauma symptoms at some time during their careers.

Pennebaker's (1990) theory and research suggest that self-disclosure may be a powerful mediation between the exposure and prevention of PTSD. However, Janoff-Bulman (1992) recommends that a delicate balance between reexperiencing and denial be maintained in traumatized victims. Such a "balancing act" also appears to be important for crisis workers. Therefore, structured, brief and focused interventions such as defusing and debriefing would seem to be appropriate (Duckworth, 1991). Also, given the inherent mistrust of "outsiders" by most crisis worker occupational groups, the training and availability of co-worker "peer counselors" seem appropriate (Solomon, 1992). Post-trauma interventions that incorporate family networks are intriguing, but largely untested to date. In most cases, the use of psychoactive medications for on-duty crisis workers is contraindicated because common side effects such as sedation or grogginess might interfere with crisis reactions/duties.

The identification-with-the-victim phenomenon provides a rationale for mandatory debriefing, and is recommended following the death or serious injury of a co-worker (e.g., firefighter, police officer) in the line of duty (Mitchell & Bray, 1990). Likewise, the suicide of a fellow emergency worker is generally considered a critical incident, and automatically triggers a debriefing in some areas (King County, 1987).

In summary, there are numerous personal and organizational barriers to the assessment and diagnosis of STS in crisis workers. Occupational "norms" and macho attitudes discourage disclosure. One important implication is that written policies regarding trauma symptoms need to be developed and implemented, thus encouraging prevention and treatment. Policies are important since most crisis workers will be exposed to trauma and will experience some STS during their careers.

REFERENCES

Alexander, D., & Wells, A. (1991). Reactions of police officers to body-handling after a major disaster: A before and after comparison. *British Journal of Psychiatry, 159*, 547–555.

American Psychiatric Association. (1987). *Diagnostic and statistical manual of mental disorders* (3rd ed., rev.). Washington, D.C.

Armstrong, K., O'Callahan, W., & Marmar, C. (1991). Debriefing Red Cross disaster personnel: The multiple stressor debriefing model. *Journal of Traumatic Stress, 4*, 581–593.

Bard, M. (1976). Immediacy and authority in crisis management: The role of the police. In H. Parad, L. Parad & H. Resnik (Eds.), *Emergency and disaster management: A mental health source book*. Borvie, Md.: Charles Press.

Beaton, R., Egan, K., Nakagawa-Kogan, H., & Morrison, K. (1991). Self-reported symptoms of stress with temporomandibular disorders: Comparisons to healthy men and women. *Journal of Prosthetic Dentistry, 65*, 289–293.

Beaton, R., & Murphy, S. (1990). Sleep disturbance and post-traumatic stress symptoms in firefighters and paramedics. Presented at annual meeting of Society for Traumatic Stress Studies, New Orleans, La.

Beaton, R., & Murphy, S.A. (1991). Social support and relationship conflict in firefighters. Presented at the Third Bi-Annual Psychosocial Nursing Conference, University of Washington, Seattle.

Beaton, R., & Murphy, S.A. (1993). Sources of occupational stress among firefighters/EMTs and firefighter/paramedics and correlations with job-related outcomes. *Prehospital and Disaster Medicine, 8*, 140–150.

Beaton, R., Murphy, S., & Pike, K. (1992a). Stress symptom factors in firefighters/paramedics. Paper accepted for presentation at APA/NIOSH Conference on Occupational Stress, Washington, D.C.

Beaton, R., Murphy, S., & Pike, K. (1992b). Symptoms of stress in male and female firefighters/paramedics. Paper presented at APA/NIOSH Conference on Occupational Stress, Washington, D.C.

Besner, H., & Robinson, S. (1982). *Understanding and solving your police marriage problems*. Springfield, Ill.: Charles C. Thomas.

Blanchard, E., Hickling, E., & Taylor, A. (1991). The psychophysiology of motor vehicle accident related PTSD. *Journal of Biofeedback and Self-Regulation, 16*, 449–458.

Boulanger, G. (1985). PTSD: An old problem with a new name. In S. M. Sonnenberg, A. S. Bauk, & J. A. Talbott (Eds.), *The trauma of war: stress and recovery in Vietnam veterans* (pp. 13–29). Washington, D.C.: American Psychiatric Press.

Burge, S. (1988). PTSD in victims of rape. *Journal of Traumatic Stress, 1*, 193–210.

Burgess, A. W., & Holstrom, L. L. (1974). Rape trauma syndrome. *American Journal of Psychiatry, 131*(9), 981–986.

Burke, R., & Weir, T. (1977). Marital helping relationships: Moderators between stress and well-being. *Journal of Psychology, 95,* 121-130.

Burno, A., Kirilloff, L., & Close, J. (1983). Sources of stress and satisfaction in emergency nursing. *Journal of Emergency Nursing, 9,* 329-336.

Campbell, D., & Stanley, J. (1963). *Experimental and quasi-experimental design for research.* Chicago: Rand-McNally.

Corneil, W. (1989). *What else can you do? A look at humor in the fire service.* Unpublished manuscript.

Corneil, W. (1992). Prevalence and etiology of PTSDs in firefighters. Presented at the Symposium on Public Safety Personnel, First World Conference on Trauma and Tragedy, The Netherlands.

Cross, H. (1990). Social factors associated with PTSDs in Vietnam veterans. In C. Meek, (Ed.), *Post-traumatic stress disorder: Assessment, differential diagnosis and forensic evaluation.* Sarasota, Fla.: Professional Resource Exchange.

Derogatis, L. (1977). *SCL-90 Administration, scoring and procedures manual I—for the revised version and other instruments of the Psychophysiology Rating Scale Series.* Baltimore, Md.

DHHS. (1990). *Seventh special report to the U.S. Congress on alcohol and health.* Rockville, Md., ADAMHA.

Duckworth, D. (1991). Information requirements for crisis intervention after disaster work. *Stress Medicine, 7,* 19–24.

Dunning, C., & Silva, M. (1980). Disaster-induced trauma in rescue workers. *Victimology: An International Journal, 5,* 287–297.

Durham, T., McCammon, S., & Allison, E. (1985). The psychological impact of disaster on rescue personnel. *Annals of Emergency Medicine, 14,* 664–668.

Dutton, L., Smolensky, M., Lorimor, R., & Leach, C. (1978). Stress levels of ambulance paramedics and firefighters. *Journal of Occupational Medicine, 20,* 111–115.

Eckenrode, J., & Gore, S. (1990). Stress and coping at the boundary of work and family. In J. Eckenrode, & S. Gore (Eds.), *Stress between work and family* (pp. 1–16). New York: Plenum Press.

Elder, G. H., & Clipp, E. C. (1988). Wartime losses and social bonding: Influences across 40 years in men's lives. *Psychiatry, 51,* 177–198.

Erikson, K. T. (1976). *Everything in its path.* New York: Simon & Schuster.

Ersland, S., Weisaeth, C., & Sund, A. (1989). The stress upon rescuers involved in an oil rig disaster. *Acta Psychiatrica Scandinavica, 80,* 38–49.

Figley, C. R. (Ed.) (1978). *Stress disorders among Vietnam veterans: Theory, research and treatment.* New York: Brunner/Mazel.

Figley, C. R. (1985). Role of the family: Both a haven and a headache. In *Role stressors and support for emergency workers.* (DHHS Publication No. 85–1408, pp. 84–94). Washington D.C.: NIMH.

Fischer, V. (1991). Combat exposure and the etiology of post discharge substance abuse problems among Vietnam veterans. *Journal of Traumatic Stress, 4,* 251-278.

Frederick, C. (1986). Psychic trauma in victims of crime and terrorism. In G. R. Vandenbos, & B. Bryant (Eds.), *Cataclysms, crises, and catastrophes: Psychology in action.* Washington, D.C.: American Psychological Association.

Gersons, B. (1989). Patterns of PTSD among police officers following shooting incidents: A two dimensional model and treatment implications. *Journal of Traumatic Stress, 2,* 247–257.

Green, B.L., Grace, M.C., Lindy, J.D., Titchener, J.L., & Lindy, J.G. (1983). Levels of functional impairment following a civilian disaster. The Beverly Hills supper club fire. *Journal of Consulting and Clinical Psychology, 51,* 573–580.

Hammer, J., Mathews, J., Lyons, J., & Johnson, N. (1986). Occupational stress within the paramedic profession: An initial report of stress levels compared to hospital employees. *Annals of Emergency Medicine, 15,* 536–539.

Hartsough, D. (1985). Emergency organizational role. In *Role stressors and supports for emergency workers.* (DHHS Publication No. ADM 85–1408) Washington, D.C.:NIMH.

Hartsough, D., & Myers, D. (1985). *Disaster work and mental health: Prevention and control of stress among workers.* Washington, D.C.: NIMH, Center for Mental Health Studies of

Emergencies.
Herbison, R., Rando, T., & Plante, T. (1984). National EMS Burnout Survey. *Journal of Emergency Medical Services, 13*, 43–47.
Holmes, T. H., & Masuda, M. (1973). Life change and illness susceptibility. Separation and Depression, *American Association for the Advancement of Science*, 161-186.
Holmes, T., & Rahe, R. H. (1967). The social readjustment rating scale. *Journal of Psychosomatic Research, 11*, 215.
Horowitz, M. (1974). Stress response syndromes: Character style and brief psychotherapy. *Archives of General Psychiatry, 31*, 769–781.
Horowitz, M. (1976). *Stress response syndromes.* New York: Jason Aronson.
Horowitz, M., Wilner, N., & Alvarez, W. (1979). Impact of event scale. A measure of subjective stress. *Psychosomatic Medicine, 41.* 209–218.
House, J. (1981). *Work, stress, and social support.* Reading, Pa.: Addison-Wesley.
Hurrell, J., Pate, A., & Kheisnnet, R. (1984). *Stress among police officers.* Pub. No. 84–108. Washington, D.C.: NIOSH, U.S. Department of Health and Human Services.
Hytten, K., & Hasle, A. (1989). Firefighters: A study of stress and coping. *ACTA Psychiatry—Scandanavia Supplement, 355*, 50–55.
Jacobsen, D. E. (1986). Types and timing of social support. *Journal of Health and Social Behavior, 27*, 250–264.
Janoff-Bulman, R. (1992). *Shattered assumptions.* New York: Free Press.
Jones, D. (1985). Secondary disaster victims: The emotional effects of recovering and identifying human remains. *American Journal of Psychiatry, 142*, 303–307.
Jurkovich, G., Campbell, D., Padrta, J., & Luterman, A. (1987). Paramedic perception of elapsed field time. *Journal of Trauma, 27*, 892–897.
Kalimo, R., Lehtonen, A., Daleva, M., & Kuorinka, I. (1980). Psychological and biochemical strain in fireman's work. *Scandinavian Journal of Work and Environmental Health, 6*, 179–187.
Karasek, R., & Theorell, T. (1990). *Healthy work.* New York: Basic Books.
Keane, T., & Wolfe, J. (1990). Comorbidity in PTSD. An analysis of community and clinical studies. *Journal of Applied Social Psychology, 20*, 1776–1788.
Keller, K., & Koenig, W. (1989). Management of stress and prevention of burnout in emergency physicians. *Annals of Emergency Medicine, 18*, 42–47.
King County, Wash. (1987). Draft of critical incident stress debriefing policy for emergency workers.
Kuhn, T. (1970). *The structure of scientific revolutions.* Chicago: University of Chicago Press.
Kulka, R., Schlenger, W., Fairbank, R., Hough, B., Jordan, C., Marmar, C., & Weiss, D. (1990). *Trauma and the Vietnam War generation: Report of the national Vietnam veterans readjustment study.* New York: Brunner/Mazel.
Kuorinka, I., & Korkonen, O. (1981). Firefighters' reactions to alarm: An ECG and heart rate study. *Journal of Occupational Medicine, 23*, 762–766.
Laube, J. (1973). Psychological reactions in disaster. *Nursing Research, 22*, 343–347.
Lifton, R. (1967). *Death in life: Survivors of Hiroshima.* New York: Simon & Schuster.
Loo, R. (1986). Post-shooting stress reactions among police officers. *Journal of Human Stress, 12*, 27–31.
Markowitz, J., Gutterman, E., Link, B., & Rivera, M. (1987, Summer). Psychological response of firefighters to a chemical fire. *Journal of Human Stress*, pp. 84–93.
Martin, C., McKean, H., & Veltkamp, L. (1986). PTSD in police and working with victims: A pilot study. *Journal of Police Science and Administration, 14*, 98–101.
Maslach, C. (1978). The burn out syndrome and patient care. In *Psychosocial care of the dying.* New York: McGraw-Hill.
Matteson, M. T., & Ivancevich, J. M. (1987). *Controlling work stress* (pp. 26–31). San Francisco: Jossey-Bass.
McCafferty, F., Domingo, G., & McCafferty, E. (1990). PTSD in the police officer: Paradigm of occupational stress. *Southern Medical Journal, 83*, 543–547.
McCammon, S., Durham, T., Allison, E., & Williamson, D. (1988). Emergency workers' cognitive appraisal and coping with traumatic events. *Journal of Traumatic Stress, 1*, 353–372.
McFarlane, A. (1988a). The aetiology of PTSDs following a natural disaster. *British Journal*

of Psychiatry, 152, 116–121.

McFarlane, A. (1988b). Relationship between psychiatric impairment and a natural disaster: The role of distress. *Psychological Medicine, 18*, 129–139.

McFarlane, A. (1988c). The phenomenology of PTSDs following a natural disaster. *Journal of Nervous and Mental Disease, 176*, 22–29.

McFarlane, A. (1988d). The longitudinal course of post-traumatic morbidity. The range of outcomes and their predictors. *Journal of Nervous and Mental Disease, 176*, 30–39.

Mileti, D., Drabek, T., & Haas, J. (1975). *Human systems in extreme environment: A sociological perspective.* Boulder: University of Colorado, Institute of Behavioral Science.

Milham, S. (1983) *Occupational mortality in Washington State, 1950–1979.* DHHS Publication No. 83–116. Washington D.C. (U.S. Department of Health and Human Services).

Mitchell, J. (1985a). Helping the helper. *Proceedings from a workshop: Role stressors and supports for emergency workers* (pp. 105–118). Rockville, Md.: National Institute of Mental Health.

Mitchell, J. (1985b, January). When disaster strikes... The critical incident stress debriefing process. *Journal of Emergency Medical Service*, pp. 36-39.

Mitchell, J., & Bray, G. (1990). *Emergency services stress.* Englewood Cliffs, N.J.: Prentice-Hall.

Murphy, S. A. (1986). Health and recovery status of victims one and three years following a natural disaster. *Trauma and its wake: Vol. 2. Traumatic stress theory, research, and intervention.* New York: Brunner/Mazel.

Murphy, S. A. (1991). Human responses to catastrophe. *Annual Review of Nursing Research, 9*, 57–76.

Murphy, S. A., & Beaton, R. (1990). Gender differences in perceived firefighter stress: Policy implications. Presented at the annual meeting of International Society for Traumatic Stress Studies, New Orleans, La.

Murphy, S. A., & Beaton, R. (1991). Counteracting effects of trauma in everyday life: Leisure patterns among firefighters. Presented at the Annual Meeting of the Society for Traumatic Stress Studies, Washington, D.C.

Myles, G., Levine, J., Ramsden, V., & Swanson, R. (1990). The impact of providing help: Emergency workers and cardiopulmonary resuscitation attempts. *Journal of Traumatic Stress, 3*, 305–313.

National Fire Protection Agency. (1988). *Annual report of firefighters deaths and injuries.* Quincy, Mass.: Author.

Penk, W., & Allen, I. (1991). Clinical assessment of (PTSD) among American minorities who served in Vietnam. *Journal of Traumatic Stress, 4*, 41–66.

Pennebaker, J. (1990). *Opening up: The healing power of confiding in others.* New York: Morrow.

Pitman, R., Orr, S., Forgue, D., de Jong, J., & Claiborn, J. (1987). Psychophysiologic assessment of PTSD imagery in Vietnam combat veterans. *Archives of General Psychiatry, 44*, 970–975.

Rahe, R. (1977). Epidemiologic studies of life change and illness. In Lipowski, Z., Lipsitt, D. & Whybrow, P. (Eds.), *Psychosomatic medicine.* New York: Oxford University Press.

Raphael, B. (1986). *When disaster strikes.* New York: Basic Books.

Raphael, B., Singh, B., & Bradbury, L. (1986). Disaster: The helper's perspective. In R. Moos (Ed.), *Coping with life crisis: An integrated approach.* New York: Plenum Press.

Raphael, B., Singh, B., Bradbury, L., & Lambert, F. (1983–1984). Who helps the helpers: The effects of a disaster on the rescue workers. *Omega, 14*, 9–20.

Robinson, R. (1986). *Health and stress in ambulance services.* Melbourne, Australia: Social Biology Resources Centre.

Sanner, P. (1983). Stress reactions among participants in non casualty simulations. *Annals of Emergency Medicine, 12*, 426–428.

Sarason, I., Levine, H., & Sarason, B. (1982). Assessing the impact of life changes. In T. Millon, C. Green, & R. Meaghen (Eds.), *Handbook of clinical health psychology.* New York: Plenum Press.

Shealy, C. (1984, Fall/Winter). Total life stress and symptomatology. *Journal of Holistic Medicine, 6*, 112–1129.

Solomon, R. (1992). *Critical incident stress debriefing in law enforcement.* In preparation.

Solomon, R., & Horn, J. (1986). Post-shooting traumatic reactions: A pilot study. In J. Reise & H. Goldstein, (Eds.), *Psychological services for law enforcement* (pp. 383–393). Washington, D.C.: U.S. Government Printing Office.

Stratton, J., Parker, D., & Snabble, J. (1984). Post-traumatic stress: Study of police officers involved in shooting. *Psychological Reports, 55,* 127–131.

Stuhlmiller, C. M. (1991). An interpretative study of appraisal and coping of rescue workers in an earthquake disaster: The Cypress collapse. Unpublished doctoral dissertation, University of California at San Francisco.

Tasto, D., Colligan, M., Skjei, E., & Polly, S. (1978). *Health consequences of shiftwork.* DHEN (NIOSH) Publication No. 78-154, Washington D.C.

Taylor, A. J. W., & Fraser, A. G. (1982). The stress of post-disaster body handling and victim identification work. *Journal of Human Stress, 8,* 4–12.

Vachon, M. (1976). Grief and bereavement following the death of a spouse. *Canadian Psychiatric Association Journal, 21,* 35–44.

Van der Kolk, B. (1988). The trauma spectrum: The interaction of biological and social events in the genesis of the trauma response. *Journal of Traumatic Stress, 1,* 273–290.

Wilkinson, C. (1983). Aftermath of a disaster: The collapse of the Hyatt Regency Hotel skywalks. *American Journal of Psychiatry, 140,* 1134–1139.

Wilkinson, C., & Vera, E. (1985). The management and treatment with disaster victims. *Psychiatric Annals, 15*(3), 174–184.

4

Working with People with PTSD: Research Implications

MARY ANN DUTTON and FRANCINE L. RUBINSTEIN

Trauma workers are professionals and paraprofessionals trained to work with persons in the aftermath of traumatic events. A traumatic stressor is defined in diagnostic terms as "when a person experienced, witnessed, or was confronted with an event or events that involved actual or threatened death or serious injury or a threat to the physical integrity of self or others" (American Psychiatric Association, p. 427). Green (1990) described the dimensions of traumatic stress as including being the recipient of a threat to one's life or bodily integrity, of severe physical injury, or of intentional injury or harm; being exposed to the grotesque; hearing of the violent or sudden loss of a loved one; witnessing or learning of violence to a loved one; learning of one's exposure or that of a loved one to a noxious agent; and causing death or severe harm to another.

Examples of trauma may include criminal victimization (e.g., sexual

---

Editor's Note: Similar to Chapter 3, this chapter focuses on the available literature on professionals who may suffer emotionally as a result of their work with people who were exposed to highly stressful events. In this chapter, however, Dutton and Rubinstein go beyond the emergency workers who work with people immediately after their exposure to traumatic events to focus on lawyers, victim advocates, judges, physicians, researchers, and mental health workers, among others. They offer a theoretical model to help account for and predict the emotional reactions, the compassion stress and compassion fatigue, of professionals in service to the traumatized.

battery, domestic violence, homicide of a family member); the suicide of a family member or friend; the Holocaust; a natural disaster (e.g., earthquake, hurricane); accidents (e.g., nuclear plant explosion, plane crash, serious car accident); combat; kidnapping or being held hostage (e.g., being held prisoner of war or hostage by terrorists, child snatching); and social violence (e.g., riots, political terrorism).

Trauma workers are persons who work directly with or have direct exposure to trauma victims, and include mental health professionals, lawyers, victim advocates, caseworkers, judges, physicians, and applied researchers, among others. Crisis workers are not included here since Chapter 3 addressed those issues separately.

The purpose of this chapter is to review the literature so as to develop an understanding of the trauma worker's secondary traumatic stress (STS) reactions, that is, the psychological effects of exposure to traumatic events through contact with survivors of trauma, as well as with perpetrators of traumatic events on others (e.g., rapist, batterer, war criminal). (We use the term *survivor* to refer to persons who have survived traumatic experiences. Survivors also have been victims, and we do not mean to minimize or negate their experiences. The use of survivor is intended to place the emphasis on the resolution and healing, rather than on the pain and suffering.) Further, this chapter presents a theoretical framework for understanding STS reactions and discusses implications for assessment, intervention, and prevention.

Secondary traumatic stress (STS) reaction is a term that has been used to describe the response by family members and friends of trauma survivors, as well as the effect of institutional treatment of victims/survivors following a catastrophic event (Stark & Flitcraft, 1988; Williams, 1984). However, this chapter focuses specifically on the impact on trauma workers of their contact with traumatic events and their sequelae through their work with persons directly involved with traumatic experiences.

SECONDARY TRAUMATIC STRESS REACTION

Description

Discussion of STS reactions or vicarious victimization among trauma workers is just beginning to appear in the literature (Courtois, 1988; McCann & Pearlman, 1990a, 1990b), but there is as yet no reported empirical evidence documenting its prevalence. Further, although reports of professional distress have appeared in the literature

(Thoreson, Budd, & Krauskopf, 1987), the treatment of this issue has been largely theoretical or anecdotal (Thoreson, Miller, & Kraukopf, 1989). Even less attention has been paid to the impact on lawyers, judges, and researchers working with trauma survivors.

The terms *vicarious victimization* (McCann & Pearlman, 1990b), *traumatic countertransference* (Herman, 1992a), and *contact victimization* (Courtois, 1988) have been used to describe reactions similar to STS. *Burnout, distressed psychologist,* and *countertransference* also describe phenomena that include features of STS reactions. However, these alternative concepts fail adequately to address their specific aspects (McCann & Pearlman, 1990b). Nonetheless, recognition of these phenomena may have been the precursor to appreciation of the more specific effect of trauma work on professional and paraprofessional workers.

Secondary traumatic stress reactions can be considered inevitable in this population (Herman, 1992a), and may occur regardless of race, gender, age, or level of training (Edelwich & Brodsky, 1980). There is a wide array of post-traumatic reactions that follow from direct exposure to traumatic or catastrophic events (Courtois, 1988; Dutton, 1992; Foy, 1992; Herman, 1992a, 1992b; Horowitz, 1986; Van der Kolk, 1987). A subgrouping of these post-traumatic reactions has been codified as post-traumatic stress disorder (PTSD) (APA, 1987), which includes intrusion (e.g., flashbacks, nightmares), avoidance (e.g., psychic numbing, amnesia), and arousal (e.g., angry outbursts, difficulty concentrating) symptoms. Additional diagnoses were considered but were not included in the DSM-IV to account for other forms of post-traumatic reaction (see Herman, 1992a, for a discussion of complex PTSD) that more adequately account for symptomatic, characterological, and increased vulnerability aspects of chronic exposure to trauma (Herman, 1992b).

Figley, in Chapter 1 of this volume, argues that trauma workers' responses to trauma should be distinguished as secondary post-traumatic reactions versus secondary post-traumatic disorders, based on the abnormality of the recovery process. The utility of pathologizing individuals' post-traumatic stress reactions of any sort is open to question. "Abnormal" or otherwise prolonged recovery from STS reactions among trauma workers, as with direct victims/survivors of traumatic events, may simply reflect features of complex PTSD referred to above. Further, the classification of some post-traumatic reactions as abnormal appears premature given the paucity of evidence concerning the course and nature of these reactions among persons in the general population. Additionally, the impact on persons with preexisting biological or social vulnerability (prior trauma, disabilities, low socioeconomic status) must be considered. Also, this may account for a more prolonged pattern of healing than might otherwise be expected.

Categories of Secondary Traumatic Stress Reaction

There is an array of reactions that trauma workers may experience in their work with trauma victims/survivors. As a means of categorization, STS reactions are described in three areas: as indicators of psychological distress or dysfunction, as changes in cognitive schema, and as relational disturbances. Dutton (1992) discussed this schema for delineating the post-traumatic reactions of battered women, for example.

Indicators of Psychological Distress or Dysfunction
One category of STS resulting from trauma work is an indication of psychological distress or dysfunction. Indicators may include:

1. Distressing emotions (Courtois, 1988; McCann & Pearlman, 1990b; Scurfield, 1985), including sadness or grief, depression, anxiety, dread and horror, fear, rage, or shame.
2. Intrusive imagery by the trauma worker of the client's traumatic material (Courtois, 1988; Herman, 1992a; McCann & Pearlman, 1990b), such as nightmares, flooding, and flashbacks of images generated during and following the client's recounting of traumatic events.
3. Numbing or avoidance of efforts to elicit or work with traumatic material from the client, including dissociation (Courtois, 1988; Herman, 1992b; McCann & Pearlman, 1990b; Silver, 1986).
4. Somatic complaints (Figley, 1986; Herman, 1992b) including sleep difficulty, headaches, gastrointestinal distress, and heart palpitations.
5. Addictive or compulsive behaviors, including substance abuse, workaholism (Boylin & Briggie, 1987), and compulsive eating.
6 Physiological arousal (McCann & Pearlman, 1990b; Van der Kolk, 1987).
7. Impairment of day-to-day functioning in social and personal roles, such as missed or canceled appointments; decreased use of supervision or cotherapy (Boylin & Briggie, 1987); chronic lateness; a decreased ability to engage in self-care behaviors, including personal therapy; and feelings of isolation, alienation, or lack of appreciation (Boylin & Briggie, 1987).

Cognitive Shifts

A second category of STS reactions experienced by the trauma workers refers to shifts in the beliefs, expectations, and assumptions that therapists hold (Janoff-Bulman, 1992; McCann & Pearlman, 1990b). McCann and Pearlman describe shifts in therapists' cognitive schemata along dimensions of dependency/trust (e.g., chronic suspicion about others); safety (e.g., heightened sense of vulnerability); power (e.g., extreme sense of helplessness or exaggerated sense of control over others or situations); independence (e.g., loss of personal control and freedom); esteem (e.g., bitterness or cynicism about others); intimacy (e.g., alienation); and frame of reference (e.g., victim blame and disorientation).

Courtois (1988) also discussed several therapist reactions, including beginning to see everyone as a victim of something, thus trivializing the experiences of others. She further described the polarized thinking reflected by one's viewing the client as "victim or survivor," thus failing to recognize both aspects of her or his experience. Viewing clients solely as victims discounts their survival skills and their use of them. Alternatively, seeing the client only as a survivor fails to recognize the price paid for surviving or the suffering endured (Courtois, 1988).

"Witness guilt" (Herman, 1992a) or "clinician guilt" (Silver, 1986), similar to bystander guilt, may plague the trauma worker who was not directly traumatized. The worker must deal with the reality that appropriate professional assistance may have been unavailable to or withheld from the direct victim of trauma. In response, the worker may feel guilty for enjoying life when she or he sees the struggle of a survivor. The novice trauma worker may feel especially guilty when the survivor reexperiences the trauma (Herman, 1992a) through necessary interview or therapeutic procedures. It is imperative, therefore, that trauma workers be attentive to the distinction between reasonable therapeutic efforts toward healing and the retraumatization that may occur in their work with victims/survivors.

Herman (1992a) described a type of victim blame that may result when a trauma worker begins to feel victimized by his or her clients whom he or she sees as threatening, manipulative, or exploitative. In order to obviate such feelings, it is important for the worker to take responsibility for herself or himself, for example, by setting appropriate limits or relinquishing responsibility for a client's unwelcome actions toward the therapist.

A related phenomenon, distorting analytic concepts, may be used by therapists to rationalize that "you get what you deserve" (Silver, 1986, p. 214). For example, failing to recognize traumatic responses (e.g., PTSD, multiple personality disorder) that result directly from exposure to trauma and attributing the survivor client's behavior to other factors (e.g., borderline personality disorder) may be the mental health professional's attempt to distance herself or himself from difficult material. Another version of this reaction is for the trauma worker to fail to attend to the "extraordinary evil of victimization," that is, the source of the trauma itself, thus preventing the maintenance of a perspective that is broader than the unique individuality of the client (Danieli, 1988). Maintaining the focus solely on the individual and avoiding attention to the traumatic experiences lead to pathologizing the survivor's reaction to trauma instead of recognizing the reaction as normal, given the circumstances.

Relational Disturbances

Secondary exposure to trauma may have an impact on trauma workers' relationships, both personal and professional. Personal relationships may suffer (Boylin & Briggie, 1987) due to increased stress or difficulty with trust and intimacy. Work with trauma survivors, especially when the traumatic event involves exploitation, abuse, or intentional violence, may increase trauma workers' sensitivity to those same dynamics in their personal relationships.

Another impact relates to the trauma worker's relationship with his or her survivor client. A commonly discussed relationship dynamic is the worker's response to the survivor, which can be either overidentification or detachment (Courtois, 1988).

The trauma worker's detachment from the survivor may result from identification with the offender, where the worker looks for culpable behaviors in the survivor (e.g., "victim blaming") and has difficulty with the victim's anger toward the offender (Herman, 1988). Distancing from the client "encourages continuation of the control mechanism of trauma survivors by, in effect, convincing them that the trauma is not over" (Silver, 1986, p. 216). It is easier to exercise authoritarian controlling behavior, even in the guise of professionalism, from a detached stance. The relatively high risk of sexual misconduct (Holroyd & Brodsky, 1977) and other boundary violations among professionals, especially in work with incest survivors (Courtois, 1988), may be more likely with therapists who detach from their own empathic emotional responses to their clients' traumatic material.

Distancing from the client may involve judging, labeling, or pathologizing the traumatic reaction (e.g., by utilizing personality disorder diagnoses), which creates the illusion that the client's reaction to the traumatic event is in some way different from that of a "normal" individual. Other forms of detachment include adopting a personal and emotional distance from the client (e.g., dissociating during appointments), being chronically late for or frequently canceling appointments, or allowing frequent interruptions during appointments. Attorneys may be particularly vulnerable to this approach since their training may not typically focus on establishing emotional contacts with their clients or on dealing with their own emotional reactions to clients.

Distancing or excessively detaching emotionally from the survivor client may enable the trauma worker to deal with her or his feelings of vulnerability or of being overwhelmed by the traumatic material by blocking out such emotional reactions. However, it leaves the client survivor again emotionally isolated and alone, detached even from those who are intent on helping. The detached trauma worker may be "intimidated by fears that the clinical investigation will trigger explosive affects in the patients, or, worse, stir up similar ones in [himself or herself]" (Titchener, 1986), and thus tread ever so lightly in this work with the traumatized individual when, especially for the psychotherapist, "a persistent, courageous advance toward the traumatic core is desperately needed" (p. 17).

Distancing as therapists' secondary response to trauma may also take the form of withdrawal from family, friends, or colleagues, perhaps out of the belief that no one could understand their distressed response to their work. In the workplace, the emotional isolation of trauma workers in their experience of such difficult and painful work contributes to the problems described here.

A different relational problem is overidentification with the survivor client to the point that the trauma worker is paralyzed by his or her reactions to the client's traumatic experience, or, alternatively, takes excessive responsibility for the client's life, perhaps in an attempt to gain control over an overwhelming situation. Overidentification with the survivor involves being "overwhelmed by feelings of helplessness and despair or with rage against the offender" that the survivor may or may not share (Herman, 1988, p. 55). A trauma worker who is so overwrought by the traumatic material at best is ineffectual and at worst potentially places the survivor client in a position of taking care of the helper. This caretaking may involve the client's withholding of details about the trauma in order to "protect" the worker.

The detrimental implications of this for psychotherapy, litigation, or research are obvious. With the overidentified psychotherapist, the survivor likely has neither safety nor the implicit permission to experience the full impact of his or her traumatic experience, since to do so may be overwhelming for the therapist, whose response then may be to rescue, derail, or otherwise impede the therapeutic process.

THEORETICAL MODEL FOR SECONDARY TRAUMATIC STRESS REACTIONS

A theoretical model is presented for explaining STS reactions among trauma workers. The model includes the following: (1) the traumatic event(s) to which the trauma worker had been exposed, (2) the trauma worker's PTS reactions, (3) the trauma worker's coping strategies for responding to the traumatic situation and to its psychological sequelae, and (4) the personal (e.g., characteristics of the trauma worker) and environmental (e.g., characteristics of the environment in which secondary exposure to the traumatic event occurred and of the recovery environment) mediators of STS reactions.

Trauma Workers' Exposure to Trauma

Following are a few typical examples of the circumstances that surround trauma workers in their involvement with their clients. However, it is not just those whose work is dominated by trauma who are affected, but also those who encounter even one experience in which they are exposed to the serious or devastating aftermath of traumatic events.

Common Scenarios

• A private-practice psychologist carries a caseload of 25 to 30 clients per week. The majority of his clients are female, and most of them have reported a history of physical or sexual abuse as a child or adolescent, rape, and/or domestic violence. Four clients are diagnosed with multiple personality disorder associated with severe early childhood abuse. Some of the alter personalities of these clients are very young and, psychologically, deeply wounded. Other alters are angry and potentially dangerous to others, including the therapist. This is not an uncommon scenario, nor is it extreme.

• Several lawyers work in a specialized Sexual Battery Unit of a state attorney's office. Each lawyer may handle numerous cases, each of which involves some form of sexual victimization of the client. The sexual batteries described include the rape of a three-year-old girl by her stepfather, in which she contracted a sexually transmitted disease; gang rape by four boys of a 16-year-old girl walking home from school; an abduction of an older woman from a grocery store parking lot who was then raped, mutilated, physically assaulted, and forced to consume drugs—all of which nearly killed her and left her with permanent physical and neurological impairment; sexual abuse of 25 children at a day-care center; and the oral, anal, and vaginal rapes and beatings at gunpoint of a woman, her husband, and their three children, following forced entry into their

home by the perpetrator while they slept. These and far more gruesome examples represent the day-to-day experience of these prosecutors.

• A psychotherapist at a Veterans Administration (VA) hospital
has 10 Vietnam combat veterans and eight Persian Gulf veterans
on her caseload. These men and women describe witnessing the
deaths and mutilations of their buddies; participating in massacres
of village people; attempting to cope with active-duty notices that
allowed 72 hours or less in which to make plans for child care,
financial support for families, and other arrangements before leaving for the Persian Gulf; and experiencing combat wounds, followed by inadequate medical attention that resulted in amputa-
tion, blindness, and other permanent disabilities. These reports of
neglect and despair are common with clients at VA hospitals and
clinics.

• A doctoral psychology student participates in a 20-hour a week
clinical practicum where she manages a caseload of six clients and
conducts a new intake evaluation each week. All of her clients are
victims/survivors of domestic violence, and some also report histories of rape and childhood physical or sexual abuse. By the end of
her 11-month placement, she has participated in more than 400
hours of clinical evaluations and interventions with clients who
have been severely traumatized, and consequently, she has been
exposed to numerous vivid stories of horror and violence. Infrequent,
but predictable, threats from battering husbands and boyfriends
expand the present danger from the client to the therapist. In addition to the psychotherapy, the therapist's testimony in court on
behalf of a battered woman client requires her to have direct contact with an abusive man who is at risk of losing his partner, children, property, job, and freedom. The man may perceive the therapist, along with the prosecutor or the woman's attorney, the jury,
and the judge, as agents in bringing about those losses, and so may
become threatening.

• A defense attorney is defending a young woman who killed her
father after years of his sexual abuse of her, his physical abuse of
her mother, and his psychological terrorism in the home through
the use of weapons or other threats. In the course of preparing a
defense, the lawyer must examine, in minute detail, the facts of the
physical and sexual abuse experienced by both the daughter and

her mother. The attorney must sit with the defendant and her mother as they recount the abusive incidents, and reexperience the trauma while doing so. The attorney may observe her reactions by the client that include emotional discomfort, dissociation, vomiting, crying, and revivification. Because of the intense, emotional nature of the information-gathering process, the attorney may be required to respond to the client's psychological defenses, including difficulty in concentrating, memory lapses, and refusal to provide needed details.

• A social worker at a forensic hospital works with incarcerated violent offenders. In the course of his work, he interviews offenders about their criminal offenses (e.g., rapes, sexually related homicides, serial killings, torturing assaults); reviews court records, including survivor interviews or evaluations and interviews with the victims' family members; reviews photographs or documents describing injuries or dead bodies and other material evidence related to the cases; and has regular contact with the offenders, who may report plans for continuing such behavior if released.

Unique Features of Exposure for Trauma Workers
The unique features of trauma workers' exposure to trauma by working with its victims/survivors or perpetrators are important in understanding their response to it. Unlike crisis workers (e.g., emergency room workers, fire rescue and disaster teams, crisis hotline workers), whose response is to the immediate effects of a catastrophic event on the survivor, trauma workers are faced with the prolonged, and often compounded, aftermath of the trauma. Thus the trauma worker's exposure to trauma has far more complex ramifications than does exposure to the traumatic event itself.

Working with the aftermath of trauma involves more than just exposure to the traumatic event (e.g., through the recounting of the event by the client and others, the client's in vivo reexperiencing of the event or revivification in the trauma worker's presence, and examining photographs of the physical injuries that followed a traumatic event). It also involves exposure to the survivor's reaction to the traumatic event (e.g., intense emotional pain, fear, rage, despair, hopelessness). In addition, there is exposure to the institutional and other social responses to the traumatized individual that revictimize her or him and over which the trauma worker may have little control (e.g., incarceration of a battered woman and separation from her children following a police call to her home in response to a complaint of domestic violence against her, unfounded sexual abuse allegations that result in returning a child to his or her alleged abuser, disregard by guards of sexual battery of refugee women held in detention while awaiting deportation).

In addition to addressing the client's experiences, Danieli (1985) suggests that the source of reaction for therapists dealing with a client's victimization is the nature of the victimization itself. Through exposure to the concept of "trauma," therapists not only become aware of their clients' pain, but also come to the realization that a particular traumatic event can occur; has occurred, perhaps repeatedly; and may recur. It is for these reasons that it is possible for a therapist, attorney, or other trauma worker exposed to the graphic details of a traumatic event, even if only once, to become traumatized. Trauma workers are further challenged with dealing simultaneously with the aftermath of prior traumatic events and the threat of continuing tragedy, in the case of domestic violence, childhood sexual or physical abuse, or hate-crime violence. The traumatized client and his or her trauma worker may both be at risk of harm from an angry batterer, a sex offender, a perpetrator of a random hate crime, or angry rioters.

Since the trauma worker's task is often quite complex, the results can be mixed and slow to appear. Any legal case requires extensive amounts of time to be spent in preparation for trial. Psychotherapy with traumatized persons can mandate long-term care, especially if the traumatic events (e.g., incest, hostage taking, domestic violence) themselves were prolonged. Intervention with violent offenders is typically long term and may involve high levels of recidivism. Consequently, the trauma worker is exposed to traumatic events repeatedly and over a significant period of time.

Typically, the goal of the crisis worker is to contain the immediate effects of trauma and to stabilize the survivor both medically and psychologically. However, a significant aspect of the task of a psychotherapist or lawyer is deliberately to facilitate recall of the traumatic event and the survivor's response in order to obtain facts on which to base legal action (e.g., lawyer, advocate, or expert witness) or to enable the therapist to deal with intrusive nightmares or other post-traumatic reactions.

The trauma worker may be in a position to learn extensive details about trauma that typically are not available from anyone other than the survivor and the perpetrator (e.g., rape, incest). When the client's own psychological coping strategies lead her or him to avoid remembering the traumatic experience(s) (e.g., psychogenic amnesia), talking or thinking about it, or encountering situations that require her or him to do so, the worker's efforts to recreate the traumatic event may be viewed by the survivor as revictimization. Without effective therapeutic efforts to deal with the psychological impact (e.g., emotional distress, despair or hopelessness, self-mutilation, or suicidal behaviors) of facilitating the memory of these traumatic events in order to (re)empower the survivor out of the trauma, she or he may be inadvertently and repeatedly revictimized by the trauma worker, who presumably is in a position to help.

The trauma worker's task requires extensive knowledge of the client's life beyond that of experiencing the traumatic event alone. The complex assignment to integrate knowledge of the client's life history, premorbid (i.e., prior to the onset of current or prior traumatic event) level of functioning, tangible and social support resources, other stressors in the client's life, and personal strengths with information about the traumatic event and the client's response to it places considerable demands on the trauma worker.

Conceptual Issues

Traumatic events vary considerably, and this variation may hold important implications for the understanding of the nature, severity, duration, and amenability to intervention for not only the primary, but also the secondary, post-traumatic reactions. Stark and Flitcraft (1988) suggested that the ongoing nature of domestic violence challenges the traumatization model's applicability for battered women. Larsen (1992) proposed a model for reconceptualizing post-traumatic effects in battered women that accounted for dimensions of domestic violence characteristic of some, but not all, other forms of trauma. These include (1) intentionality, (2) secrecy, and (3) chronicity. Although initially described for the battered woman, they are also relevant for the trauma worker.

Other dimensions of the traumatic experience that are suggested as useful for the understanding of both primary and secondary traumatic stress reactions include the following.

1. Level of unpredictability of traumatic events (e.g., trauma worker's expectation of encountering traumatic material).
2. Source of traumatic experience (e.g., personal behavior of client toward trauma worker versus exposure to traumatic photographs or written material).
3. Relationship with perpetrator (e.g., client versus stranger).
4. Extent to which the trauma involved the violation of assumptions about the world or others (e.g., traumatic event by someone who was expected to be safe versus someone expected to be unsafe).

5. Level of death threat involved.
6. Level of professional development (e.g., graduate student or intern verses experienced professional) or developmental age of the trauma worker (e.g., adolescent versus older adult volunteer at children's shelter) at the time of exposure to traumatic events.
7. Whether any form of threat continues in the present.
8. Presence of "mind control" (e.g., manipulative threats to trauma worker) as a component of the traumatic experience.
9. Whether the trauma worker experienced the exposure to trauma individually (e.g., solo practitioner) or as part of a group (e.g., specialized sex crimes unit involving more than one attorney).
10. Whether the trauma worker was a witness to or had knowledge of a traumatic event that happened to someone else (e.g., evaluation interview) or was a direct survivor (e.g., assaulted by angry client).
11. Level of intimacy of traumatic experience (e.g., sexual versus nonsexual).

Research is needed to consider STS reactions as a function of the nature and "dose" of exposure to traumatic events. Considerable work is required to delineate the potential implications for direct and secondary victims/survivors of the variations in traumatic events described above.

Coping Strategies

Recognizing the trauma worker's efforts to cope with being exposed to trauma, both through hearing about the traumatic events and by more direct exposure (e.g., threats by angry family members, observing horrifying photographs or physical evidence), is an important component in understanding trauma workers' STS reactions. Coping responses have been found to relate to levels of stress (Antonovsky, 1990). Trauma workers' coping responses, which themselves are influenced by the workers' personal (e.g., abuse) histories, thus are hypothesized to influence the development and course of STS reactions. Trauma workers who have learned ways to cope with difficult personal issues (e.g., memory of traumatic events, grief experience surrounding loss) may find these strategies useful for managing the STS reactions associated with their work involving trauma victims as well.

Trauma workers' coping responses may be considered in two categories: personal and professional. Personal strategies might include taking time for play in addition to work, developing a network of emotionally supportive personal relationships, taking time for self-exploration and attending to personal needs, and using personal therapy as a means of coping with the effects of working with trauma. Professional strategies refer to using peer supervision and consultation, working in a professional setting with others rather than in isolation, and diversifying one's professional practice. Empirical evidence is required to test the effectiveness of these coping strategies singly and in combination.

Mediating Factors

Both individual and environmental factors are hypothesized to mediate trauma workers' reactions to indirect exposure to traumatic events via their clients. These are discussed in the following.

Individual Factors
Individual mediating factors may include (1) inner strengths or resources (e.g., high self-esteem; extensive professional experience, education, or training); (2) personal or professional vulnerabilities (e.g., emotional insecurity, loneliness, prior traumatization, inexperience or lack of adequate education or training); (3) "countertransference" or personal/emotional reactions to the survivor, separate from STS reactions (e.g., identification with client as youngest child in family, as a single mother or father, or as another midwesterner living in an eastern city; personal attraction to client or feelings of repulsion based on appearance, age, or ethnicity); and (4) general satisfaction or dissatisfaction with professional and personal life (e.g., satisfaction with profession as a lawyer or psychologist, dissatisfaction with marital relationship).

Hellman, Morrison, and Abramowitz (1987) found variables measuring experience to predict level of work-related stress for psychotherapists after social desirability, gender, and four therapeutic-style factors were accounted for. In a similar study, Rodolfa, Kraft, and Reilley (1988) found less experience to be related to greater stress among professionals and trainees.

Environmental Factors
Environmental factors hypothesized to mediate trauma workers' STS reactions include (1) personal and professional social support (e.g., supportive professional network, strong friendship or family relationships); (2) other stressors in the trauma worker's life (e.g., divorce; death in family; financial, legal, or medical difficulties); (3) institutional or professional response to trauma worker (e.g., being ridiculed or labeled as pathological by other professionals for being affected by clients' trauma, knowledge of institutional response to client's trauma or traumatic

events); and (4) the social, political, and economic context in which the professionals work and live.

Hellman, Morrison, and Abramowitz (1986) derived a five-factor solution accounting for 89% of the variance in work-related stresses for psychotherapists based on work-related areas: therapeutic relationship, scheduling difficulties, professional doubt, work overinvolvement, and personal depletion. These authors also derived a five-factor solution predicting 84% of the variance in work-related stresses based on stressful patient behaviors: negative affect, resistances, psychopathological symptoms, suicidal threats, and passive-aggressive behaviors. Similar results were found by Deutsch (1984) for predicting self-reported stress through stressful client behaviors: suicidal statements, expression of anger toward the therapist, severe depression, clients' lack of motivation, and premature termination.

Cultural and social factors (e.g., gender, ethnicity, cultural differences) impact on how emotions are expressed (Brown & Root, 1990; Gibbs, 1984). Likewise, these factors influence the way in which trauma workers respond emotionally to their work with victims/survivors. Knowledge of the trauma worker's cultural and social norms for acknowledging and expressing emotion is central to understanding his or her response to trauma work. The influence of the social definition of gender, ethnicity, culture, and age, for example, cannot be overlooked in the study of trauma workers' STS responses.

IMPLICATIONS

This section briefly discusses the implications of STS reactions for assessment and diagnosis, intervention, and prevention.

Assessment and Diagnosis

For the protection of both trauma victims/survivors and trauma workers, the detection of STS is a priority whenever trauma workers are routinely exposed to traumatic events as part of their work (e.g., workers in battered-women's shelters, trauma therapists, special prosecutors or judges dealing with domestic violence or sexual abuse). Detection could be facilitated through increased training (e.g., graduate or law school, continuing professional education, regular debriefing sermons, in-service training) so that trauma workers themselves can detect indicators of STS in an early stage. Normalizing the trauma workers' secondary traumatic reactions (which, of course, may vary widely) as inevitable creates a work or training environment in which detection can be less stigmatized and thus facilitated through collegial interactions.

Procedures for the formal assessment and diagnosis of STS reactions require development. Currently, methods for assessing PTSD (see Dutton, 1992, and Foy, 1992, for a discussion of assessment methods) may serve as useful for this purpose until more specific procedures for the assessment of STS reactions of trauma workers (e.g., behavior or symptom checklists, structured interviews) are further developed. Further discussion is needed regarding the threshold of severity of secondary traumatic reactions in diagnostic prractices and the usefulness of such distinctions (see Chapter 1 of this volume).

Intervention

With notable exception (McCann & Pearlman, 1990b), models of intervention with STS among trauma workers have yet to be widely developed, although greater discussion has taked place with regard to burnout (Lyall, 1989; Rawnsley, 1989; Scott & Haw, 1986) and distressed psychologists (Thorenson, Miller, & Krauskopf, 1989), from which directions for intervention may be adapted.

Strategies for responding to STS reactions may be grouped into three areas: work-related strategies, informal strategies, and personal strategies. Work-related strategies may include adjusting one's caseload to include a diversity of clients, thus reducing one's amount of contact with severely traumatized clients. Alternatively, diversifying one's work-related activities beyond direct contact with trauma victims/survivors (e.g., teaching or supervision, research, consultation) may provide sufficient distance to reduce the impact of working exclusively with severe trauma. Another work-related strategy is the availability of supervision consultation and/or peer support that allows for the emotional safety necessary for trauma workers to talk about their STS reactions in an environment that provides support and comfort. Supportive supervision has been found to correlate with relieving stress in mental health professionals (Savicki & Cooley, 1987).

Informal strategies include general self-care activities, such as maintaining strong personal support networks of family and friends, developing diverse interests, and seeking positive experiences outside of work (Edelwich & Brodsky, 1980).

Personal strategies may involve the trauma worker's own use of personal psychotherapy (Boylin & Briggie, 1987; Fleischer & Wissler, 1985; McCann & Pearlman, 1990b) to address not only the various effects of STS reactions, but also the factors that may mediate their impact (e.g., concomitant stressors) or that render the trauma worker initially more vulnerable (e.g., prior abuse history). These strategies may address trauma workers' idealized expectations about their work and the excessive responsibility they may take for their clients' improvement or success, as well as for failures or lack of progress. The development of increased personal awareness is essential in order that trauma workers can monitor the impact of their work and respond effectively in a timely manner.

Prevention

The central effort toward the prevention of STS reactions is to prevent the traumatic events that lead to them. Sidel (1992) indicated that it is the responsibility of those who deal with traumatic events also to implement primary prevention. Prevention of both primary and secondary traumatic events requires prevention of the events themselves. Although some traumatic events are not preventable (e.g., natural disasters), many others potentially are (e.g., war, mass destruction of people such as in the Holocaust, rape, battering, incest, murder, other forms of violence). Prevention efforts toward ending these traumatic events necessarily involve political, social, and economic action and reform. Primary prevention of secondary or primary traumatic stress effects requires nothing less.

Secondary prevention of STS reactions may involve training trauma workers (e.g., law, medical, or graduate schools) to identify, anticipate, and prepare for coping with these effects. Effective coping with STS effects may require both professional and personal social support networks to create a layer of greater resiliency to these effects. Awareness and knowledge of personal issues are essential for both monitoring and responding effectively to STS reactions. A trauma worker with a personal history as a perpetrator of abuse is unlikely to be in a position to work effectively with many trauma victims without concerted attention to those issues. The impact of such a history on STS reactions is unclear at this point. Trauma workers with personal histories of traumatization (e.g., abuse history, being a survivor of a natural disaster) are likely to require deliberate personal attention to their own healing process in order to manage most effectively the difficult task of coping with STS reactions. With such personal healing, trauma survivors are placed in a unique position of empathy that may bestow on them a considerable advantage in engaging in trauma work.

REFERENCES

American Psychiatric Association. (1994). *Diagnostic and statistical manual of mental disorders* (4th ed., rev.). Washington, D.C.: Author.

Antonovsky, A. (1990). Pathways leading to successful coping and health. In M. Rosenbaum (Ed.), *Learned resourcefulness: On coping skills, self-control, and adaptive behavior*. New York: Springer.

Boylin, W. M., & Briggie, C. R. (1987). The healthy therapist: The contribution of symbolic-experiential family therapy. *Family Therapy, 14*(3), 247–256.

Brown, L. S., & Root, M. P. P. (Eds.). (1990). *Diversity and complexity in feminist therapy*. New York: Harrington Park Press.

Courtois, C. (1988). *Healing the incest wound: Adult survivors in therapy*. New York: Norton.

Danieli, Y. (1985). The treatment and prevention of long-term effects and intergenerational transmission of victimization: A lesson from Holocaust survivors and their children. In C. R. Figley (Ed.), *Trauma and its wake: The study and treatment of post-traumatic stress disorder* (pp. 295–313). New York: Brunner/Mazel.

Danieli, Y. (1988). Treating survivors and children of survivors of the Nazi Holocaust. In F. M. Ochberg (Ed.), *Post-traumatic therapy and victims of violence* (pp. 278–294). New York: Brunner/Mazel.

Deutsch, C. J. (1984). Self-reported sources of stress among psychotherapists. *Professional Psychology: Research and Practice, 15*(6), 833–845.

Dutton, M. A. (1992). *Empowering and healing the battered woman: A model of assessment and intervention*. New York: Springer.

Edelwich, J., & Brodsky, A. (1980). *Burn-out: Stages of disillusionment in the helping professions*. New York: Human Sciences Press.

Fleischer, J. A., & Wissler, A. (1985). The therapist as patient: Special problems and considerations. *Psychotherapy, 22*(3), 587–594.

Figley, C. R. (1983). Catastrophes: An overview of family reaction. In C. R. Figley & H. I. McCubbin (Eds.), *Stress and the family: Vol. 2.Coping with catastrophe* (pp. 3–20). New York: Brunner/Mazel.

Figley, C. R. (1986). *Trauma and its wake: Vol. 2. Traumatic stress theory, research, and intervention*. New York: Brunner/Mazel.

Foy, D. (Ed.). (1992). *Treating PTSD: Procedure for combat veterans, battered women, adult and child sexual assault*. New York: Guilford Press.

Gibbs, M. S. (1984). The therapist as imposter. In C. M. Brody (Ed.), *Women therapists working with women: New theory and process of feminist therapy*. New York: Springer.

Green, B. (1990). Defining trauma: Terminology and generic stressor dimensions. *Journal of Applied Social Psychology, 20*(20), 1632–1642.

Hellman, I. D., Morrison, R. L., & Abramowitz, S. I. (1986). The stresses of psychotherapeutic work: A replication and extension. *Journal of Clinical Psychology, 42*, 197–205.

Hellman, I. D., Morrison, R. L., & Abramowitz, S. I. (1987). Therapist experience and the stresses of psychotherapeutic work. *Psychotherapy, 24*(2), 171–177.

Herman, J. L. (1992a). *Trauma and recovery*. New York: Basic Books.

Herman, J. L. (1992b). Complex PTSD: A syndrome in survivors of prolonged and repeated trauma. *Journal of Traumatic Stress, 5*(3), 377–391.

Holroyd, J., & Brodsky, A., (1977). Psychologists' attitudes and practices regarding erotic and nonerotic physical contact with patients. *American Psychologist, 32*, 843–849.

Horowitz, M. J. (1986). *Stress response syndromes* (2nd ed.). Northvale, N.J.: Jason Aronson.

Janoff-Bulman, R. (1992). *Shattered assumptions: Towards a new psychology of trauma*. New York: Free Press.

Larsen, B. (1992). The traumatic effects of battering: A conceptualization. Unpublished manuscript, Nova University.

Lyall, A. (1989). The prevention and treatment of professional burnout. *Loss, Grief and Care, 3*(1/2), 27–32.

McCann, I. L., & Pearlman, L. A. (1990a). *Psychological trauma and the adult survivor: Theory, therapy, and transformation*. New York: Brunner/Mazel.

McCann, I. L., & Pearlman, L. A. (1990b). Vicarious traumatization: A framework for understanding the psychological effects of working with victims. *Journal of Traumatic Stress, 3*(1), 131–149.

Rawnsley, M. M. (1989). Minimizing professional burnout: Caring for the care givers. *Loss, Grief and Care, 3*(1/2), 51–57.

Rodolfa, E. R., Kraft, W. A., & Reilley, R. R. (1988). Stressors of professionals and trainees at APA-approved counseling and VA medical center internship sites. *Professional Psychology: Research and Practice, 19*(1), 43–49.

Savicki, V., & Cooley, E. J. (1987). The relationship of work environment and client contact in burnout in mental health professionals. *Journal of Counseling and Development, 63*, 249–252.

Scott, C., & Haw, J. (Eds.). (1986). *Heal thyself: The health of health care professionals.* New York: Brunner/Mazel.

Scurfield, R. M. (1985). Post-trauma stress assessment and treatment: Overview and formulations. In C. R. Figley (Ed.), *Trauma and its wake: The study and treatment of post-traumatic stress disorder* (pp. 219–256). New York: Brunner/Mazel.

Sidel, V. (1992, June). Primary prevention of traumatic stress caused by war. Coplenary presented at the World Conference of the International Society for Traumatic Stress Studies, Amsterdam, The Netherlands.

Silver, S. M. (1986). An inpatient program for post-traumatic stress disorder: Context and treatment. In C. R. Figley (Ed.), *Trauma and its wake: Vol. 2. Traumatic stress theory, research, and intervention* (pp. 213–231). New York: Brunner/Mazel.

Stark, E., & Flitcraft, A. (1988). Personal power and institutional victimization: Treating the dual trauma of woman battering. In F. M. Ochberg (Ed.), *Post-traumatic therapy and victims of violence* (pp. 115–151). New York: Brunner/Mazel.

Titchener, J. L. (1986). Post-traumatic decline: A consequence of unresolved destructive drives. In C. R. Figley (Ed.), *Trauma and its wake (Vol. 2).* New York: Brunner/Mazel.

Thorenson, R. W., Budd, F. C., & Kraukopf, C. J. (1987). Alcoholism among psychologists: Factors in relapse and recovery. *Professional Psychology: Research and Practice, 18*, 497–503.

Thorenson, R. W., Miller, M., & Kraukopf, C. J. (1989). The distressed psychologist: Prevalence and treatment considerations. *Professional Psychology: Research and Practice, 20*(3), 153–158.

Van der Kolk, B. A. (1987). *Psychological trauma.* Washington, D.C.: American Psychiatric Press, Inc.

Williams, J. E. (1984). Secondary victimization: Confronting public attitudes about rape. *Victimology: An International Journal, 9*(1), 66–81.

5

Sensory-Based Therapy for Crisis Counselors

CHRYS J. HARRIS

When giving consideration to the developmental psychology of Erik Erikson, crises may be viewed as fundamental parts of life. According to Slaikeu (1984), "Crisis is a time when 'everything is on the line,' so to speak. Previous means of coping and managing problems break down in the face of new threats and challenges. The potential for good or bad outcomes lies in the disorganization and disequilibrium of crisis."

While most people attempt to limit crises in their lives, trauma workers, who intentionally put themselves into daily disorganization and disequilibrium, often find it difficult to do this. Because trauma workers administer to trauma victims and operate in the aftermath of traumatic events (known to trauma workers as critical incidents), it should be anticipated that they will confront unintended, unexpected, and deleterious effects. Traumatologists refer to this as secondary traumatic stress (STS). These detrimental consequences, if not recognized and dealt with

Editor's Note: This chapter identifies innovative methods for assessing and treating professionals and volunteers who respond in emergencies, including therapists, counselors, and Red Cross workers. Harris defines secondary traumatic stress as the unintended, often unexpected and deleterious, emotional consequence derived from exposure to (or the aftermath of) traumatic events known as critical incidents; and describes a model for understanding its etiology. Sensory-based therapy, along with two treatment paradigms, is discussed.

appropriately, can cause work-related issues ranging from job ineffectiveness to job loss, from minor emotional issues to suicide.

This chapter focuses on several treatment methodologies for ameliorating the effects of STS on trauma workers.

TRAUMA WORKERS

The National Organization for Victim Assistance (NOVA) (1991) identifies nine categories of trauma workers:

1. Immediate responders (firefighters and law enforcement personnel).
2. Later responders (medical, paramedic, and ambulance personnel).
3. Unexpected responders (passersby, others in the event).
4. Emergency room personnel.
5. Body recovery, identification, and burial personnel.
6. Crisis intervenors (clergy and medical and mental health professionals).
7. Voluntary personnel (Red Cross, Salvation Army, and shelter caregivers).
8. Remote responders (equipment maintenance personnel).
9. Emergency support personnel (dispatchers).

A new category of trauma workers not yet identified by NOVA is called "victim advocates." In the state of South Carolina, these victim advocates work in various capacities. Many are found in each of the 13 judicial circuits and predominantly deal with victims of criminal activity. Law-enforcement victim advocates work within 19 law enforcement agencies and deal with the victims of any law enforcement response. Further, the state offers assistance to crime victims through the South Carolina State Office of Victim Assistance (SOVA).

At the time of this writing, the Rodney King trial had just concluded and Los Angeles was cleaning up after the devastation. What were the actual or potential detrimental emotional repercussions for trauma workers who worked during the Los Angeles riots (critical incidents)? The news reports would have us believe that such consequences probably included feelings of helplessness or frustration over their lack of success in saving life and property. There was confusion over responsibility issues and political issues, and about who was in charge. There was evidence of anger and hostility concerning the deaths, at the event itself, at interference with duties (e.g., snipers shooting at firefighters). Anger and hostility were expressed as a result of harassment, because of the public ventilation of anger, and at personal issues (loss of stock or facilities). There was worry and helplessness due to the victimization of the self and significant others. We could anticipate that there would be worry and feelings of helplessness with regard to such issues as image and peer perception, decision making, the conflict of job versus feelings, and concern on the part of those trauma workers who waited instead of participating (they were not on the front lines). We may speculate that there was emotional pain from dealing with death and severe wounds, about the pointlessness or uselessness of the event, and over a pileup of distinctly separate traumas during the term of the crisis.

SECONDARY TRAUMATIC STRESS

In this author's experience, trauma workers go through several phases as they attempt to manage the aftermath of each critical incident in which they are involved (see Figure 1). The first phase is confronting the STS. This phase consists of a series of deliberate and natural behaviors and feelings that should be associated with the trauma worker's attempt to manage the psychological response immediately following the critical incident. Since the trauma worker was not a primary victim of the critical incident, the effects that will be experienced are said to be "secondary," that is, it is the consequences of the critical incident that lead to the traumatic stress, not the actual critical incident.

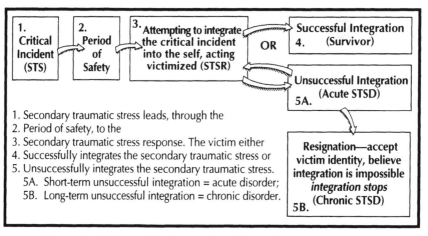

Figure 1. Eitiology of the integration of secondary traumatic stress

The second phase is the period of safety. This is when the trauma worker can say, "It [the trauma work, the critical incident, and the aftermath] is finally over!" The period of safety was introduced by Horowitz (1976) as an explanation for that time when the traumatic event was physically over but the emotional consequences remained to be integrated into one's self (STS is present). The period of safety signals the onset of the secondary traumatic stress reaction (STSR) phase.

The third phase, STSR, is the phase in which the trauma worker does the actual mental labor of assimilating and accommodating the experience into the model of the world. (This term comes from Lewis and Pucelik [1982] and is used to describe their assertion that one does not perceive reality, one perceives a neurological model of reality.) It involves a series of deliberate and natural behaviors and feelings that can be associated with the trauma worker's attempt to integrate the memories of the trauma work performed, the critical incident, and the aftermath. This phase is of paramount importance, as it is the phase in which the trauma worker either remains in or moves toward emotional mobility by successfully integrating the STS; or, if unsuccessful, moves toward emotional immobility. The real significance of this phase can be seen when we examine a parallel phase in the diagnosis of post-traumatic stress disorder (PTSD).

The latest edition of the *Diagnostic and Statistical Manual of Mental Disorders (DSM IV)* (American Psychiatric Association, 1994) does not allow PTSD to be diagnosed for 30 days following exposure to a traumatic event. Presumably this is necessary because the victim requires time to do the work of assimilating and accommodating the memories of the event into a view of self and life. Trauma workers also need time to do their emotional assimilation and accommodation. As we will see later, it is the STSR phase in which prevention-oriented crisis intervention can be a great benefit.

The final phase is the integration phase. It is during this phase that the trauma worker either successfully or unsuccessfully integrates the STS, depending on how the memories of the trauma work, the critical incident, the aftermath, and other related issues are managed. Successful integration requires effective psychological assimilation and accommodation of the trauma work, the critical incident, and the aftermath into the self with little or no emotional remnant. Unsuccessful integration results in secondary traumatic stress disorder (STSD).

The hallmark of STSD is the secondary victimization of the trauma worker. Acute STSD involves continual attempts (and failures) of the trauma worker to integrate the STS. Failure to integrate is not condoned because of a reluctance to acquiesce to becoming victimized. The trauma worker will be a reluctant victim throughout this phase, since there is a constant effort to become a survivor.

Chronic STSD involves the resignation of the trauma worker to being victimized. Attempts at integration stop and survivorship is no longer sought. It may appear that there are attempts to continue integration, but these are largely oriented to reducing the effects of the victimization rather than to assimilating and accommodating the critical incident.

Characteristics

There are a number of characteristics that may account for the development, sustenance, preventability, and treatability of the secondary traumatization that may arise in trauma workers. Such characteristics include culture, race, interpersonal competence, and experience with psychological trauma, specifically the STS reaction. The attributes of traumatic stress reaction include recurring memories of the event, problems dealing with recurring memories, and the stress reaction's having an effect on important relationships.

NOVA (1991) provides a cultural matrix suggesting that there are 11 issues that define cultural identity. These include the attitudes toward (1) family, (2) spirituality, (3) birth, (4) death, (5) marriage, (6) gender, (7) dress, (8) children, (9) politics, (10) authority, and (11) freedom.

They also identify 13 issues that are sources of cultural identity: (1) race/ethnicity, (2) religion, (3) age, (4) gender, (5) geographic orientation, (6) nation, (7) rural/urban, (8) language, (9) sexual, (10) education, (11) profession, (12) politics, and (13) economics.

Parson (1985) proposes that ethnicity is a cardinal factor in organizing experience. He submits that it is paramount in how one seeks assistance, defines the problem(s), assesses the cause of psychological difficulties, understands symptoms, perceives the potential for recovery (of self or others), and views crisis-intervention and therapy. McGoldrick (1982) implies that ethnicity defines how people differ in their views of the world. This includes how they experience pain, what they label as symptoms, how they communicate about pain and symptoms, what they believe about the cause of their illness, how they view those who help (physicians, therapists, etc.), and what treatment they desire or expect.

The following case studies illustrate specific ethnic patterns for coping with STS related to two separate traumatic events that occurred in South Carolina.

Case Studies

(*Note:* These case studies may not be indicative of STS management for other Puerto Ricans or African Americans.)

1. R.G. (born and raised in Puerto Rico) was an ambulance driver
who was involved in the aftermath of Hurricane Hugo on a volunteer basis. After several days of transporting animal bodies and
observing the devastation, R.G. had difficulties with "the great
amount of pain and suffering." He was placed on physician-
advised medical leave, during which he was seen at his church on
a number of occasions. He returned to work after two weeks of
absence and resumed his normal duties.

While at a debriefing after the hurricane, R.G. revealed that he
had handled his STS through means consistent with his upbring-
ing, medical advice, and the church. Garcia-Preto (1982) reports
that many Puerto Ricans attribute stressful predicaments to external factors, and they will seek a physician's advice. If the problem
is not medical and the physician cannot "cure" it, the problem is
considered spiritual. Spiritual issues are dealt with by the clergy or
by a spiritist.

2. C.W. (African American) lives near the railroad tracks in
Camden, South Carolina, where an Amtrak derailment recently
occurred. He ran to the site of the accident and began to help in
any way he could. He saw a number of bodies and body parts, as
well as a great deal of pain and suffering. C.W. was extremely
impressed with the "twisted wreck and lots of blood." He reported
that he "prayed a lot at church" and that he "talks with Grandma"
about the incident.

White (1984) suggests that "most Black adults live in a three-gener-
ational space." As an illustration of this conclusion, C.W. found a
great deal of comfort in the wisdom he attributes to his grandmother,
who lives with him (and his mother and two sisters). He indicated
that he could always talk to her about anything, and she was always
there for him. It was his grandmother who urged C.W. to pray in
church to have "the Lord lessen the burden" of the memories.
Mendes (1982, p. 204) advises that religion is a psychosocial dynamic
in the African-American culture, and that the faith of the "believers
can promote or hinder their mental health." In C.W.'s case, it would
appear that his mental health was promoted.

A number of authors (e.g., Darling, 1983; Holroyd & Lazarus, 1982;
Janoff-Bulman, 1985) imply that emotional traumatization is an individual problem. The question then arises: how can the social dictates of the
victim's long-established cultural precepts be laminated onto the newly
instituted individual perception(s) of trauma in order to effect appropriate interventions?

It is difficult to account for the social dictates of long-established cultural precepts. Accounting for every cultural factor utilized in the organization of trauma would vary from person to person and culture to culture. Further, such an accounting could fail to assess those who deviated from their cultural norm or fell outside the parameters of identified cultural standards. Additionally, we have no methodology to employ such findings in determining trauma organization.

The work of McGoldrick (1982) and Parson (1985) suggests that we can utilize ethnicity as a potential measure that encompasses a great deal of one's cultural heritage. In support, NOVA (1991) recommends a trauma intervention comprising (1) an ethnic search for the meaning of suffering and pain; (2) an ethnic exploration of potential tools for intervention, such as systematic relaxation, oblique experience techniques, and therapy involving the family; (3) ethnic disclosures of values and styles relating to communication; and (4) an ethnic exploration of how to reduce isolation and existential aloneness; of the provision of opportunities for learning and experiencing self and others; and of appropriate methods of helping individuals to develop control and increase self-esteem and self-regulation. The establishment of reliability and validity measures for such an ethnic-oriented methodology of intervention will require more research.

It may be easier to account for the newly instituted individual perception of trauma. Perception is sensory based, so it can be determined what one saw, heard, felt (internal feelings, as well as what one touched), tasted, and smelled. The trauma worker can explain the personal model of the world by describing attitudes, values, beliefs, scripts from the family and individual methods of sorting the environment (by positive/negative, general/detail, sameness/difference, approach/avoidance, internal/external, etc.). One can assess therapeutically the trauma worker's response to the trauma, the previous traumas encountered, the work environment, the work relations, the family, the community, and others regarded as important. It is this model of the world and the individual's perception of the trauma that form the basis for an effective program to prevent STSD in individual trauma workers.

INTERVENTIONS

There are two appropriate times to offer outside intervention when a trauma worker is integrating STS. The first is during the STSR phase (see Figure 1), and the second is during the integration phase when there is STSD. When the intervention is during the STSR phase, the intervention is considered preventive (preventing the onset of STSD) and should not usurp the trauma worker's ability to integrate his or her own emotions. In fact, the intervention is designed to be less invasive so as to enhance the worker's ability to assimilate and accommodate the trauma. Enhancement is viewed as strengthening the trauma worker's coping skills as compared with a more generative intervention in cases where the worker may have few or no coping skills and so these have to be therapeutically generated (replaced or created).

When the intervention is done during the STSD phase, it is considered more invasive and is designed to identify barriers to integration, to eliminate or neutralize the barriers, and to foster assimilation and accommodation of the trauma.

Prevention

Probably the most effective preventive intervention for trauma workers is a group intervention called critical incident debriefing (CID). The newly forming State Crisis Response Team in South Carolina defines CID as a process of education, ventilation, validation, and preparation regarding the psychological and emotional impacts of a traumatic life event. Clark (1988) proposes that the intention of CID is fourfold: (1) to provide support for trauma workers after a critical incident, (2) to provide referral sources for a variety of needs, (3) to provide follow-up assistance, and (4) to conduct educational programs about critical incident stress (CIS). For all intents and purposes, CIS and STS are commensurate with each other.

Currently, there are two major national models and numerous regional and local models of CID. The two national models, the NOVA model and the Mitchell model (Jeffery Mitchell, Ph.D., University of Maryland, Baltimore County), vary slightly, but appear to accomplish the same goals: fostering STS relief and enhancing the trauma worker's attempt to integrate the critical incident into the individual model of the world.

Those who do the debriefing are usually members of a crisis response team (CRT) who have been specifically trained to do CID. This training can be received through the national models or from qualified individuals (this author recommends individuals who have had national training). The training usually deals with how to do CID, as well as how to start, manage, and utilize a CRT.

The CID usually begins no earlier than 48 hours and no later than one week after the critical incident. This period varies from model to model, and the difference appears to lie in the interpretation of how long a trauma worker must wrestle with emotional issues before taking advantage of outside intervention. The debriefing centers on the trauma workers (usually a team of trauma workers) and is sensory based, encouraging them to report what each saw, heard, felt (external and internal), smelled, and tasted. A flip chart is kept so that all responses can be written down (usually in an abbreviated format). The chart is used to summarize the session. More often than not, only one or two CID interventions are required to enhance the trauma workers' ability to facilitate integration of the STS into their models of the world.

The CID process does not always enhance STS integration for all who participate in such sessions. Still, it may be too early for interventions other than those that are preventive in nature. In that event, the next step chosen is to enhance STS integration by adding didactic information (presented on a level the trauma worker can understand) to define strategic segments of the trauma worker's struggle to integrate STS. Usually this is accomplished during more traditional therapy sessions (in the therapist's office). As a side note, preventive intervention that is not group oriented will tax even the most experienced therapist. The goal is to help the victim reestablish immediate coping (Slaikeu, 1984) while maintaining a good self-esteem (Figley, 1984). This intervention, like the CID, should not usurp the trauma worker's ability to integrate emotions.

A five-step preventive intervention model such as shown in Table 1 can be used to help keep the intervention oriented to enhancing the skills the trauma worker has rather than to engender new skills. The major didactic issues that are introduced include (but are not limited to) understanding systemic relations, social support, self-protection issues, phases of the struggle to integrate memories, and more sensory-based tasks. Systemic relations include having the trauma worker discuss the biologic, marital, and work/family systems and the connections within each system and between the systems. The major focus of the connection within the family systems can be explained through social support.

Figley (1987) proposes that social-support resources can be critical to a victim's recovery process. Accordingly, the trauma workers' families (biological, marital, and work) can be viewed as essential features in the integrating process. Therefore, it is valuable to teach trauma workers about their systemic relations and how the five components of social support can benefit. These five social-support components are encouragement, advice, emotional aid, tangible aid, and companionship (Figley, 1983).

Protection issues are important in that they help the trauma worker to concentrate on what must be done immediately to protect the self both emotionally and physically. Topics of discussion include present

TABLE 1[*]
Individual-Oriented Preventive Intervention
for Secondary Traumatic Stress Response

Stage of Psychological Intervention	Therapeutic Intervention	Objective
1. Psychological contact	• Invite the client to talk • Listen to the client's facts • Watch for feelings • Try to calm intense feelings • Teach methodology for the self-management of stress	• Client to be heard, supported, understood, and accepted • Client to accept initial coping as appropriate • To bulid rapport
2. Explore dimensions of the problem	• Inquire about the immediate past with attention to past positive coping skills • Inquire about the present functioning with attention to strengths and weaknesses	• To identify issues that should be addressed immediately • To identify issues that should be addressed later • To develop communication skills
3. Examine possible solutions to the client's problems	• Inquire about what the client has tried so far • Focus on what works and why and what does not work and why • Explore what the client can do now	• Alternative solutions for issues that are of an immediate nature • Alternative solutions for issues that are not of an immediate nature
4. Assist in taking concrete action	• Assist the client in taking action on the contents gleaned from the previous three stages • Focus on taking action on the most immediate needs • Teach problem-solving techniques	• To take the best steps given the timing and the situation • To confront barriers to solving problems • To ensure success
5. Follow-up	• Recommend support (family, relatives, friends, etc.) • Allow client to make follow-up appointment(s) if deemed necessary • Consider other trained therapists	• Client will view others as potential social support • Client will view therapist as part of social support

[*] Adapted with permission from Harris (1991), "A Family Crisis Intervention Model for the Treatment of Post-Traumatic Stress Reaction," *Journal of Traumatic Stress, 4* (2), p. 204.

responses to the critical incident, past responses to other critical incidents, and systemic responses to the trauma worker's state of being.

The stages of the struggle to integrate the memories of the critical incident are defined for the trauma worker so he or she can move into a process that will help determine what has been accomplished and what is left to accomplish. The first stage is called stability. The therapist helps the trauma worker define (consistent with the trauma worker's model of the world) the specific particulars that lead to stable or unstable activity. Stable activity is concerned with behaviors that promote rationality and balance in one's life. The goal is to move in the direction of achieving *stability*.

The second stage is *adjustment*. The therapist helps the trauma worker identify what must be done to assimilate and accommodate the critical incident. An alternative definition involves the trauma worker's identifying specific particulars (consistent with his or her model of the world) that allow for positive or negative adjustment. The goal is to move in the direction of positive adjustment.

The third and final stage is *adaptation*. The therapist helps the trauma worker to identify specific particulars (again, consistent with his or her model of the world) that allow for adaptation of the critical incident either negatively or positively. The goal is to adapt positively.

It is important to note that the trauma worker moves through these stages at his or her own pace and reports success or failure according to his or her perception of integration. In other words, moving through these stages is client centered and client guided.

Most of this intervention is done by sensory-based methods. As in CID, the trauma worker is encouraged to respond from a personal model of the world in terms of what was seen, heard, felt, thought, smelled, and tasted—hence the sensory-based paradigm.

Treatment

As mentioned earlier, the other point of intervention in the process of integrating STS is when the trauma worker has failed to assimilate and accommodate the critical incident, the trauma work, and the aftermath. If the trauma worker exhibits a specific set of symptoms (not unlike those described in DSM-IV for PTSD), then there may be a diagnosis of STSD. An assumption can be made that the trauma worker has few or no coping skills to enhance, so the intervention required is engendering rather than enhancing. In other words, the intervention becomes oriented toward replacing or creating coping skills that can be used to integrate the STS.

Figley (1984) states that an "efficient" therapy for PTSD is one that systematically uncovers, processes, and resolves traumatic memories.

We can speculate that this should hold true for an STSD therapy. In fact, at present and in this author's experience, there is little, if any, difference between the treatment processes for PTSD and for STSD.

Like PTSD, STSD is an individual disorder. It involves individual appraisal of self and environment, personal assessment of vulnerability, and an intimate evaluation of one's emotional condition. An effective treatment program for treating STSD in trauma workers should involve both individual-oriented assessment and treatment stages.

Since there is currently no standard by which to make a diagnosis of STSD, we can initiate treatment based on other criteria. Harris (1991) suggested that a victim who is being treated for exposure to a traumatic event should be assessed for certain characteristics. We can use these characteristics in our efforts to treat trauma workers. The first characteristic to assess is that the trauma worker is experiencing recurring memories of either the critical incident, the trauma work that was performed, or something in the aftermath of the critical incident. The second characteristic to assess is that the trauma worker is having problems managing the recurring memories. The third characteristic is that the trauma worker is experiencing relationship problems (at work, home, or elsewhere) as a direct result of attempts to manage these recurring memories. Throughout the assessment of these three characteristics, we would expect the trauma worker to identify that the memories were intrusive, invasive, or some combination of both. When specific criteria are established to diagnose STSD, then we will seek to recognize the disorder prior to beginning treatment.

After assessment, the STSD treatment this author utilizes and would recommend combines a PTSD treatment model (e.g., the algorithmic approach [Figley, 1984]) combined with the previously described sensory-based treatment model. The goals of the algorithmic approach, stated in the present terminology of treating STSD, are as follows:

1. All aspects of the critical incident can be recalled by the trauma worker with little or no emotional response.
2. The trauma worker is able to explain why the STS happened and the emotional response(s) to it.
3. The trauma worker can differentiate the critical incident in both positive and negative ways.
4. The trauma worker is symptom free.
5. The trauma worker's self-esteem is equal to or better than it was prior to treatment.

When the focus is sensory based and the trauma worker explores the personal model of the world in therapy, he or she gains experience and an understanding of how the world is perceived and can gain insight into how others may perceive their worlds. The sensory based model of intervention is a valuable aid to help the trauma worker to answer the victim questions Figley (1984) proposes in his trauma-resolution stage: What happened? Why did it happen? Why did I act as I did then? Why have I acted as I have since then? What will I do if it happens again?

Finally, the components of the STSD therapy include the trauma worker's perception of the critical incident, of the victims, and of the self. The trauma worker should identify feelings and any methods of stress management employed. The therapy should look at the trauma worker and his or her strengths, weaknesses, barriers to problem solving, barriers to systemic cohesiveness (connectedness with family, friends, co-workers, etc.), and barriers to systemic rapport (harmony with family, friends, co-workers, etc.). It is useful for the trauma worker to identify immediate needs and future needs, and how one will know when the needs are met.

Last, but not least, the trauma worker will need to identify a healing theory that is ecologically sound for the self—in other words, a healing theory that can be stated in the positive, that is under the control of the trauma worker, and that is testable or measurable as far as achieving results is concerned. The healing theory is the key for the trauma worker to feel secure when going back to the job and the world.

CONCLUSIONS

Many trauma workers from various agencies have made statements to and asked questions of CRT debriefers similar to the following.

• "I am not supposed to feel this way. These feelings are not in my job description!"

• "How can I work if I'm always going to have this kind of response?"

• "I have to be strong for the others, so I need to hide my feelings."

• "Am I in the wrong line of work?"

• "Why does helping others carry such a large emotional price tag?"

These statements and questions are legitimate responses to STS and conspicuously emphasize the fact that trauma work is an emotional, stress-inducing occupation (to say nothing of the physical stress involved). It is imperative that trauma workers' powers-that-be heed the plea to acknowledge the emotional consequences that may inhibit the vital work that these men and women perform. Out of this understanding, preventive measures can be established to ensure that trauma workers will be able to meet their emotional needs (at work and at home) to integrate job-induced STS.

REFERENCES

American Psychiatric Association. (1994). *Diagnostic and statistical manual of mental disorders*, (4th ed.). Washington, D.C.: Author.

Clark, D.F. (1988, November). Debriefing to defuse stress. *Fire Command*, pp. 33–35.

Darling, R.B. (1983). The birth defective child and the crisis of parenthood. In E.J. Callahan & K.A. McCluskey (Eds.), *Life-span developmental psychology: Nonnormative life events* (pp. 115–143). New York: Academic Press.

Figley, C.R. (1983). Catastrophes: An overview of family reactions. In C.R. Figley & H.I. McCubbin (Eds.), *Stress and the family: Vol. 2., Coping with catastrophe* (pp. 3–20). New York: Brunner/Mazel.

Figley, C.R. (1984). Treating post traumatic stress disorder: The algorithmic approach. *Newsletter of the American Academy of Psychiatry and the Law, 9*, 25–26.

Figley, C.R. (1987). Post-traumatic family therapy. In F. Ochberg (Ed.), *Post-traumatic therapy* (pp. 83–109). New York: Brunner/Mazel.

Garcia-Preto, N. (1982). Puerto Rican families. In M. McGoldrick, J.K. Pearce, & J. Giordano (Eds.), *Ethnicity and family therapy* (pp. 164–185). New York: Guilford Press.

Harris, C.J. (1991). A family crisis-intervention model for the treatment of post-traumatic stress reaction. *Journal of Traumatic Stress. 4*, 195–207.

Holroyd, K.A., & Lazarus, R.S. (1982). Stress, coping, and somatic adaption. In L. Goldberger & S. Breznitz (Eds.), *Handbook of stress* (pp. 21–35). New York: Free Press.

Horowitz, M.J. (1976). *Stress response syndromes.* New York: Jason Aronson

Janoff-Bulman, R. (1985). The aftermath of victimization: Rebuilding shattered assumptions. In C.R. Figley, (Ed.) *Trauma and its wake* (pp. 15–35). New York: Brunner/Mazel.

Lewis, B.A., & Pucelik, R.F. (1982). *Magic demystified.* Lake Oswego, Oreg.: Metamorphous Press.

McGoldrick, M. (1982). Ethnicity and family therapy: An overview. In M. McGoldrick, J.K. Pearce, & J. Giordano (Eds.), *Ethnicity and family therapy* (pp. 3–30). New York: Guilford Press.

Mendes, H.A. (1982). The role of religion in psychotherapy with Afro-Americans. In B.A. Bass, G.E. Wyatt, & G.J. Powell (Eds.), *The Afro-American family: Assessment, treatment and research issues* (pp. 203–210). New York: Grune & Stratton.

National Organization for Victim Assistance. (1991). *Community Crisis Response Training Institute participants' manual for Pickens, South Carolina.* Washington, D.C.: Author.

Parson, E.R. (1985). Ethnicity and traumatic stress: The intersecting point in psychotherapy. In C.R. Figley (Ed.), *Trauma and its wake* (pp. 314–337). New York: Brunner/Mazel.

Slaikeu, K.A. (1984). *Crisis intervention: A handbook for practice and research.* Boston: Allyn & Bacon.

White, J.L. (1984). *The psychology of blacks: An Afro-American perspective.* Englewood Cliffs, N. J.: Prentice-Hall.

6

Debriefing and Treating Emergency Workers

SUSAN L. McCAMMON AND
E. JACKSON ALLISON, JR.

"They, who risk their lives and their welfare to assist others, should not be neglected" (Miles, Demi, & Mostyn-Aker, 1984, p. 329).

Despite the enthusiasm and commitment of crisis workers, many professionals in the field have expressed alarm over attrition, from the field and the potential for burnout in those who remain. Studies of occupational stress in emergency medical services (EMS) workers have examined factors contributing to burnout, such as organizational variables, role perceptions, and working conditions (Allison, Whitley, Revicki, & Landis, 1987; Cydulka, Lyons, May, Shay, Hammer, & Mathews, 1989; Revicki, Whitley, Landis, & Allison, 1988). Neale (1991) investigated work stress in emergency medical technicians (EMTs) and found higher levels of burnout, stress, and strain, and lower coping skills than in samples of other occupational groups. The effects of secondary traumatization on emergency workers have been documented by Beaton and Murphy (see Chapter 3 of this volume).

Editor's Note: This chapter expands the focus to include the debriefing and treatment not only of trauma workers, as in the last chapter, but also of medical personnel. McCammon and Allison, with many years of research and education experience with this population, suggest methods for preventing secondary traumatic stress and stress disorder. These methods focus on the normality of confronting secondary stress in this line of work. The post-trauma interventions focus on ventilation and integrating the traumatic experiences into the overall competence of the workers.

Since we are still in the early stages of learning about the impact of chronic stressors in this rapidly developing health care specialty, as well as the effects of being responders to traumatic events, we know very little about the effectiveness of our attempts to promote trauma resolution and healthy coping strategies in emergency workers. In this chapter, we review models for providing stress management and trauma resolution interventions for emergency caregivers, both prehospital and hospital-based. We focus especially on medical caregivers, but will also discuss Red Cross workers, police officers, firefighters, and other protective service workers who are first responders to traumatic events.

Within the past two decades, emergency medical services have evolved and expanded tremendously with the development of basic and advanced life support services. Graham (1981) noted that in 1970 few ambulance attendants had any specialized training beyond basic first aid procedures, and in some states, a valid chauffeur's license was the only required credential. In contrast, in the United States in 1992, there were 450,000 technicians trained at the EMT level and 100,000 prehospital life-support personnel, including paramedics. From one resident in emergency medicine in 1970 (Graham, 1981), today there are 96 residency training programs in the country, with approximately 800 resident graduates annually (Graduate Medical Education, 1992). There are also 75,000 emergency nurses nationally. In addition, literally thousands of volunteers from the Red Cross and other agencies respond to disasters in the United States every year.

In the early 1980s, various writers acknowledged the emotional effect of rescue work and lamented the lack of training to address this concern. Based on participant observation and interview data, Mannon (1981) observed: "Indirect evidence suggests that there is little in the training that is directed toward the socio-emotional problems of working with critical and dying patients: whatever coping strategies that are developed, will evolve out of street experience, and socialization from more experienced crewmates" (p. 23).

Graham (1981) noticed a reluctance to label the psychological impact of the work as a source of distress. "When EMS people admit to emotional exhaustion, they usually deny that it comes from the tragedy and horror they witness. Instead they blame the hassles . . . . Lacking any systematic training, education or even any very good advice on how to handle the emotional overload of their work, EMS people are on their own with the heartbreak and the hassles. Lacking a protocol, they wing it" (p. 28).

Nevertheless, some of those in the field have recognized that "simply talking about the feelings a person is somewhat aware of" could be helpful (Nydam, 1983, p. 45). Nydam suggested the use of small groups to do "Rescue Rehash." He proposed using a simple formula of sentence completion to promote discussion. "The mission made me feel... because . . . ." Following a hotel skywalk collapse, Miles and colleagues (1984) warned, "The stoic rescue worker, who appears unaffected by a disaster, may have many unmet needs related to the disaster, and if these needs are not addressed, the rescue worker may suffer impaired health, impaired relationships, or other behavioral dysfunction" (p. 329). The workers reported that talking and sharing was the most helpful intervention modality. Miles and co-workers emphasized the need for a preventive intervention program for rescue workers following a major disaster, including both immediate debriefing sessions and ongoing support groups.

Raphael (1986) and Dunning (1988) have offered comprehensive discussions of intervention strategies for the psychosocial care of emergency workers. We will use their framework in which programs are organized according to the timing of intervention: programs that could be implemented prior to, during, or following the traumatic event.

INTERVENTIONS BEFORE EXPOSURE TO TRAUMA

Stress Audit

A systematic assessment of the sources and degree of job stresses and the way in which they are manifest is the first step in planning for improving the work environment and addressing the concerns of workers. Bailey, Steffen, and Grout (1980) developed a Stress Audit questionnaire to identify "stressors" and "satisfiers" of nurses on intensive-care units, which they found a useful tool for this purpose. Possible indicators of psychological injury include illness, changes in personnel turnover patterns, requests for transfer, absenteeism, and job performance (Dunning, 1988). This information can then form the basis for developing remediation plans.

Training and Education

Incorporating information on stress and its management, as well as on the physical and psychological impact of trauma, into emergency worker training programs can serve two purposes. In addition to providing valuable information, the training can lay the groundwork for collaboration between mental health and emergency workers. As Raphael (1986, pp. 248–250) noted, "Practical workers such as rescue personnel and police, or those in charge of the disaster response organization, may view mental health services as unnecessary, a luxury, or even a nuisance . . . . Many organizations will be resistant to the psychological component of disaster management and counterdisaster activity unless they have had recent experience of human behavior during a catastrophe and perhaps also some awareness of recent developments in this field."

Mitchell and Bray (1990) observed that "human elements training" before a crisis event can help emergency personnel deal more effectively with the distressed people they are serving, as well as decrease serious stress reactions in themselves and other workers. Topics in human elements training include crisis intervention skills, stress management skills, coping with difficult patients and situations (mentally ill, obstetrical, violent, or dying patients; injuries resulting from drug overdose, rape, fires, shootings, stabbings or assaults, poisonings, and exposure), communication and conflict resolution skills, assisting families of the dead, disaster psychology, and peer support services (Brownstone, Shatoff, & Duckro, 1983; Cydulka et al., 1989; Mitchell & Bray, 1990; Neale, 1991).

Information should also be provided about the process of debriefing and the existence of other support services. Dunning (1988) suggested that by including a discussion of psychological injury with other, more commonly recognized types of duty-related injury, emergency workers may be more receptive to preventive and rehabilitative programing. "Psychological injury is thus not singled out as something unusual or more serious, but is seen as something that can normally happen in the course of performing one's job" (p. 289).

Emergency worker training should review health maintenance strategies (adhering to a proper diet, exercising, stopping smoking and chewing tobacco, and attending to spiritual and other aspects of life beyond the job) (Mitchell & Bray, 1990). Educational articles confirming the importance of caring for one's self (in order to offer better care for others) have been published in EMS and public safety trade journals (Hinds, 1988; Schmuckler, 1991a, 1991b; Shelton, 1991).

Among specific stress management techniques that could be included in training programs are enhancement of stress awareness, deep muscle relaxation, stress inoculation, and development of a mental attitude of "detached concern" (Hunter, Jenkins, & Hampton, 1982). Hoge and Hirschman (1984) evaluated a brief psychological training program for EMT part-time volunteers and documented that participants acquired skills in anxiety reduction, behavioral limit setting, and referral. Having the technical skills, along with being prepared to perform them under difficult circumstances, and being properly equipped can reduce or prevent many stress reactions (Mitchell & Bray, 1990). Finally, opportunities for professional growth and development enhance job satisfaction, according to Whitley, Revicki, Allism, and Landis (1990).

Training for supervisors and administrators is important to help develop management, leadership, communication, and conflict resolution skills (Cydulka et al., 1989; Mitchell & Bray, 1990; Whitley et al., 1990). As Mitchell and Bray noted, a more interactive leadership style may fit today's emergency workers better than it did those of years past.

Education of the public and attention to the social system that provides care are needed. Ho (1988) has called for public education regarding the intended functions of an emergency department and has appealed for the more rational use of emergency visits; EMTs find non-emergency calls upsetting (Neale, 1991).

Policy Development Planning

Hospitals are required by the Joint Commission on Accreditation of Healthcare Organizations (JACHO) to maintain a disaster plan and to conduct semiannual disaster exercises (Aghababian, 1986). Usually, the emergency department is the center of this activity. Aghababian delineated the ways in which patient care changes during disasters, discussed the role of the emergency physician, and made recommendations for disaster preparedness planning. Mitchell and Bray (1990) discussed the need for written policies for the use of mental health services during a disaster.

Additional planning needs have been summarized by Dunning (1988), such as the use of predisaster stress audits to guide the assignment of personnel to especially stressful tasks. Policy development should also include attention to developing policies for notifying families in the event of injury of emergency personnel, and protocols for handling line-of-duty deaths and funerals, dignitary visits, and the media (Mitchell & Bray, 1990).

Preplanned Mental Health Services

Establishing access to referral, counseling, and therapy services is often accomplished through employee assistance programs and chaplain programs. Family life programs and spouse support programs can also be valuable in educating, encouraging, and counseling family members of emergency workers (Mitchell & Bray, 1990). Advance planning and training must be completed to establish post-trauma debriefing and follow-up procedures, which are discussed in a later section of this chapter.

INTERVENTIONS DURING TRAUMA EXPOSURE

Orientation to the Trauma Site

Paton (1992, 1994) discussed the importance of preparing workers before their exposure to a trauma site. In his comparison of the Scottish inexperienced volunteers and experienced firefighters who responded to a devastating earthquake in Armenia, he found a higher incidence of problems for the firefighter group than for the volunteers (as measured by the Impact of Event Scale) (Paton, 1990). He suggested that the difference could be attributed to discrepant cognitive schemata as well as the preparation of the volunteer group. Preparation activities included a review of films of previous disasters that portrayed the devastation of natural disasters and created realistic expectations regarding the likelihood of effecting rescue, team building, and briefing by an advance group, which allowed for realistic expectations about the situation in Armenia. He also noted the need to brief workers on the cultural and religious climate of countries they are about to enter.

Rest and Respite

First line supervisors are often able to identify early signs of emotional upset and can relieve workers in a particularly stressful assignment (Dunning, 1988). Mitchell and Bray (1990) recommended that providing an opportunity for rest, having the worker talk with someone at the scene, or rotating him or her to another assignment be considered before removing a distressed worker from the scene. They offered many practical suggestions for stress management during extended trauma exposure.

On-scene Support Services

On-scene support services are usually provided to obviously distressed personnel on a one-on-one basis. Interventions may range from ascertaining whether someone has been injured to bringing a cup of water, listening to what has happened, or sitting by silently.

Following his work on the collapse of the Cypress structure of the I-880 freeway during the San Francisco earthquake, Foreman (1990) discussed the use of "decompression." This is accomplished in one-to-one discussions, or by talking in small work groups, during breaks and immediately following rotation off-site. It involves normalizing and validating the workers' reactions, and allowing them to ventilate frustrations and intense emotions. Attempts are made to defuse survivor guilt, self-doubt, and conflicts by helping the worker reframe emotional reactions.

Demobilization

A demobilization is held after emergency units disengage from operations in a major incident. Participants are not asked to discuss the incident. A presentation on critical incident stress is made and suggestions for stress management are given. An opportunity for asking questions or for a private discussion is provided. Those being demobilized are given the chance to eat and rest before returning to duty or going home. The demobilization process lasts about half an hour, with about two thirds of this time reserved for resting and eating (Mitchell & Bray, 1990).

INTERVENTIONS FOLLOWING EXPOSURE TO TRAUMA

Debriefing Models

Critical incidents are defined as "any events that have sufficient emotional power to overcome the usual coping abilities of emergency personnel who are exposed to them" (Mitchell & Bray, 1990, p. 140). Such events are not limited to catastrophic disasters. Mitchell and Bray (1990, p. 140) listed the following events as typical of those that may cause distress for emergency personnel.

- Line-of-duty death
- Serious injury to emergency personnel
- Serious multiple-casualty incident
- Suicide of an emergency person
- Traumatic deaths of children
- Serious injuries to children
- Events that attract excessive media interest
- An event involving victims known to the emergency person
- An event that has an unusually powerful impact on the personnel

Based on the work of Davidson (1979) and Wagner (1979a, 1979b), a formally structured postincident debriefing session is recommended as an intervention acceptable to public safety and emergency workers (Dunning, 1988). Dunning described two approaches to debriefing: the didactic and the emotional. The protocols for a number of debriefing models are summarized in Table 1, and a brief description of each fol-

TABLE 1

Conceptual Components of Post-Trauma Stress Debriefing Models

Debriefing Model	Review of Events	Ventilation of Feelings	Education, Integration, and Mastery	Closure
Didactic debrief	None	None	• Give information • Prepare for counseling	None
CISD	• Fact phase • Thought phase	• Reaction phase • Symptom phase	Teaching phase	Reentry phase
Psychological debrief	Experience of disaster	Positive and negative aspects and feelings	• Discuss meaning • Offer guidance • Explore relationship with workers, own family, and those helped	Relinquish disaster role
Continuum of care	Telling the story	Looking at and understanding the consequences of survival	• Building of coping skills • Cognitive restructuring • Contracting	• Closing and evaluating • Plan for follow-up • Short-term counseling as needed
NOVA	Tell about experience during event and in aftermath	Predict possible emotions to come	Identify coping skills: reinforce methods; suggest alternative strategies for negatives	• Review session • Plan
MSDM	Disclosure of events	Feelings and reactions	Coping strategies	Termination • Positive discussion of work accom-plished • Prepare for leaving and transition • Final Q & A session • Referral as needed

lows. In addition to the educational component of the didactic debrief, the emotional debriefing models share common features.

Although the various models were developed to address the needs of different populations, all the models involve structuring opportunities for participants to review the events of the traumatic situation and ventilate feelings; learn skills for integrating and mastering the event; and learn to identify, enlist, and accept help from their support systems.

Didactic Debrief

The didactic, or teaching, approach is designed to provide information about common psychological, behavioral, and physical reactions of trauma workers (Dunning, 1988). When workers (and their family members) are acquainted with typical responses to disaster duty, either they can accept their symptoms as normal or, if the symptoms are overwhelming, they may feel it acceptable to seek appropriate mental health services. During the didactic debrief, there is no attempt to perform therapy, but the groundwork is laid to build rapport with the mental health coleader, who would be available for future counseling.

If workers know that flashbacks or nightmares are normal reactions to particular events, they will not view such events with as much alarm. If they understand that the symptoms are common and predictable, their emergence will not be as distressing, and hence will not be as likely to be exacerbated by anxiety or refusal to seek resolution (p. 300).

Critical Incident Stress Debriefing

The history of critical incident stress debriefing (CISD) has been described by Mitchell (1988). Military debriefing, especially during World War II and in subsequent work by the Israeli defense forces, is given substantial credit for the development of group psychological debriefings. Police psychologists, hospital-based mental health professionals, and postdisaster intervenors have contributed to the development of CISD. A decade ago Mitchell (1983) articulated the CISD process, and more recently (Mitchell & Bray, 1990), he summarized its current format. Although primarily developed for use with public safety personnel, the model is also employed in community and school settings.

In the CISD Introduction, the team leader reviews the ground rules and explains the process of the debriefing. During the *Fact Phase*, participants describe their job during the event and provide facts regarding what happened. The *Thought Phase* introduces more personal elements as members of the group describe their first thought during the event. In the *Reaction Phase*, members usually move from cognitive to emotional processing; they respond to such questions as, "What was the worst thing about the event?" Then, moving back to a more cognitive level, participants discuss their cognitive, physical, emotional, and behavioral symptoms during the *Symptom Phase*. In the *Teaching Phase*, the team members are educated about stress reactions and ways to alleviate them. Finally, in the *Reentry Phase*, members may make supportive contracts or plan follow-up activities. A summary statement is made by a CISD team member and group participants have the opportunity to speak.

An important aspect of the CISD process, as well as of other debriefing models, such as the Federal Bureau of Investigation's Stress Response Program (Horn & Reese, undated), is the involvement of peer support personnel. Carefully screened peers are selected from among law enforcement officers, firefighters, EMS workers, dispatchers, or other emergency workers. Peer support personnel may initiate contact with responders to an incident, assess the need for defusings or debriefings and help to conduct them, provide on-scene support services, assist in educational activities, and serve as referral guides (Mitchell & Bray, 1990).

Psychological Debrief

Raphael (1986) described the preventive aim of the psychological debriefing—to deal with the inevitable stresses of emergency work so that subsequent problems do not arise. In formal group sessions, the facilitator is careful not to imply that the workers have not coped well or that he or she is "psychoanalyzing" them. Initial questioning explores initiation into the disaster role and initial feelings. The workers' experiences and roles in the disaster are explored. Psychological perceptions and reactions, including frustrations and negative experiences, are ventilated and explored in depth.

Positive aspects are also discussed to provide balance and assist workers in integrating the experience and gaining perspective. Relationships with co-workers and family members are discussed, as well as the stresses of empathy with the people they assisted. Finally, disengagement from the disaster is discussed in terms of relinquishing the disaster role and making the transition back to the daily routine. The CISD is usually offered one to three days following the event. It generally takes about three hours and ideally serves from four to 20 (possibly up to 60) participants.

Defusing

A defusing is a shorter (30 to 45 minutes), less formal, and less structured version of CISD that occurs within a few hours of the event (Mitchell & Bray, 1990). The defusing allows for some ventilation, along with the provision of information on stress. It may eliminate the need for a formal debriefing or may enhance the debriefing that follows.

Continuum of Care

The continuum of care proposed by Bergman and Queen (1986a, 1986b) includes debriefing sessions. (The other elements of the continuum are duty-related trauma training, peer support, and post-trauma counseling.) Their psychological debriefing process (Bergman & Barnett-Queen, undated) begins with *Setting the Stage*, which includes an introduction, discussion of the agenda, and the setting of ground rules. In *Telling the Story*, participants describe their experiences. In the next component, *Looking at the Consequences of Survival*, participants describe their critical incident stress consequences. During *Understanding the Consequences of Survival*, the debriefers normalize the stress consequences and discuss appropriate coping skills for survivors. This discussion is followed by the *Contracting for Recovery* component, in which participants devise a plan for reducing the likelihood of long-term stress consequences, especially emphasizing the importance of social support. The *Closing and Evaluating* component allows for review of the process, educational materials, and follow-up plans. Participants then make a written evaluation of the debriefing.

Community Response Team Group Debriefing Techniques

The National Organization for Victim Assistance (NOVA) (Young, 1991) provides training for Community Crisis Response Teams, and was designed for interventions with primary victims. Its debriefing model specifies a pair of debriefers, a leader, and a support person who serves as the group's scribe. The debriefing process is similar to that of previously described models. Following the establishment of ground rules, the participants talk about their experiences during the event and in its aftermath. They predict the range of emotions they are likely to encounter in the coming days and months, and are helped to identify positive coping techniques. The session is concluded with a review, the expression of the participants' concerns, and the distribution of handouts.

Multiple Stressor Debriefing Model

Following the 1989 San Francisco earthquake, Armstrong O'Callahan, and Marmar (1991) developed the Multiple Stressor Debriefing Model (MSDM) for conducting exit interviews with Red Cross and other emergency personnel. The MSDM is a modification of Mitchell's CISD protocol; adaptations were made to address the multiple stressors encountered by the workers. For example, some workers came directly to San

Francisco after responding to Hurricane Hugo. In the first stage of the debriefing, *Disclosure of Events*, workers were allowed to discuss several incidents that had affected them. In the *Feelings and Reactions* stage, they ventilated their distress in encountering such things as victims' dissatis-faction with relief efforts. In the *Coping Strategies* stage, they discussed methods of coping while still in the stressful situation and after returning home. During the *Termination* stage, participants discussed positive aspects of their experience, said good-bye to one another, and talked about the transition of returning home.

Evaluation of Debriefings

While a number of informants over the past decade have testified to the value of debriefing following a traumatic incident, evaluation of its effec-tiveness remains mainly at the anecdotal level. Currently, a study funded by the National Institute of Mental Health is being undertaken by Charles Marmar and others of the San Francisco VA Medical Center to study res-cue worker responses to the I-880 freeway collapse. In this study, the impact of debriefing is being examined. Until evaluative studies are com-pleted, accounts of debriefing outcomes provide clinical insights that should prove helpful in working with other emergency responders.

Hytten and Hasle (1989) credited the opportunity for debriefing as con-tributing to the favorable coping of many firefighters to a hotel-fire rescue operation. Nearly half of the men reported that the event was the worst experience they had ever had, and 10% were identified as having clinical-ly significant stress reactions. Nevertheless, "80% thought that they had coped with the job well to fairly well and for as many as 66% the rescue action represented something positive to them in retrospect" (p. 50).

All of those surveyed reported they had talked extensively about their experience with others, either at a formal debriefing session or with a group of fellow workers. Of 39 men who participated in debriefing, 38 found the experience helpful. They said the debriefing was useful pro-fessionally and reported that it increased their self-confidence. However, there was no difference in Impact of Event scores seven to 21 days post-disaster between those who were formally debriefed and those who talked informally with their colleagues.

Following their work using the MSDM with Red Cross relief teams, Armstrong and colleagues (1991) concluded that the debriefings were helpful in reducing stress symptom disorders and increasing worker effectiveness. For future disaster responders, they recommended weekly group meetings (an orientation briefing and a midassignment group), concluding with an exit group using the MSDM.

Dyregrov and Mitchell (1992), in commenting on insights gained from a CISD following a bus disaster involving both child and adult victims, noted that while emotional distancing is a helpful strategy at the trauma scene, later it is most helpful to confront one's impressions and reactions. The CISD provided a structured way for talking through the experience. Dyregrov and Mitchell observed that on the day of the event, or on the day that work is completed, the emergency worker may still be in the emotionally distanced mode. Individual support should be provided until a formal debriefing is arranged within the next few days.

Post-trauma Counseling

The importance of follow-up to debriefing has been emphasized by Barnett-Queen and Bergman (1988) and Mitchell and Bray (1990). After a debriefing, some workers may benefit from post-trauma counseling. This is usually completed in three to four sessions (Barnett-Queen & Bergman, 1988). Sometimes, a second debriefing may be needed, and attention should be paid to anniversary dates (Mitchell & Bray, 1990).

Eye Movement Desensitization and Reprocessing

Solomon (1991) has proposed that eye movement desensitization and reprocessing (EMDR) may be a treatment of choice for critical incident trauma. This procedure involves the induction of specific eye movements in the context of cognitively reprocessing traumatic images. He reported, "Following a critical incident EMDR can be effective in rapidly desensitizing traumatic feelings, reducing physiological tension, reducing traumatic symptomology, and shifting cognitive beliefs" (p. 1).

Based on his experience as a police department psychologist and consultant to the critical incident program of a major railroad, Solomon found that EMDR can rapidly reduce the emotional impact of traumatic situations. He provided case studies of police officers and detectives, which show that by his adding EMDR to his usual intervention procedures, his clients accomplish in one to four sessions what used to take three to 12 sessions. Further, he reported that post-treatment scores on the Impact of Events Scale are significantly lower for people who are given EMDR as compared with those who are not. Currently, investigations are under way to study the use of EMDR systematically. If the efficacy of this procedure is confirmed, it may prove an important tool in the treatment of traumatized emergency workers.

Reporting

Finally, another post-trauma responsibility of a psychology/psychiatry disaster management group is collecting, compiling, and reporting on the experience (Swedish National Board of Health & Welfare, 1991). A description of intervention processes and outcomes may provide information about events and trauma response sequelae that future workers might encounter.

NEEDED RESEARCH

Dunning (1990) observed that the major impediment to a comprehensive approach to trauma resolution in emergency workers is that "existing research is virtually nonexistent." She recommended that further research be encouraged to examine three criteria for efficacy in responding to trauma: reducing transitory emotional distress, reducing personal or occupational problems after the event, and identifying mechanisms that restore or maintain one's sense of control or sense of competence during or after a traumatic incident.

McCammon, Durham, Allison, and Williamson (1988) and Genest, Levine, Ramsden, and Swanson (1990) studied coping strategies of emergency responders. While they did identify some helpful cognitions and coping behaviors, further research is needed to investigate the mediating effect of coping variables on traumatic impact. As Dunning (1990) has noted, little has been done to enlist workers' self-protective mechanisms and support networks prior to and during a traumatic event.

Keller and Koenig (1989) recommended the development of a longitudinal study to identify characteristics of workers with low burnout rates. And Whitley and Allison (1989) have called for a study to investigate the exacerbating effect of responding to disaster in a job that is normally stressful. Long-term outcomes for rescue workers and the variables that influence these outcomes should also be studied, according to Miles and colleagues (Miles et al., 1984). However, they warned of the risk associated with follow-up research, such as the recall of painful material linked with the disaster experience. In their study, participants could return a postcard requesting one of the investigators to call. Three respondents asked to be called and one was seen for counseling.

The United Nations has declared the 1990s to be the International Decade for Natural Disaster Reduction. Among its goals is the advancement of scientific and technical knowledge to reduce social disruption from natural hazards. Perhaps the advances of the decade will include a reduction in risk of mental injury to workers deployed to traumatic events. Raphael (1986) has commented on the power of the themes of human disaster response: "Courage rather than cowardice; compassionate human concern of one for the other; and resilience in the face of overwhelming stress (p. 310)." The work of emergency responders exemplifies these themes, and these workers deserve the most supportive work settings and systems we can provide.

REFERENCES

Aghababian, R. V. (1986). Hospital disaster planning. *Topics in Emergency Medicine, 7*(4), 46–54.

Allison, E. J., Whitley, T. W., Revicki, D. A., & Landis, S. S. (1987). Specific occupational satisfaction and stresses that differentiate paid and volunteer EMS. *Annals of Emergency Medicine, 16,* 676–679.

Armstrong, K., O'Callahan, W., & Marmar, C. R. (1991). Debriefing Red Cross disaster personnel: The multiple stressor debriefing model. *Journal of Traumatic Stress, 4,* 581–593.

Bailey, J. T., Steffen, S. M., & Grout, J. W. (1980). The stress audit: Identifying the stressors of ICU nursing. *Journal of Nursing Education, 19*(6), 15–25.

Barnett-Queen, T., & Bergman, L. H. (1988). Implementing posttrauma programs. *Fire Engineering, 141*(9), 52–58.

Bergman, L. H., & Barnett-Queen, T. (undated). Critical incident stress debriefings: Debriefing process. Unpublished manuscript.

Bergman, L. H., & Queen, T. R. (1986a, April). Critical incident stress: Part I. *Fire Command,* 18–20.

Bergman, L. H., & Queen, T. R. (1986b, May). Critical incident stress: Part II. *Fire Command,* 52–56.

Brownstone, J.E., Shatoff, D. K., & Duckro, P. N. (1983). Reducing stress factors in EMS: Report of a national survey. *Emergency Health Services Review, 2*(1), 35-53.

Cydulka, R. K., Lyons, J., Moy, A., Shay, K., Hammer, J., & Mathews, J. (1989). A follow-up report of occupational stress in urban EMT-paramedics. *Annals of Emergency Medicine, 18,* 1151–1156.

Davidson, A. D. (1979). Air disaster: Coping with stress. *Police Stress, 1*(2), 20–22.

Dunning, C. (1988). Intervention strategies for emergency workers. In M. Lystad (Ed.), *Mental health response to mass emergencies.* New York: Brunner/Mazel.

Dunning, C. (1990). Mental health sequelae in disaster workers: Prevention and intervention. *International Journal of Mental Health, 19*(2), 91–103.

Dyregrov, A., & Mitchell, J. T. (1992). Work with traumatized children—psychological effects and coping strategies. *Journal of Traumatic Stress, 5,* 5–17.

Foreman, W. C. (1990, October). Traumatic incidents at work—cases. Presented at Work-Related Trauma Workshop, at the sixth annual meeting of the Society for Traumatic Stress Studies, New Orleans, La.

Genest, M., Levine, J., Ramsden, V., & Swanson, R. (1990). The impact of providing help: Emergency workers and cardiopulmonary resuscitation attempts. *Journal of Traumatic Stress, 3,* 305–313.

Graduate Medical Education. (1992). *Journal of the American Medical Association, 268*(9), 1170–1176.

Graham, N. K. (1981, January). Done in, fed up, burned out: Too much attrition in EMS. *Journal of Emergency Medical Services,* pp. 24–29.

Hinds, C. (1988). The heat of burnout: How to reduce stress. *Emergency Medical Services, 17*(10), 52–54.

Ho, K. (1988). Stress among emergency medical staff. *Canadian Medical Association Journal,* *139,* 1034–1035.

Hoge, M. A., & Hirschman, R. (1984). Psychological training of emergency medical technicians: An evaluation. *American Journal of Community Psychology, 12,* 127–131.

Horn, J. M., & Reese, J. T. (undated). The Federal Bureau of Investigation's traumatic incident stress response program. Unpublished paper, Quantico, Va.

Hunter, K., Jenkins, J. O., & Hampton, L. A. (1982). Burnout among providers of emergency health care. *Crisis Intervention, 12*(4), 141–152.

Hytten, K., & Hasle, A. (1989). Fire fighters: A study of stress and coping. *Acta Psychiatric Scandinavian Suppl. 355, 80,* 50–55.

Keller, K. L., & Koenig, W. J. (1989). Management of stress and prevention of burnout in emergency physicians. *Annals of Emergency Medicine, 18,* 42–47.

Mannon, J. M. (1981, May/June). Aiming for "detached concern"—how EMTs and paramedics cope. *Emergency Medical Services,* pp. 6–23.

McCammon, S., Durham, T. W., Allison, E. J., & Williamson, J. E. (1988). Emergency workers' cognitive appraisal and coping with traumatic events. *Journal of Traumatic Stress, 3,* 353–372.

Miles, M. S., Demi, A. S., & Mostyn-Aker, P. (1984). Rescue workers' reactions following the Hyatt Hotel disaster. *Death Education, 8,* 315–331.

Mitchell, J. T. (1983). When disaster strikes... The critical incident stress debriefing process. *Journal of Emergency Medical Services, 8*(1), 36–39.

Mitchell, J. T. (1988). Stress: The history, status and future of critical incident stress debriefings. *Journal of Emergency Medical Services, 13*(11), 46–47, 49–52.

Mitchell, J., & Bray, G. (1990). *Emergency services stress: Guidelines for preserving the health and careers of emergency services personnel.* Englewood Cliffs, N.J.: Prentice Hall.

Neale, A. V. (1991). Work stress in emergency medical technicians. *Journal of Occupational Medicine, 33,* 991–997.

Nydam, R. J. (1983, February). Rescue trauma threshold. *Emergency,* pp. 35, 45.

Paton, D. (1990). Assessing the impact of disasters on helpers. *Counselling Psychology Quarterly, 3,* 149–152.

Paton, D. (1992). Disaster research: The Scottish dimension. *The Psychologist, 5,* 533–538.

Paton, D. (1994). Disaster relief work: An assessment of training effectiveness. *Journal of Traumatic Stress, 7,* 275–288.

Raphael, B. (1986). *When disaster strikes: How individuals and communities cope with catastrophe.* New York: Basic Books.

Revicki, D. A., Whitley T. W., Landis, S. S., & Allison, E. J. (1988). Organizational characteristics, occupational stress, and depression in rural emergency medical technicians. *Journal of Rural Health, 4* (2), 73–83.

Schmuckler, E. (1991a). How to avoid becoming a statistic. *Peace Officer, 41*(1), 91–101.

Schmuckler, E. (1991b). Don't become a statistic. *Emergency Medical Services, 20*(9), 26–32.

Shelton, R. (1991). Staying in service. *Emergency Medical Services, 20*(9), 20–25.

Solomon, R. M. (1991, September). Eye movement desensitization and reprocessing: Treatment of choice for critical incident trauma. Presented at the Eighth Users' Stress Workshop, San Antonio, Texas.

Swedish National Board of Health and Welfare. (1991). *Psychological, psychiatric and social management of disaster.* Modin-tryk, Stockholm.

Wagner, M. (1979a). Airline disaster: A stress debrief program for police. *Police Stress, 2*(1), 16–20.

Wagner, M. (1979b, August). Stress debriefing—flight 191: Department program that worked. *Police Star,* pp. 4–8.

Whitley, T. W., & Allison, E. J. (1989). Stress in EMS: Opportunities and directions for future research. *Annals of Emergency Medicine, 18,* 1247–1248.

Whitley, T. W., Revicki, D. A., Allison, E. J., & Landis, S. S. (1990). Predictors of job satisfaction among rural emergency medical technicians. *Prehospital and Disaster Medicine, 5,* 217–224.

Young, M. (1991). *Community crisis response team training manual.* Washington, D.C. National Organization for Victim Assistance.

7

Treating the "Heroic Treaters"

MARY S. CERNEY

"Trauma" comes from the Greek word meaning "injury." Haynal (1989) describes three characteristics of trauma: (1) It is "linked to frustrated *desires*," accentuating the (2) "*helplessness*" of the individual to achieve them, and it is (3) "situated in the relationship with the *other*" (p. 316). Freud (1955) said that trauma occurs when the ego is overwhelmed "as a consequence of an extensive breach being made in the protective shield against stimuli" (p. 31). Because each person's experience of trauma is so different, there is much discussion about what may or may not constitute trauma (Furman, 1986; Yorke, 1986). Nevertheless, authors generally agree that a "traumatic event is one in which the person is flooded with intense stimulation that he or she cannot control" (Thompson & Kennedy, 1987, p. 195).

The author expresses her appreciation to the professional staff of the Division of Scientific Publications at the Menninger Clinic, especially to Philip R. Beard and Mary Ann Clifft for providing editorial assistance in the preparation of the final draft of this manuscript.

Editor's Note: In this chapter, Mary Cerney discusses the special burdens of therapists who treat patients suffering from traumatic stress. As an experienced therapist and educator, she helps the reader appreciate the factors that appear to contribute to secondary traumatic stress. She then explores how such stress overlaps with transference and countertransference and suggests effective methods for counteracting its powerful effect on those whom she calls the "heroic treaters."

Not everyone reacts in the same manner to what objectively may be labeled as traumatic events. Many conditions, including physical and psychological development, age, and the specific circumstances in which the trauma occurred, influence how and whether an individual will respond to a particular traumatic event. The same inference may be made in regard to therapists who work with traumatized individuals. In addition to these factors, the personal and professional experiences of therapists affect their response to the tragic stories of their patients. Therapists' reactions resemble those of individuals who have witnessed tragedies, natural or created catastrophes, and acts of violence (Mitchell, 1985). But most powerful and shattering to these therapists is their sense of personal outrage and disillusionment. What they hear becomes a violent attack on their own sense of integrity and view of the world—their internal schema (McCann & Pearlman, 1990a). As suggested by the editor of this series, I will use the term "secondary trauma" when referring to this phenomenon.

NATURE OF TRAUMA

Some patients tend to be protective of their therapists, repeating the phenomena typical of the patients' lives. As in the past, such a patient may sacrifice personal needs for the well-being and comfort of another—now the therapist. At the slightest hint of displeasure or disbelief on the part of the therapist, the patient will avoid that particular painful topic and go on to a more acceptable subject. The problem of being believed extends even to patients' not believing it themselves, despite the persistence of troublesome memories. These patients are frequently reluctant to permit the material to surface into their own consciousness, because the traumatic experience may be so difficult for them to believe, may create such sheer terror in remembering, and may fill patients with guilt and the expectation of blame. Once there, it still takes a very trusting individual to share this material with another.

For many individuals, the cruelty and sadistic atrocities that are enacted on innocent children, or on victims of any age, race, or nationality, are difficult to fathom, much less believe. When confronted with such horror, therapists themselves can become traumatized by what they hear and experience in therapy. Like individuals who witness a tragic event happening to others and suffer intense feelings of guilt and responsibility for not having prevented it, these therapists are faced with "survivor guilt" (Niederland, 1981, p. 420). As witnesses to tales of unbelievable cruelty and the obvious pain of the shared revelation, therapists may undergo the dissolution of previously cherished concepts and views of the world and of human beings. Furthermore, they may be psychically shattered by the loss of these beliefs and by the consequences of this loss—a less trusting mode of interaction with others and a sense of hopelessness at the enormity of the therapeutic undertaking.

It is not surprising or unexpected that therapists should themselves become traumatized. As English (1976) has noted, "If one wayward child can impair the morale of a whole family, it therefore stands to reason that ten disturbed patients are going to take their toll on the therapist" (p. 197). And these therapists frequently have many more than ten such individuals in their practice.

UNDERLYING CRITICAL CONCEPTS

Four central psychodynamic concepts underlie a sound understanding of why therapists may be vulnerable to secondary trauma: transference, countertransference, projective identification, and identification. It is beyond the scope of this chapter to review comprehensively the current—and sometimes differing—views of these phenomena. Each will be discussed specifically as it concerns the subject at hand.

Transference

A growing literature speaks to the diagnostic and therapeutic advantages of understanding transference and countertransference phenomena (Allen, 1991; Epstein & Feiner, 1979; Giovacchini, 1985; Greenberg & Mitchell, 1983; Kernberg, 1965; Levy, 1990; McDougall, 1979; McElroy & McElroy, 1991; Meissner, 1991; Racker, 1957; Stolorow, 1992; Walker, 1991; Winnicott, 1949) as they arise within a therapeutic relationship. Transference phenomena occur in all aspects of life. Individuals may react to certain persons in authority as though they were their parents, or to colleagues as though they were siblings or other important figures from early childhood. Generally, these reactions can be handled without jeopardizing relationships or jobs. They may even enhance both working and social relationships, repairing early experiences.

The more traditional concept of transference confines it to the therapeutic relationship, describing the patient's view of the treater. In this scenario, the patient responds initially "as if" the treater were the "all-caring" parent for whom the patient has been searching. Soon, however, this positive transference evolves into what is termed the *negative transference*, in which the patient, despite the reality of what is actually occurring, sees the therapist as the "all-abusive" parent, sibling, relative, neighbor, or stranger. Diagnostically, the development of transference can facilitate and illuminate the therapeutic understanding of what is hidden within the patient, his or her deep (perhaps unconscious) desires, the inner pain, and the feelings of rage and guilt that arise from real or perceived mistreatment. Within the context of the transference experience, the patient's early relationships can be examined, understood, reframed, and, in time, healed.

Patients in the neurotic range of psychopathology can tell, despite their feelings to the contrary, the difference between the "real" therapist and the "transference " experience. Even though the patient experiences the therapist as mother, father, or persecutor, he or she recognizes that the therapist is not actually his or her mother, father, or persecutor.

The distinction between the real persons and the transference figures, however, may fade when working with patients in the borderline and psychotic ranges. In a psychotic transference, the patient is convinced that the therapist is the cruel, rejecting mother, father, or persecutor of previous experience. When dealing with trauma victims, particularly those who have multiple personalities, the therapist may encounter psychotic "alters" in an otherwise neurotic individual, thus creating particularly difficult transference paradigms. At such times, therapists who are having personal difficulties may experience the negative transference more acutely.

In working with traumatized individuals, therapists soon encounter not only perceptions of themselves as persecutors and sadistic torturers (Pines, 1986; Rustin, 1980), but also their own feelings of disgust and revulsion. For example, therapists working with Holocaust survivors and their descendants report their patients' view of them as brutal torturers, and their own feelings of being those brutal torturers. In a reversal of roles, these therapists can experience despair, terror, and helplessness as they become the victims and as their patients assume the roles of cruel tormentors and persecutors (Pines, 1986).

Countertransference

Despite clear evidence supporting the therapeutic value of an awareness and acknowledgment of countertransference feelings and the insight that can be generated, many therapists still feel inept and inadequate when they become aware of their own countertransference feelings and behavior. Instead of having such insights as, "Now, I understand what the patient is experiencing," or "My own feelings are getting in the way of my work. I need to look at them and understand where they are com-

ing from," many sincere and competent clinicians are plagued by con-
demning thoughts such as, "I made a mistake," and "If I really understood what was happening, I wouldn't have had this problem."

Countertransference feelings, if not recognized, can raise havoc in
treatment. Newberry (1985) wrote of countertransference feelings ranging from overestimating to underestimating the trauma experienced by
Vietnam veterans as a result of the public condemnation not only of the
war, but also of the soldiers who participated in the conflict.

The reactions of male and female therapists may differ according to
their gender. Upon hearing of a patient's being assualted, a female therapist may respond with her own feelings of vulnerability and fear. Her
own experiences may come to mind and cloud her thinking. She may
become overly protective of her patient. A therapist who is male, on the
other hand, may feel guilty for being a man or for his own past sexual
aggressions, rape fantasies, or attraction to the patient. Male therapists
may perceive a need to prove that they are "good" men, not like the
assailant, and they may be tempted to offer physical support or to
become overly protective of the patient, and of women in general (Colao
& Hunt, 1983).

In supervision, Bill reported how distressed and frightened his
patient had become after a painful sexual experience with a previous
therapist. She said she could feel comfortable addressing the trauma
only if she could sit on the floor next to Bill's chair, wrap her arms
around his legs, and lay her head in his lap. Bill knew that this scenario
was inappropriate, but he struggled with how to support his patient
most effectively.

These patients are in such pain, and so skilled in communicating it,
that inexperienced and even experienced therapists can accede in good
faith to such patients' inappropriate requests. At these times, it is difficult for therapists to recognize that what these patients are searching for
is not what they ask for. They are desperately looking for someone who
can maintain appropriate boundaries and, in so doing, prove that they,
the patients, are not the perpetrators, and so are not responsible for their
abuse, as they have been led to believe.

Therapists can experience particular difficulty in hearing patients'
descriptions of atrocities perpetrated not only on the patients, but, as in
the case of Vietnam veterans, also on innocent populations (S.L.
Bradshaw, Jr., personal communication, August 25, 1992; Bradshaw,
Ohlde, & Horne, 1991; Brende & Parson, 1985; Haley, 1974). The same
thing can happen when hearing of the rituals performed by satanic cults.
Countertransference has the potential to play a key role in the treatment
of trauma victims (Abarbanel, 1979; McCombie & Arons, 1980;

McCombie, Bassuk, Savitz, & Pell,1976; Schuker, 1979). However, instead of serving as a resource for insight into the victims' psychodynamics, countertransference "has often exacerbated and entrenched victims' psychodynamics and has limited research and treatment" (Rose, 1986, p. 818). Countertransference feelings can, under the guise of giving comfort, repeat the trauma of previous experience.

Projective Identification

In the course of the therapy, a patient will often experience feelings of being persecuted by even the gentlest of therapists. When these persecutory feelings become unbearable, the patient tends to project them outward, often with such intensity that the therapist internalizes the feelings to the point of identifying with them, and then acts accordingly, as a persecutor, even though that is not his or her usual style. The therapist may become rude, insulting, and at times cruel to the patient. Both individuals suffer: The patient again undergoes the trauma of being victimized, and the therapist's self-perception of being a kind, understanding person may be severely damaged (Catherall, 1991).

This phenomenon, called "projective identification," was introduced by Melanie Klein (1946). It has been used to refer to a variety of different, but usually complementary, conceptualizations (Schafer, 1968, Segal, 1964). Ogden (1979) is perhaps clearest in conceptualizing projective identification as referring to a "group of fantasies and accompanying object relations having to do with the ridding of the self of unwanted aspects of the self; the depositing of those unwanted 'parts' into another person; and finally, with the 'recovery' of a modified version of what was extruded" (p. 357).

Horwitz (1983), however, in speaking of projective identification in dyads and groups, postulated that the defense of projective identification, unlike that of projection, "stems from a variety of motivations and not just the wish to rid oneself of unwanted impulses like aggression and sadism. Wishes to dominate, devalue, and control—based on primitive envy and the wish to cling parasitically to the valued object—are among the other motives" (p. 261). Like any other concept, projective identification has many ramifications and can occur in many situations other than one-to-one therapy.

Identification

Identification is different from empathy, in which the therapist "feels" with the patient without losing distance. Greenson (1967) has observed that there are many different kinds of identifications: "some are partial, some total; some transitory, some permanent; some accessible to consciousness, some inaccessible; some ego syntonic and some ego dystonic" (p. 245). In working with trauma victims, it is easy to identify with their rage and desire for revenge, thus intensifying their feelings rather than helping them to work through and beyond them, which is necessary if resolution is ever to be achieved.

Overidentification may be a problem for a therapist when a patient comes from a background that is similar in terms of culture, social values, and experience. On the other hand, the therapist may tend to minimize, negate, or invalidate aspects of a patient's experience if the patient comes from a different background (Fischman, 1991; Fischman & Ross, 1990). Ethnicity, language, sex, and nationality can be barriers to a true therapeutic alliance. Wilson (1989) has pointed out that psychotherapy will not be effective if the therapist does not understand the ethnic and cultural factors that affect the patient's processing of the traumatic event. The same is true in working with therapists who have experienced secondary trauma.

THERAPISTS OF TRAUMA VICTIMS

English (1976) wrote, "The therapist must be fully conscious of the needs of his or her patient, and fully aware of the tactics he uses in an attempt to repair himself. If he is not, the therapist may find he has taken over the pathology of his patient within himself to such an extent that the therapist himself feels 'sick' " (p. 191). The affront to the sense of self experienced by therapists of trauma victims can be so overwhelming that, despite their best efforts, the therapists begin to exhibit the same characteristics as their patients. That is, they experience a change in their interaction with the world, themselves, and their families. They may begin to have intrusive thoughts, nightmares, and generalized anxiety. They themselves need assistance in coping with their trauma.

Henry (1966) claimed that "the career of a mental health professional, at least those in direct therapeutic work, is a commitment to a *lifestyle*, as well as an investment in a line of work" (p. 54). Changes reflected in the therapist due to his or her experiences in therapeutic work are bound to be reflected in interactions with the world outside therapy.

Although Henry referred particularly to a way of viewing the world (i.e., the therapist's theoretical orientation), what he said also applies to the changes within therapists as a result of their work.

McCann, Sakheim, and Abrahamson (1988) contend that as therapists find their internal schemata changing, particularly regarding their idiosyncratic view of the world and how people interact, their own interactions with the outside world also change. McCann and colleagues reported that as a result of working with victims of sexual abuse, some members of their group became more vigilant concerning their own families and more suspicious of other children's parents. These feelings were discussed and worked through in case supervision groups. If these feelings had been unattended to and unresolved, they could have had a detrimental effect on the lives of these therapists, on their families and loved ones, and on their work with patients.

Therapists are often unaware that their patients may have suffered severe trauma in the past, either because the patients have never had the courage to tell them, or because they do not remember it. Not believing the traumatic event themselves, or feeling that they caused it, patients may be reluctant to reveal such incidents until they are comfortable and in a more accepting environment. The same holds true for therapists suffering from secondary trauma.

Two or three trauma patients in a practice may be manageable, but rarely does a therapist treat only two or three such patients. As the therapist becomes more effective with these patients, his or her reputation grows, leading to more referrals and thus increasing the therapist's difficulty in limiting the number of such patients. The pleading of these patients, their families, or a therapist's colleagues can be so poignant, and the intensity of a patient's suffering so compelling that many therapists think they can handle just "one more patient." But there is always just one more patient, until even the best therapists burn out or suffer "psychic overload," which can take them out of the front lines of work with such patients, if not out of the field entirely.

With burnout, these therapists may experience such a revulsion to their patients' trauma or such an identification with their patients' pain and outrage that all objectivity is lost, along with the ability to be helpful. Some therapists can sink into a deep depression, which isolates them from the support of others. They may be plagued by dreams, nightmares, and intrusive thoughts similar to those their patients reported. As these therapists become overwhelmed, their behavior with relatives and friends may become isolative or offensive. At this point, these therapists themselves have become traumatized and require professional help.

Some therapists, may find certain kinds of trauma more difficult to deal with than others. The rituals described by traumatized victims as practiced in some satanic cults, for example, can be so sadistic and horrifying that it is practically impossible for therapists to maintain the balance of empathy and objectivity necessary to facilitate the working through of these experiences. Furthermore, working with trauma patients may activate therapists' previously repressed memories of being similary abused themselves, which may have escaped detection in their personal therapy. Until therapists come to terms with their own memories and their own trauma, their work with trauma victims cannot proceed.

PREVENTIVE MEASURES FOR TRAUMA THERAPISTS

Therapeutic Realism

Therapists should not allow themselves to feel that they must be able to treat every kind of patient, regardless of diagnosis, or to handle an unlimited number of patients. Giovacchini (1985) cautions, "Some therapists can treat patients others cannot. No one can treat all patients, and our personal orientation and reactions figure prominently in our capacity to conduct psychotherapy" (p. 450). Despite this warning, which is proclaimed repeatedly in every psychotherapy training class, studies continue to find that many therapists hold the irrational belief that they must operate at peak efficiency and competence at all times with all patients (Deutsch, 1984; Forney, Wallace-Schutzman, & Wiggers, 1982). This belief can be a contributing factor to a therapist's experience of secondary trauma. Therapy is not what it once was, nor were the problems we encounter today prepared for in yesterday's psychotherapy training curricula. Widespread but hitherto concealed abuse is now being acknowledged and is demanding resolution. Because not enough therapists are skilled in treating the post-traumatic stress disorder (PTSD), the few therapists who do this work are swamped with referrals. Despite their best efforts, they are still unable to meet the demand for their services. Consequently, they may become traumatized not only by the content of their patients' traumatic experiences, but also by their inability to serve all who need their help.

Supervision–Consultation

Much secondary trauma can be avoided or its effects ameliorated if therapists seek regular supervision or consultation. Within the supervisory process, blind spots can be detected, overidentification corrected, alternative treatment procedures discussed and evaluated, and the therapist's overextension or overinvolvement analyzed and understood.

Group supervision can be very helpful in working with trauma victims. As group members listen to how the presenter is handling a particular case, they gain insight into their own cases in a way that can avoid much countertransference clouding. Presenters also frequently report that they gain insight into their own cases as they present them.

Viewing another therapist's patient and listening to how that therapist is handling material generated in therapy can facilitate the recognition of similarities to one's own patients. This process allows therapists to view their own therapy as others might view it, without the blind spots they might encounter in directly examining their own cases in the privacy of their offices.

McCann and Pearlman (1990b), in citing examples of how therapists react to work with particular trauma patients, emphasized the importance of case supervision as a way of dealing with affect overload and the intrusive imagery that can disrupt the therapist's life. The importance of supervision and discussion with colleagues cannot be overemphasized.

Establishing a Balance

All therapists should establish and maintain a balance between their professional and personal lives, but for trauma therapists, this is imperative. When the needs of professional life intrude on a therapist's personal life, the result is damage not only to the therapist, but also to the members of the therapist's family and to the therapist's friends. Frequently overworked and overtraumatized themselves, these therapists may traumatize their families by their chronic unavailability and emotional withdrawal, perhaps in much the same way that trauma victims sometimes traumatize those around them.

In treating a patient who had been sexually abused by her father as a child, Jane, a therapist, became aware that she, too, has been an incest victim. She sought treatment and began to uncover memory after memory of sexual abuse. Over and over, she described her memories in great detail to her friends. Every conversation began and ended with what she was uncovering. Her friends began to report dreams and nightmares of their friend being in great pain, but in the dreams they were always impeded from helping her, just as they were in real life. Many of her friends sought help themselves to deal with this situation. Jane also began to see evidence of sexual abuse in her husband, children, and friends. In essence, she was destroying her family life, her friendships, and her personal life. Issues of sexual abuse intruded on every aspect of her life, both professional and personal, including her interactions with patients, colleagues, and friends.

Maintaining a satisfactory personal life enables therapists to have fun, to enjoy themselves alone and in the company of others, to laugh, and to renew their faith in the goodness of most humans. Maintaining a balanced personal life also enables them to approach their professional work with renewed zest and a freshness that inspires a reawakening of hope in their patients.

Maintaining Physical and Mental Health

Listening to others hour after hour is strenuous work under any circumstances. Listening to facilitate the working through of trauma requires a stamina that can be maintained only by therapists who are in good mental and physical health. Staying healthy both mentally and physically requires a regime of regular exercise and play, a balanced diet, and sufficient rest. Time is needed to nourish one's physical needs, personal needs, and professional needs. To maintain the boundaries necessary for good mental and physical health, therapists may have to prioritize their commitments, and even terminate some of them.

TREATMENT MODALITIES FOR THERAPISTS

Because therapists who suffer secondary trauma exhibit many of the same symptoms that their patients do, some of the same treatment methods can be effective. Traumatized therapists may be reluctant to enter treatment, however, because this would seem to be an indictment of their clinical ability. Instead, burned out and wounded, they may choose to abandon work with trauma victims. Thus therapists who enter treatment require treating therapists who are accepting, nonjudgmental, and empathic without being overawed. In other words, they require the same kind of therapist that the trauma victim requires.

The treating therapist must identify the basic elements of the trauma. No doubt there will be aspects of transference, countertransference, and identification. Once identified, these issues must be worked through. But most prominent among the difficulties therapists will face in treatment will be the trauma resulting from the assault on their perceptions of the world and of the people who inhabit that world. McCann and Pearlman (1990a) utilize constructivist theory as a way of understanding and synthesizing what trauma patients are undergoing. The same theoretical understanding applies to the trauma experienced by therapists. This theory explicates a very commonsense view of why people report different experiences even when their situations are identical. Each person has a unique constellation of physical, psychological, and environmental experiences that make up and affect that person at any given moment as he or she creates a personal internal schema to make sense out of what is happening. Despite certain commonalities, no one absorbs, reacts, or integrates any experience exactly as another person does. No single individual encounters a life event with the same constellation and repertoire of experiences as any other individual. Consequently, each individual's experience of any given moment is unique.

Except for anecdotal accounts, no studies were found in the literature describing work with therapists who had become traumatized as a result of their work with trauma patients. There are numerous references to the countertransference reaction of the therapist (Colao & Hunt, 1983; Fischman, 1991; Ganzarain, 1991; Ganzarain & Buchele, 1989; Peebles-Kleiger, 1989), but no reports of work with therapists who suffer from secondary trauma.

I have treated a number of therapists suffering from secondary trauma using basically the same techniques I use with trauma victims. Determining how to proceed with such an individual depends on a careful evaluation of what the patient is experiencing and what is precipitating that experience. In many situations, the recommendation of case supervision may be sufficient to resolve the problem. At other times, a more in-depth process may be necessary, particularly if the current reaction is uncovering the patient's own previously repressed abuse or other unresolved issues. In the following, I review some techniques for working through trauma and how they may be helpful with the therapist suffering from secondary trauma.

Hypnosis

Stutman and Bliss (1985) found that combat veterans with severe PTSD demonstrated high hypnotic susceptibility and an above-average capacity for mental imagery. Much of what is disturbing to trauma patients is imagery in the form of nightmares, intrusive recollections, and the repeated memories that accompany their recollections. It is, therefore, not surprising that hypnotherapy increasingly is being used in work with trauma victims. It can be an invaluable technique in recovering and resolving traumatic memories for both the trauma patient and the traumatized therapist.

Hypnosis, however, poses several problems independent of the skill of the therapist. A recognized authority, Horevitz (1983), noted the "heightened rapport of hypnosis," which facilitates the development of "unique, emotionally charged relationships" (p. 143). He is not alone in this opinion. Earlier, Guze (1956) likened the hypnotic state to the infant's primitive responsiveness to parental figures, which Solovey de Milechnin (1956) described as a *"return to the peculiar equilibrium in corti-cal/subcortical activity that characterizes mental functioning at an early age"* (p. 39). Peebles-Kleiger (1989) states that when the therapist and patient share this emotional field, there is access to primitive, unconscious emotional contents in both therapist and patient, with the possibility of transmitting unconscious material back and forth between them. The hypnotic situation is likely to evoke intensification of responses in both therapists and patients, particularly in the area of transference and countertransference (Fromm, 1968; Orne, 1965; Spiegel, 1959). Thus therapists who use hypnosis in this work are at risk of assuming the same symptoms as their patients. It may be that the same quality that enables therapists to be effective in hypnotic techniques and work with trauma victims may also make them vulnerable to secondary trauma.

Technique is very important in the use of hypnosis, but the outcome may depend more on the characteristics of the hypnotist than on that individual's technical skill (Gill & Brenman, 1959). Good hypnothera-pists have the same characteristics as good therapists. They are sensitive to the patient's needs and are able to "dance" with the patient, that is, they accommodate procedures to what the patient can handle and at a pace that the patient can follow.

Imagery

According to Paivio (1986), it is the imagery system of memory that is most likely to be affected in trauma. This finding applies both to trauma victims and to their therapists. Horowitz (1983) and McCann and Pearlman (1990b) cite vignettes of therapists who reported nightmares, flashbacks, and intrusive memories similar to those of their patients.

Imagery, although more popular in recent times, is not a newcomer to the therapist's armamentarium of effective techniques. Among the early clinicians to suggest the use of visual imagery were Breuer and Freud (1955), Ferenczi (1950), and Jung (1959). Today imagery has experienced a revival and has gained considerable respectability under the leader-ship of respected clinicians and researchers (Horowitz, 1983; Sheikh, 1983; Singer & Pope, 1978).

Many clinicians use imagery in their work with trauma victims as a way of desensitizing the traumatic memory. Grigsby (1987), however, prefers to intensify the feeling, and then to suggest that the patient imagine a differ-ent outcome to clarify other facets of his or her emotional response.

Grove and Panzer (1991) employ what they term "clean language" in their work with imagery. Their work focuses on linguistically based techniques, which enable the therapist to access information contained in primary process language. By not imposing secondary process language and thinking on the patient, the therapist enables the patient to gain access to his or her own inner world and to experience whatever is necessary. For example, the question, "How can I help?" reframed as a "clean" question, would be, "What would be helpful?" The first question focuses on the therapist, whereas the second question focuses on the patient. As Panzer (1991) explains, "The use of clean language can elicit trance without induction, enable the client to discover the infrastructure of his [or her] complaint, permit the therapist to communicate with the client's non-conscious functions. A healing evolution of the memories, metaphors, symbols, and semantic constructs underlying the client's disturbance is facilitated" (p. xi).

My use of imagery bears some resemblance to that of Grove and Panzer. It differs in that it is guided at particular points, although it, too, obtains direction from the patient. Like Grove and Panzer, I do not use induction; instead, when asked to image, patients spontaneously go into the level of trance required. When patients present a nightmare, dream, memory, flashback, or intrusive thought, they are asked to redream the dream or go over the experience again. At the point at which the abuse is about to begin, I suggest they freeze the scene so that they can program how the scenario is to proceed. They are then asked if they would like to enter the scene—be it dream, memory, or flashback—as an adult. Or they may bring anyone they wish into the drama with them. Thus they have the opportunity to say what they could not say earlier, to express feelings of anger and regret, to inquire into the motivation of the perpetrator, to search for the "why" behind the abuse. As the work continues, they are invited to consider alternative views of understanding the experience, which ultimately facilitates letting go of painful, wounding aspects of the memory. Restructuring the internal experience and reframing the understanding of this experience can lead to significant breakthroughs in treatment (Cerney, 1985, 1988, 1989; Cerney & Buskirk, 1991).

Timing is of the essence in the use of imagery. Patients are not always able to handle imagery, or may even prefer other techniques. They should not be forced. Horowitz (1983) stresses that "image techniques should be related to a larger, well-formulated plan for how a patient may change" (p. 305).

The effectiveness of imagery can seem almost miraculous. Individuals frequently make significant progress in only a few sessions.

The intricacies of how and why it works so effectively when it does work are not clearly known. Meichenbaum (1978) suggests that three psychological processes explain the effectiveness of all imagery-based therapies. Sheikh (1983) summarizes these as: "(1) the feeling of control which the client gains as a result of the monitoring and rehearsing of various images; (2) the modified meaning or changed internal dialogue that precedes, attends, and succeeds examples of maladaptive behavior; and (3) the mental rehearsal of alternative responses that lead to the enhancement of coping skills" (p. 423).

SUMMARY

Therapists who work with trauma victims are subject to significant stress and are vulnerable to what is now being called "secondary trauma." This particular traumatization comes from being exposed to a reality that is beyond ordinary comprehension and seems unbelievable to the uninitiated. As therapists begin to accept the credibility of what they are hearing, their own moorings in reality may be shaken, if not shattered. Their internal schemata, as described by McCann and Pearlman (1990a), are altered or destroyed, and they, too, become traumatized as they seek to construct a new reality for themselves.

What appears to be most helpful to therapists who work with trauma victims is for them to acknowledge that they cannot treat every patient. They must also be connected with their peers in support groups and supervision groups. They must not isolate themselves. To maintain some opportunity to express their feelings of pain, guilt, and responsibility, they need to discuss their cases regularly with their colleagues and supervisors. In an accepting atmosphere, these traumatized therapists can gain support and assistance in rebuilding their view of the world—albeit a different view.

In addition, therapists should limit their practice and take time to refresh themselves in their private lives through leisure and relaxation. It is important for these therapists, as for everyone, not only to continue to develop a sense of humor, but also to be able to laugh. Someone once described laughter as "internal massage." In the area of trauma, it is difficult to find anything to laugh about, but in a group there are always clever others who can make us laugh appropriately. We just need to listen to them and allow them the freedom to help us laugh at ourselves. It is silly for any one of us to think we have all the answers or the only way of resolving the trauma question! We should also admit that we will make mistakes. We need to take ourselves less seriously.

Maintaining good physical health is a necessity. Without stamina, we cannot tolerate the stress that working with trauma victims entails. A balance of work and play, supported by a balanced diet with appropriate exercise and sufficient rest, will resolve many a stressful situation.

In our efforts to deal with the issue of trauma, it would be helpful to remember the words of Reinhold Niebuhr (1952): "Nothing that is worth doing can be achieved in our lifetime; therefore we must be saved by hope. Nothing which is true or beautiful or good makes complete sense in any immediate context of history; therefore we must be saved by faith. Nothing we do, however virtuous, can be accomplished alone; therefore we are saved by love" (p. 63).

REFERENCES

Abarbanel, G. (1979). The sexual assault patient. In R. Green (Ed.), *Human sexuality: A health practitioner's text* (2nd ed., pp. 226–241). Baltimore: Williams & Wilkins.
Allen, D.M. (1991). *Deciphering motivation in psychotherapy.* New York: Plenum.
Bradshaw, S.L., Jr., Ohlde, C.D., & Horne, J.B. (1991). The love of war: Vietnam and the traumatized veteran. *Bulletin of the Menninger Clinic, 55,* 96–103.
Brende, J.O., & Parson, E.R. (1985). *Vietnam veterans: The road to recovery.* New York: Plenum.
Breuer, J., & Freud, S. (1955). Studies on hysteria. In J. Strachey (Ed. and Trans.). *The standard edition of the complete psychological works of Sigmund Freud* (Vol. 2, pp. vii–xxxi, 1–311). London: Hogarth Press. New York: Basic Books. (Original work published 1893–1895).
Catherall, D.R. (1991). Aggression and projective identification in the treatment of victims. *Psychotherapy, 28,* 145–149.
Cerney, M. (1985). Imagery and grief work. *Psychotherapy, 2*(1), 35–44.
Cerney, M. (1988). "If only..." Remorse in grief therapy. *Psychotherapy Patient, 5*(1/2), 235–248.
Cerney, M. (1989). Use of imagery in grief therapy. In J.E. Shorr, M. Wolpin, P. Robin, & J.A. Connella (Eds.), *Imagery V* (pp. 105–119). New York: Plenum.
Cerney, M.S., & Buskirk, J.R. (1991). Anger: The hidden part of grief. *Bulletin of the Menninger Clinic, 55,* 228-237.
Colao, F., & Hunt, M. (1983). Therapists coping with sexual assault. *Women and Therapy, 2,* 205–214.
Deutsch, C.J. (1984). Self-reported sources of stress among psychotherapists. *Professional Psychology: Research and Practice, 15,* 833–845.
English, O.S. (1976). The emotional stress of psychotherapeutic practice. *Journal of the American Academy of Psychoanalysis, 4,* 191–201.
Epstein, L., & Feiner, A.H. (Eds.). (1979). *Countertransference.* New York: Jason Aronson.
Ferenczi, S. (1950). On forced phantasies. In J. Rickman (Ed.), *Further contributions to the theory and technique of psycho-analysis* (pp. 68–77). London: Hogarth Press. (Original work published 1924.)
Figley, C.R. (1983). Catastrophes: An overview of family reaction. In C.R. Figley & H.I. McCubbin (Eds.), *Stress and the family: Vol. 2. Coping with catastrophe* (pp. 3–20). New York: Brunner/Mazel.
Fischman, Y. (1991). Interacting with trauma: Clinicians' responses to treating psychological aftereffects of political repression. *American Journal of Orthopsychiatry, 61,* 179–185.
Fischman, Y., & Ross, J. (1990). Group treatment of exiled survivors of torture. *American Journal of Orthopsychiatry, 60,* 135–142.

Forney, D.S., Wallace-Schutzman, F., & Wiggers, T.T. (1982). Burnout among career development professionals: Preliminary findings and implications. *Personnel and Guidance Journal, 60*, 435–439.

Freud, S. (1955). Beyond the pleasure principle . In J. Strachey (Ed. and Trans.), *The standard edition of the complete psychological works of Sigmund Freud* (Vol. 18, pp. 1–64). London: Hogarth Press. (Original work published 1920.)

Fromm, E. (1968). Transference and countertransference in hypnoanalysis. *International Journal of Clinical and Experimental Hypnosis, 16*, 77–84.

Furman, E.E. (1986). On trauma: When is the death of a parent traumatic? *Psychoanalytic Study of the Child, 41*, 191–208.

Ganzarain, R. (1991, February). Transference and countertransference are challenges in treating incest. *Psychiatric Times, 8*(2), 36–37.

Ganzarain, R., & Buchele, B. (1989). Countertransference when incest is the problem. In R. Ganzarain (Ed.), *Object relations group psychotherapy: The group as an object, a tool, and a training base* (pp. 111–132). Madison, Conn.: International Universities Press.

Gill, M.M., & Brenman, M. (1959). *Hypnosis and related states: Psychoanalytic studies in regression.* New York: International Universities Press.

Giovacchini, P.L. (1985). Countertransference and the severely disturbed adolescent. *Adolescent Psychiatry, 12*, 449–467.

Greenberg, J.R., & Mitchell, S.A. (1983). *Object relations in psychoanalytic theory.* Cambridge, Mass.: Harvard University Press.

Greenson, R.R. (1967). *The technique and practice of psychoanalysis* (Vol. 1). New York: International Universities Press.

Grigsby, J.P. (1987). The use of imagery in the treatment of posttraumatic stress disorder. *Journal of Nervous and Mental Disease, 175*, 55–59.

Grove, D.J., & Panzer, B.I. (1991). *Resolving traumatic memories: Metaphors and symbols in psychotherapy.* New York: Irvington.

Guze, H. (1956). The involvement of the hypnotist in the hypnotic session. *Journal of Clinical and Experimental Hypnosis, 4*, 61–68.

Haley, S.A. (1974). When the patient reports atrocities: Specific treatment considerations of the Vietnam veteran. *Archives of General Psychiatry, 30*, 191–196.

Haynal, A. (1989). The concept of trauma and its present meaning. *International Review of Psycho-Analysis, 16*, 315–321.

Henry, W.E. (1966). Some observations on the lives of healers. *Human Development, 9*, 47–56.

Horevitz, R. (1983). Hypnosis for multiple personality disorder: A framework for beginning. *American Journal of Clinical Hypnosis, 26*, 138–145.

Horowitz, M.J. (1983). *Image formation and psychotherapy.* New York: Jason Aronson.

Horwitz, L. (1983). Projective identification in dyads and groups. *International Journal of Group Psychotherapy, 33*, 259–279.

Jung, C.G. (1959). *The archetypes and the collective unconscious,* In R.F.C. Hall (Trans.), *The collected works of C.G. Jung* (Vol. 9, P. 1). New York: Pantheon.

Kernberg, O.F. (1965). Notes on countertransference. *Journal of the American Psychoanalytic Association, 13*, 38–56.

Klein, M. (1975). Notes on some schizoid mechanisms. In *Envy and gratitude and other works, 1946–1963* (pp. 1–24). New York: Delacorte Press/Seymour Laurence. (Original work published 1946.)

Levy, S.T. (1990). *Principles of interpretation* (rev. ed.) Northvale, N.J.: Jason Aronson. (Original work published 1984.)

McCann, I.L., & Pearlman, L.A. (1990a). *Psychological trauma and the adult survivor: Theory, therapy, and transformation.* New York: Brunner/Mazel.

McCann, I.L., & Pearlman, L.A. (1990b). Vicarious traumatization: A framework for understanding the psychological effects of working with victims. *Journal of Traumatic Stress, 3*, 131–149.

McCann, I.L., Sakheim, D.K., & Abrahamson, D.J. (1988). Trauma and victimization: A model of psychological adaptation. *Counseling Psychologist, 16*, 531–594.

McCombie, S.L., & Arons, J.H. (1980). Counseling rape victims. In S.L. McCombie (Ed.), *The*

rape crisis intervention handbook: A guide for victim care (pp. 145–171). New York: Plenum.
McCombie, S.L., Bassuk, E., Savitz, R., & Pell, S. (1976). Development of a medical center rape crisis intervention program. *American Journal of Psychiatry, 133,* 418–421.
McDougall, J. (1979). Primitive communication and the use of countertransference. In L. Epstein & A.H. Feiner (Eds.), *Countertransference* (pp. 267–303). New York: Jason Aronson. (Original work published 1978.)
McElroy, L.P., & McElroy, R.A., Jr. (1991). Countertransference issues in the treatment of incest families. *Psychotherapy, 28,* 48–54.
Meichenbaum, D. (1978). Why does using imagery in psychotherapy lead to change? In J.L. Singer & K.S. Pope (Eds.), *The power of human imagination: New methods in psychotherapy* (pp. 381–394). New York: Plenum.
Meissner, W.W. (1991). *What is effective in psychoanalytic therapy: The move from interpretation to relation.* Northvale, N.J.: Jason Aronson.
Mitchell, J.T. (1985). Healing the helper. In *Role stressors and supports for emergency workers* (pp. 105–118). Rockville, Md.: National Institute of Mental Health.
Niebuhr, R. (1952). *The irony of American history.* New York: Charles Scribner's Sons.
Newberry, T.B. (1985). Levels of countertransference toward Vietnam veterans with post-traumatic stress disorder. *Bulletin of the Menninger Clinic, 49,* 151–160.
Niederland, W.G. (1981). The survivor syndrome: Further observations and dimensions. *Journal of the American Psychoanalytic Association, 29,* 413–425.
Ogden, T.H. (1979). On projective identification. *International Journal of Psycho-Analysis, 60,* 357–373.
Orne, M.T. (1965). Undesirable effects of hypnosis: The determinants and management. *International Journal of Clinical and Experimental Hypnosis, 13,* 226–237.
Paivio, A. (1986). *Mental representations: A dual coding approach.* New York: Oxford University Press.
Panzer, B.I. (1991). Preface. In D.J. Grove & B.I. Panzer, *Resolving traumatic memories: Metaphors and symbols in psychotherapy* (pp. ix–xii). New York: Irvington.
Peebles-Kleiger, M.J. (1989). Using countertransference in the hypnosis of trauma victims: A model for turning hazard into healing. *American Journal of Psychotherapy, 43,* 518–530.
Pines, D. (1986). Working with women survivors of the Holocaust: Affective experiences in transference and countertransference. *International Journal of Psycho-Analysis, 67,* 295–307.
Racker, H. (1957). The meanings and uses of countertransference. *Psychoanalytic Quarterly, 26,* 303–357.
Rose, D. S. (1986). "Worse than death": Psychodynamics of rape victims and the need for psychotherapy. *American Journal of Psychiatry, 143,* 817–824.
Rustin, S.L. (1980). The legacy is loss. *Journal of Contemporary Psychotherapy, 11,* 32–43.
Schafer, R. (1968). *Aspects of internalization.* New York: International Universities Press.
Schuker, E. (1979). Psychodynamics and treatment of sexual assault victims. *Journal of the American Academy of Psychoanalysis, 7,* 553–573.
Segal, H. (1964). *Introduction to the work of Melanie Klein.* New York: Basic Books.
Sheikh, A.A. (Ed.). (1983). *Imagery: Current theory, research, and application.* New York: Wiley.
Singer, J.L., & Pope, K.S. (Eds.). (1978). *The power of human imagination: New methods in psychotherapy.* New York: Plenum.
Solovey de Milechnin, G. (1956). Concerning a theory of hypnosis. *Journal of Clinical and Experimental Hypnosis, 4,* 37–45.
Spiegel, H. (1959). Hypnosis and transference: A theoretical formulation. *Archives of General Psychiatry, 1,* 634–639.
Stolorow, R.D. (1992). Closing the gap between theory and practice with better psychoanalytic theory. *Psychotherapy, 29,* 159–166.
Stutman, R.K., & Bliss, E.L. (1985). Posttraumatic stress disorder, hypnotizability, and imagery. *American Journal of Psychiatry, 142,* 741–743.
Thompson, C.L., & Kennedy, P. (1987). Healing the betrayed: Issues in psychotherapy with child victims of trauma. *Journal of Contemporary Psychotherapy, 17,* 195–202.
Walker, L.E. (1991). Post-traumatic stress disorder in women: Diagnosis and treatment of battered woman syndrome. *Psychotherapy, 28,* 21–29.

Wilson, J.P. (1989). *Trauma, transference and healing: An integrative approach to theory, research, and post-traumatic therapy.* New York: Brunner/Mazel.
Winnicott, D.W. (1949). Hate in the counter-transference. *International Journal of Psycho-Analysis, 30,* 69–74.
Yorke, C. (1986). Reflections on problem of psychic trauma. *Psychoanalytic Study of the Child, 41,* 221–236.

8

Treating Therapists with Vicarious Traumatization and Secondary Traumatic Stress Disorders

LAURIE ANNE PEARLMAN and
KAREN W. SAAKVITNE

Psychotherapists who work with trauma survivors in general, and with adult survivors of childhood sexual abuse in particular, face a special set of issues as they evaluate and address the impact of their work on themselves. These issues relate both to the personal and social meanings of interpersonal violence and child sexual abuse and to the qualitative experience of working therapeutically with clients who are struggling to heal from the devastating impact of such abuse. In this chapter, we discuss ways of addressing the transformative effect on the therapist of doing psychotherapy with adult survivors of childhood sexual abuse, an effect that we call vicarious traumatization. While our focus is on the impact of working with these particular clients, the concepts presented pertain equally to the therapist who works with other traumatized populations.

The concept of vicarious traumatization, introduced by McCann and Pearlman (1990a) and elaborated elsewhere (McCann & Pearlman,

Editor's Note: This chapter focuses special attention on vicarious traumatization, secondary traumatic stress disorder (STSD) and other stress disorders that arise among therapists who work with survivors of childhood sexual abuse. Of special note here is the application of the constructivist self development theory.

1990b; Pearlman & Saakvitne, in press), provides a theoretical framework for understanding the complicated and often painful effect of trauma work on the therapist. This framework provides an essential guide to systematic treatment.

The term secondary traumatic stress disorder (STSD) has been used elsewhere in this volume to describe the responses individuals have to hearing about others' traumatic experiences. Vicarious traumatization includes the symptomatology of STSD in the context of profound changes in the therapist's sense of meaning, identity, world view, and beliefs about self and others. But while there is overlap between them, the terms *secondary traumatic stress* and *vicarious traumatization* differ in focus and emphasis in ways we will discuss below. Nevertheless, despite these conceptual differences, the treatment approaches for vicarious traumatization also are appropriate for STSD.

VICARIOUS TRAUMATIZATION

Vicarious traumatization refers to a transformation in the therapist's (or other trauma worker's) inner experience resulting from empathic engagement with clients' trauma material. That is, through exposure to clients' graphic accounts of sexual abuse experiences and to the realities of people's intentional cruelty to one another, and through the inevitable participation in traumatic reenactments in the therapy relationship, the therapist is vulnerable through his or her empathic openness to the emotional and spiritual effects of vicarious traumatization. These effects are cumulative and permanent, and evident in both a therapist's professional and personal life.

Working as a therapist with sexual abuse survivors profoundly affects us as therapists and as human beings. While it is work we enter into by choice, and continue because of a commitment to our clients and because of the tremendous rewards we can experience, we must recognize that it affects us personally. This is not the responsibility of our clients, nor is it in any way an indictment of them. It is, rather, an occupational hazard that must be acknowledged and addressed.

By definition, the effects of vicarious traumatization on an individual resemble those of traumatic experiences. They include significant disruptions in one's sense of meaning, connection, identity, and world view, as well as in one's affect tolerance, psychological needs, beliefs about self and others, interpersonal relationships, and sensory memory, including imagery. This concept of vicarious traumatization is based in constructivist self development theory (CSDT) (McCann & Pearlman, 1990c), a developmental, interpersonal theory explicating the impact of trauma on an individual's psychological development, adaptation, and identity.

To define vicarious traumatization further, it is a new term developed to describe a particular phenomenon we have observed consistently in therapists who treat trauma survivors, which is marked by profound changes in the core aspects of the therapist's self, or psychological foundation. These alterations include shifts in the therapist's identity and world view; in the ability to manage strong feelings, to maintain a positive sense of self and connect to others; and in spirituality or sense of meaning, expectation, awareness, and connection; as well as in basic needs for and schemata about safety, esteem, trust and dependency, control, and intimacy. In addition, the therapist is vulnerable to intrusive imagery and other post-traumatic stress symptomatology as he or she struggles to integrate trauma material and these profound personal changes.

Two sets of factors contribute to a therapist's vicarious traumatization: (1) specific characteristics of the therapy and its context, including characteristics of the clients, the nature of the work itself, and the political, social, and cultural context within which both the traumatic events and the therapy take place; and (2) particular characteristics and vulnerabilities of the therapist and the way he or she works. In the former category, contributing factors include working with clients whose abuse histories and psychological adaptations are not widely accepted or understood (such as survivors of incest, sadistic abuse, or cult abuse, and clients with dissociative disorders); working with clients who continue to be exposed to danger, as with the incest survivor who is in a battering relationship or is still vulnerable to his or her childhood perpetrator; facing the undeniable reality of society's tolerance of the damaging emotional, verbal, physical, and sexual abuse of children and its prevalence (Straus & Gelles, 1986; Vissing, Straus, Gelles, & Harrop, 1991); working in a climate of misogyny, racism, heterosexism, and victim blaming; and negotiating the therapeutic dilemmas often posed by clients who live in a chronic state of suicidal depression and who frequently engage in self-mutilation. All of these challenging aspects of trauma work set the stage for vicarious traumatization for the trauma therapist.

Therapist factors that contribute to vicarious traumatization include the therapist's own history of childhood sexual or other abuse; the therapist's high ideals, rescue fantasies, and overinvestment in meeting all of his or her clients' needs, which can result in inadequate self-care and oblivion to warning signs of vicarious traumatization; inadequate training in psychotherapy in general and trauma therapy in particular; insufficient supervision by experienced trauma-therapy supervisors; and a decontextualized sympathetic connection with the abused child which can open the therapist to overidentification and/or paralysis. Fundamentally, a therapist's sense of self is a crucial factor that allows the therapist to attend to his or her own emotional, spiritual, psychological, and physical needs. A strong sense of self and self-respect will allow a therapist to take the necessary preventive and ameliorative steps detailed later in this chapter.

Finally, we want to differentiate vicarious traumatization from two related terms, burnout and secondary traumatic stress (STS). Burnout has been applied to trauma therapists, as well as to many other individuals in social service or helping jobs identified as high stress with low rewards, or in situations in which the workers' minimal goals (Rotter, 1954), the minimum necessary for work-related satisfaction, are unachievable. Burnout is related to the situation, but does not incorporate the interaction of the situation with the individual that is essential in vicarious traumatization. One study in progress is attempting to validate this distinction (Gamble, Pearlman, Lucca, & Allen, work in progress).

Vicarious traumatization differs from STS in focus and context. The latter term is based on a diagnostic conceptualization of post-traumatic stress disorder (PTSD). Consistent with the version of PTSD given in the fourth edition of the *Diagnostic and Statistical Manual of Mental Disorders* (DSM-IV), such a conceptualization focuses on observable symptoms, and while acknowledging context and etiology, gives them less attention. In contrast, the vicarious-traumatization concept presumes a particular developmental and constructivist model of personality, one in which meaning and relationship are integral parts of any human experience. These two conceptualizations are not orthogonal to one another; the STS approach focuses primarily on the symptoms, while the vicarious-traumatization approach focuses on the individual as a whole, placing observable symptoms in the larger context of human adaptation and quest for meaning.

TRAUMA WORK VERSUS GENERAL PSYCHOTHERAPY

Vicarious traumatization is unique to trauma work. We differentiate it from the "soul sadness" that all therapists can develop as a result of doing psychotherapy with clients who are struggling with depression and despair (Chessick, 1978). We also differentiate vicarious traumatization from the fatigue that can result from working in a profession that requires therapists to maintain careful empathic attunement, selflessness, and the capacity to form connections with, and respectfully hold projections, affect, and transference from, a range of clients.

What is it about trauma work that places special demands on therapists? First, traumatic events such as childhood sexual abuse are painfully real and part of our larger world and society. If we are to help our survivor clients, we cannot protect ourselves from acknowledging this reality as we listen to their stories. The social and professional denial of child sexual abuse (Herman, 1992) erodes as we enter our clients' worlds, and we are left with the powerful affects stirred as we face this reality on a daily basis.

Second, as therapists to trauma survivors, we inevitably become aware of the potential for trauma in our own lives. Traumatic events can happen to any one of us or our loved ones at any time; it is almost intolerable, however, to accept the fact that our lives can be permanently changed in a moment. The concomitant sudden experience of losing control, losing a sense of connection with others, being pushed beyond one's perceived ability to cope, having one's frame of reference (i.e., sense of identity, world view, moral principles, life philosophy, and spirituality) change is then a terrifying but undeniable possibility for all of us. The presence of a survivor client in our office is an inescapable reminder of our own personal vulnerability to traumatic loss.

Third, for the many therapists who are themselves adult survivors of child sexual abuse, the adult survivor client is a reminder of the therapist's own painful experience. Opening up a client's trauma memories or exploring the disruptions in the self and in relationships that follow childhood sexual abuse evokes the therapist's personal experience and pain. This process results in particular countertransference responses which, if not understood and analyzed, can derail the therapy and thus undermine the therapist's self-esteem and professional identity (Saakvitne, 1991).

Fourth, clients who have been profoundly hurt and betrayed in early trusting relationships bring to the therapy relationship powerful emotional needs and a highly developed sense of mistrust. They present enormous pain and distress and yet are often unable to be soothed, given their despair and vigilance. These clients are often compelled unconsciously to reenact both within and outside the therapy relationship earlier painful, abusive, and denigrating relationships.

Fifth, whether through reenactments or projections of expectations of harm learned in earlier relationships, survivor clients often cast the therapist in malevolent, dangerous, or exploitative roles that may assault the therapist's identity. The affects that the client needs the therapist to hold may challenge the therapist's long-standing defenses. The therapist then may find it difficult to maintain a therapeutic stance as she or he mobilizes self-protection against the intolerable affects, memories, or experiences aroused by the therapeutic work. These defenses can result in

increased unanalyzed countertransference, failed or stalemated therapies, boundary violations, increased shame and self-reproach, and
increased vicarious traumatization.

In addition, in our role as trauma therapists, we must also be, in
effect, bystanders and helpless (although not silent) witnesses to damaging and often cruel past events. This helplessness to change what happened in the past transforms us, challenges our helper identities, and
can lead us defensively to devalue survivor clients (Staub, 1989). In
addition, we are often helpless witnesses to current reenactments of
traumatic memories, which can be an excruciating experience. These
reenactments can be expressed at many levels: behavioral, emotional,
and physiological (Van der Kolk, 1989), as well as interpersonal, both
within the therapy through transference and countertransference, and
outside of the therapy in the client's current relationships.

It is, however, both inevitable and potentially therapeutic that we at
times must participate in our clients' unconscious reenactments as they
show us, through the therapy relationship, what happened in previous
relationships. While we can comment on and interpret this behavior, we
are often helpless to prevent it. Our role, to provide an accepting relationship within which the survivor can come to understand and integrate her or his trauma experience, is vital, yet limited. We must struggle against our wish to be more powerful and to exert more protective
control in our clients' lives. The rage and grief we may feel about the
intentional harm done to our clients must be contained and used con-
structively. Rather than helping our clients fight their battles, we must
work with them, through the therapeutic relationship, to enable them
first to understand, and then to conduct, their own struggles in their
own ways. This limitation can place a strain on the trauma therapist,
whose identity may include a sense of self as rescuer.

The final aspect of trauma therapy that sets the stage for special
effects on the therapist is the permanence of traumatic events. In our lex-
icon, trauma results in a permanent change in one's frame of reference,
or enduring ways of understanding self and the world (McCann &
Pearlman, 1990c). Certainly one can come to hold traumatic experiences
differently, and this is an important goal of trauma therapy. But the reality of a permanent loss, whether of innocence, loved ones, bodily integrity, hope, or trust, cannot be denied. Again, our trauma survivor clients
continuously invite us to acknowledge this painful reality, and in doing
so, open us up to our own grief.

In summary, all of these challenges to our sense of ourselves and our
beliefs about the world and the people in it present unique demands for us,
as trauma therapists, and make us susceptible to vicarious traumatization.

Countertransference and Vicarious Traumatization

Quite broadly, countertransference can be understood as the therapist's responses to a particular client and all that client represents to the therapist (including the client's material, presentation, and transference to the therapist, and the therapist's transference to the client), whereas vicarious traumatization refers to the cumulative impact of trauma work on the therapist, across clients. Elsewhere we elaborate upon the special countertransference issues that arise in working with adult survivors of child sexual abuse, as well as the interaction between countertransference and vicarious traumatization (Pearlman & Saakvitne, in press). In brief, vicarious traumatization increases the therapist's susceptibility to certain countertransference responses. If one is suffering from vicarious traumatization, one's countertransference responses may be less readily recognizable and can become problematic in the therapy with adult survivors.

Vicarious Traumatization and Childhood Sexual Abuse

While vicarious traumatization can affect therapists and others working with any traumatized population, here we are interested in the specific form that takes in the therapist who is working with adult survivors of childhood sexual abuse. The shared cultural meanings of incest and childhood sexual abuse influence our perceptions of our survivor clients and their struggles. Some of the aspects of child abuse that have an impact on us, elaborated elsewhere by Saakvitne (1990), include the incest taboo, that is, the universal wish to deny incest; our need to see parents and caretakers as benevolent; grief about the loss of the innocence of childhood; shock and outrage that children are cruelly victimized; the meanings of doing work that can elicit voyeurism, erotic transferences, and sometimes sexually stimulating material; and the gender-related meanings of sexual abuse material for the various possible groupings of male and female clients, perpetrators, therapists, and supervisors. The presence of these issues in the therapy is part of what sets the stage for vicarious traumatization.

THE PROBLEM

The Costs of Vicarious Traumatization

Vicarious traumatization takes a serious toll on both the therapist and the client, as well as on the organizations and the society that provide the context for their work together. The profound personal costs to the therapist can include depression, despair, and cynicism; alienation from friends, colleagues, and family; professional impairment, often resulting in premature job changes; and a host of psychological and physical symptoms similar to those experienced by untreated trauma survivors.

In addition, the therapist with unacknowledged vicarious traumatization can retraumatize clients and otherwise harm them in both overt and subtle ways. When a therapist's emotional and psychological needs are not addressed in appropriate ways outside his or her work, they can become more focal in the therapy relationship than the client's needs (Fromm-Reichmann, 1950). This imbalance can result in violations of therapeutic frame and boundaries, such as forgotten appointments, unreturned phone calls, or inappropriate contact with clients between sessions, as well as the more serious violations of abandonment, professional mistreatment, and sexual or emotional abuse of clients. We know that incest survivors are at particular risk of being sexually abused by psychotherapists (Armsworth, 1989). Such abuse inevitably confirms the beliefs many survivor clients hold about their own lack of self-worth, their culpability for their own victimization, and their omnipotence or seductiveness.

Many adult survivors of child sexual abuse have been given diagnoses that have powerful negative connotations, such as borderline personality disorder (Herman, Perry, & van der Kolk, 1989; Westen, Ludolphe, Misle, Ruffins, & Block, 1990). When it carries with it blame, shame, and hopelessness, the diagnosis is potentially harmful or abusive. We believe that the use of such diagnoses comes out of clinicians' frustration and despair and their need to externalize their sense of helplessness and futility (Vaillant, 1992). The damaging use of diagnoses can signify the vicariously traumatized therapist's loss of hope, which can lead him or her to blame and abandon the survivor clients.

At a broader level, the therapist's disillusionment and mistreatment of clients diminish the profession and demoralize professional colleagues. Individuals feel discouraged about entering treatment, often confirming the worst fears of survivors of sexual abuse that all relationships are at best neglectful, and more likely are abusive, and that there is no safe place. Coupled with the disturbing number of trauma therapists who have not had sufficient training in either trauma therapy or psychotherapy theory and techniques, these failures by mental health practitioners have opened the profession to critical scrutiny and censure.

Vicarious traumatization also can impair supervisors and affect their supervisees, both directly and indirectly. Supervisors may be withdrawn and fail to take adequate interest in their supervisees' development. They may fail to model adequate personal and professional self-care, and can be at risk of violating boundaries in supervisory as well as therapy relationships.

In their organizations, traumatized therapists are less effective team members. They may feel tired and unwilling to contribute to projects, such as case conferences, that benefit clients, or endeavors, such as professional networking, that contribute to the growth of the organizational support for their work. They may be unavailable to colleagues who want to consult them about cases or need them in other ways. They may be cynical or excessively critical or judgmental, thus diminishing their colleagues' professional esteem. The impaired clinician may require and draw extra support from colleagues, which may be unacknowledged by either party. Cynicism, a hallmark of vicarious traumatization, can permeate the organization, resulting in disrespect for clients, therapists, and the process of psychotherapy, as well as mismanagement of such issues as confidentiality, billing, and scheduling. Vicarious traumatization also leads to high staff turnover, which is harmful to the morale and well-being of any organization.

Finally, the social cost of vicarious traumatization is difficult to measure, but critical; it is reflected in the tragic transformation of hope to cynicism. As trauma therapists and researchers, we carry hope for the human capacity to heal from the effects of trauma. If we lose this hope, the legacy of trauma becomes more ominous, leaving survivors alone with the grief and despair that follow traumatic loss. Overall, cynicism represents a loss to society of positive energy, optimism, and hope. When helpers lose their faith and fervor, despair paralyzes the world.

The Scope of the Problem

While it is impossible to provide a statistical estimate of the extent of vicarious traumatization among psychotherapists who work with adult survivors of child sexual abuse, by definition, all trauma therapists are at risk. The construct was only recently defined (McCann & Pearlman, 1990a; Pearlman & Saakvitne, in press), and is still insufficiently operationalized. We do not yet know all the factors that contribute or may ameliorate vicarious traumatization. We have widespread confirmation of the clinical validity of the construct from hundreds of clinicians to whom we presented these ideas in workshops and talks, as well as some early research findings.

A recent survey of trauma therapists has provided data that may give us preliminary answers to some of these questions (Pearlman & Mac Ian, submitted for publication). Many of these therapists showed significantly disrupted beliefs about self and others, one hallmark of vicarious traumatization, as well as psychophysiological symptoms and experiences of intrusion and avoidance of clients' trauma material. A recent study of vicarious traumatization among female mental health professionals by Schauben and Frazier (1995) also found that working with sexual abuse survivors affected therapists' schemata, as well as resulting in other symptoms of vicarious traumatization. Follette, Polusny, and Milbeck (1994) studied general symptoms and trauma symptoms in mental health and law enforcement professionals. They found trauma symptoms in mental health professionals correlated with level of personal stress, use of "negative coping" strategies, and negative clinical response to sexual abuse cases.

To our knowledge, there is not yet a literature on the treatment of vicariously traumatized therapists of adult survivors of child sexual abuse, a fact that undoubtedly reflects the recency of our recognition and acknowledgment of the problem. There is a literature on burnout among psychotherapists and, of course, a large literature on countertransference. Yet neither of these bodies of writing offers treatment possibilities that address the breadth of the problem of vicarious traumatization. This deficiency may stem from the shame therapists feel about acknowledging their pain or distress, or perhaps it is a reflection of the despair therapists feel about their ability to heal themselves.

Therapists may not know where to turn for help, and, as a group, are too often reluctant to acknowledge their need for help until their distress becomes so great that they leave the field (Mahoney, 1991). If we are to continue to provide psychotherapy for adult survivors of childhood sexual abuse, we must overcome our denial of its impact on us as therapists and develop effective treatments for ourselves, as well as for our clients. Our failure to do so could contribute, over time, to the abandonment through denial of the issue of child sexual abuse, a solution that society and the profession have adopted before as reflected by our field's recurrent amnesia for its reality (Herman, 1992).

In the remainder of this chapter, we propose an assessment and treatment model that we hope will further the goal of ethical treatment of survivors, through respectful self-care for therapists and trauma workers.

ASSESSING VICARIOUS TRAUMATIZATION

In this section, we describe the manifestations and assessment of vicarious traumatization, providing a guideline for its evaluation in oneself, in a supervisee, or in a client who is a psychotherapist.

Conceptual Dimensions for Assessment

Constructivist self development theory, the context for the construct of vicarious traumatization, emphasizes the progressive development of a sense of self and world view in response to life experiences. Trauma disrupts the self in specific ways, disrupting frame of reference (or identity, world view, and spirituality); impairing the individual's capacities to tolerate affect, maintain a sense of self, and maintain an inner sense of connection with others; disrupting central needs and beliefs about self and others, and, therefore, one's interpersonal relationships; impairing the ego resources; and altering the individual's sensory memory systems. Vicarious traumatization similarly can affect these aspects of the therapist's self.

Frame of Reference: Identity, World View, and Spirituality

Perhaps the most fundamental disruption the trauma therapist will experience is the disruption of frame of reference, including the individual's sense of identity, central beliefs about the world, and spirituality.

The loss of a familiar sense of identity is a disturbing and often unanticipated by-product of one's work as a trauma therapist. We can come to question who we are as therapists, as men or women, as parents, as humans. The genders of the victim and the perpetrator, as well as the social context of a paternalistic, often misogynist, society will shape gender-related conflicts in both the client and the therapist (Saakvitne & Pearlman, 1993). This work can lead us to question our gender roles, our self-esteem, and our own histories. We can question whether we ourselves have experienced childhood sexual abuse, or have repressed other memories or feelings. Therapists who are actively questioning their identities and are not making progress in this process may be suffering from vicarious traumatization. A sense of oneself as jaded, confused, or depleted can reflect an identity disruption.

The second aspect of frame of reference that is invariably affected by trauma is world view, the way we understand the world, including causality, life philosophy, and moral principles. For example, central world-view beliefs that can be challenged include the beliefs that people behave according to a set of values, that the world is fundamentally just, that people can influence outcomes in their lives, that the future is bright, and so forth. Given the prevalence and acceptance of violence, cruelty, and bigotry to which we are exposed as trauma therapists, the emergence of cynical beliefs about the world, such as the tenet that life events are random or that people are basically malevolent or selfish, is not uncommon (Janoff-Bulman, 1985, 1989) and is a central symptom of vicarious traumatization.

Both identity and world-view disruptions are reflected in the encompassing realm of spiritual impoverishment. We have come to believe over time that the most malignant aspect of vicarious traumatization is the loss of a sense of meaning for one's life, a loss of hope and idealism, a loss of connection with others, and a devaluing of awareness of one's experience. This constellation of experience seems best described as spirituality (Neumann & Pearlman, manuscript in preparation). For some, spiritual needs are addressed through religion, while others maintain a private, nontheistic belief system that provides a context for joy, hope, wonder, meaning, and connection. We believe this larger sense of meaning and connection is crucial for psychological well-being in general, and a critical tool for anyone trying to face the darkness of childhood sexual abuse. Disruptions in this realm may be the most troubling, and perhaps the least explored, aspect of the experience of both trauma survivor and trauma therapist.

Disruptions in Self Capacities
    Self capacities are the inner or intrapersonal abilities that allow us to maintain a continuous, relatively positive sense of self, and are critical for self-soothing and affect tolerance. They have three components: (1) the ability to maintain a positive sense of self, (2) the ability to modulate strong affect, and (3) the ability to maintain an inner sense of connection with others.
    Signs that these capacities may be disrupted include overextending oneself; overindulging or compulsively consuming to manage or avoid affect (e.g., overeating, substance abuse, binge shopping); frequent or intense self-criticism, or a movement from self-criticism to self-loathing; difficulty tolerating strong feelings or hypersensitivity to emotionally charged stimuli (including an inability to read the newspaper or watch movies because they are disturbing, or, conversely, a numbing or insensitivity to emotional material that formerly would have evoked a response); and a sense of isolation in the world and disconnection from loving others, both interpersonally and in one's inner world. Certain adaptations, such as immersing oneself in work, numbing, or intellectualizing, can disguise this pain. These manifestations of vicarious traumatization may be more difficult to recognize, yet their appearance is equally dangerous for therapist and client. The development of self capacities is often the central work in psychotherapy with survivor clients, and for this reason, the therapist's own self capacities must be well developed and maintained.

Disruptions in Needs, Beliefs, and Relationships
    Certain basic psychological needs (safety, trust, esteem, control, and intimacy) that motivate behavior are particularly susceptible to change through traumatic experiences (McCann, Sakheim, & Abrahamson,

1988; Pearlman, Mac Ian, Johnson, & Mas, 1992). Based on life experiences, people develop beliefs founded in these needs and their ability to meet them, which, in turn, shape their perceptions of new life experiences. When, as a result of trauma, an individual believes certain basic needs cannot and will not ever be met (e.g., "I am never safe," "People are not trustworthy," "I am not worthy of being loved"), these beliefs shape relationships, identity, and access to hope or despair.

A therapist can find his or her beliefs about self and others strongly affected by trauma work. In a recent study, one area of disruption that related to exposure to trauma material for therapists was that of other esteem; therapists who reported more exposure to clients' trauma material also exhibited more disruptions in their esteem for others in general (Pearlman & Mac Ian, manuscript in preparation). Negative schemata about self and others can be heard in the therapist's statements about other people, including clients, colleagues, friends, and family members. It is important to notice shifts in these beliefs, as we may move, for example, from believing we are reasonably safe most of the time to believing that we are constantly threatened by potential harm; from believing that we can trust our judgment in most situations to believing that we cannot trust ourselves in clinical or nonclinical situations. These shifts may represent accurate interpretations of our world; it would be unwise to feel safe in dangerous situations. However, they may alternatively represent vicarious traumatization: a newly developing inability to feel safe even in situations in which there is a reasonably low likelihood of danger. Important signs of disrupted needs and schemata include an increased sense of personal vulnerability or capacity to do harm (safety), a decreased sense of trust in one's perceptions or judgments or in others (trust), a devaluing of oneself or others (esteem), an increased need for control or decreased sense of control over self or others (control), and a decreased sense of connection with self or others (intimacy).

A formal assessment of schemata can be made using the TSI Belief Scale, an 80-item Likert-scaled questionnaire measuring disruptions in beliefs related to the five central need areas identified above (Pearlman, Mac Ian, Johnson, & Mas, 1992). Taking this test periodically can provide interesting feedback to the clinician on the changes in her or his beliefs about self and others over time.

Effects on Interpersonal Relationships

Vicarious traumatization has a profound effect on a therapist's interpersonal relationships; if one believes that others are not trustworthy or valuable, for example, it is difficult to have rewarding relationships. Similarly, one's beliefs about oneself can also lead to interpersonal disruptions. Signs that suggest vicarious traumatization may be affecting a therapist's relationships include (1) social withdrawal, whether because of feeling different, knowing something others do not know (a common effect of traumatic experiences on survivors), or feeling depleted and exhausted; (2) inability to tolerate the wide range of feelings necessary to maintain intimate relationships; (3) feeling alienated from intimate friends and sexual partners because of the unique nature of the work; and (4) inability to enjoy common forms of entertainment, including movies and television. One can become less available to others in one's own life because of the demands of clients, colleagues, or work. We may be more likely to want to talk with colleagues than with friends or family members because of the restrictions of confidentiality or our wish for understanding and empathy. The potential to develop a greater sense of connection with colleagues than with family (Friedrich, 1990) can result in serious interpersonal difficulties for the therapist, as well as in a failure to nurture and develop non-work-related aspects of the therapist's life.

Therapists can experience an imbalance among needs, in which one or two needs become dominant. For example, a therapist with an overriding need for intimacy or an inability to be alone may take advantage of inappropriate situations; rather than seek appropriate mature intimate relationships, he or she might attempt to meet intimacy needs through clients, whom the therapist feels will be more accepting. Another therapist might develop an overriding need for safety that governs all of his or her activities, including clinical work, and extends into the therapist's personal life, perhaps making him or her an overprotective parent or creating agoraphobia.

When our needs are out of balance, we can find it difficult to recognize any but our own salient needs in our clients, leading to a reenactment of clients' childhood experiences of functioning as a mirror for others and not being seen as separate, unique persons. This pattern also demonstrates one way in which vicarious traumatization can influence and interact with countertransference, resulting in a compromised or stalled therapy.

Ego Resources

Ego resources are abilities that enable the individual to meet psychological needs and to relate to others; they can be disrupted by trauma and by the work of trauma therapy. For example, one's judgment can be impaired by disrupted beliefs that result in an inability to foresee consequences accurately. We can find it more difficult to establish mature relations with others; to maintain appropriate boundaries in relationships, professional and personal; and to make self-protective judgments. It is important to explore such changes and to question how they may be related to our work.

Imagery

Finally, disruptions in memory are a hallmark of the aftermath of trauma (Brett & Ostroff, 1985; McCann & Pearlman, 1990c; Van der Kolk, 1989). Like our clients, we can experience such disruptions in sensory memories. Many trauma therapists experience intrusions of their clients' traumatic imagery that can be profoundly disturbing. When the intrusive images or sensations are sexual and emerge during sexual activity, the therapist may feel that his or her intimate life is no longer the province of the therapist and his or her partner. This dilemma can be difficult to discuss with one's sexual partner, or, if one does discuss it, can result in interpersonal conflict. The Impact of Event Scale (IES; Horowitz, Wilner, & Alvarez, 1980) is a systematic way of assessing the extent to which one is being affected by intrusive imagery and thoughts, or perhaps actively avoiding such intrusions. In our study of trauma therapists, the IES discriminated trauma therapists with a personal trauma history from those without one. The former group was more likely to experience clients' trauma material as intrusive (Pearlman & Mac Ian, manuscript in preparation).

Trauma History

The TSI Life Event Questionnaire (Mac Ian & Pearlman, 1992) now contains items concerning the effects of hearing another person's trauma material. In addition, it assesses the therapist's own trauma history, which appears to be a major contributing factor to the experience of vicarious traumatization (Pearlman & Mac Ian, manuscript in preparation). Where significant differences on mental health measures were found, they consistently showed those with a trauma history having more difficulties.

Behavior Changes

Vicarious traumatization also can be manifest in behavior changes. To assess the behavioral manifestation of disrupted cognitive schemata, we developed a behavior change checklist, which we administered in our trauma-therapist study. Our trauma-therapist sample reported, as a result of their work with trauma survivors, an increase in a variety of behaviors (such as talking to oneself in self-critical ways, going out to avoid being alone, dropping out of community affairs, and rejecting one's partner's sexual advances) that correlated significantly with over-all schema disruptions (Pearlman & Mac Ian, submitted for publication).

Summary

To date, our strongest assessment tool is our own ability to reflect on our experience and to hear what important others in our lives tell us about our functioning. There is a definite need for additional measures of vicarious traumatization. While we have measures of disrupted cognitive schemata (the TSI Belief Scale), distress related to hearing another's trauma material (TSI Life Event Questionnaire), and intrusive imagery (Impact of Event Scale), there are as yet no measures for the common disruptions in meaning, in identity, in interpersonal relationships, and in ego resources that reflect vicarious traumatization. Work is currently in progress on the Life Orientation Inventory, a measure of the spiritual damage that can come about through psychological trauma and through working with trauma survivors (Neumann & Pearlman, manuscript in preparation) and on a questionnaire measure of self capacities (Pearlman, Dieter, & Black, work in progress).

TREATING VICARIOUS TRAUMATIZATION

Interventions by the Therapist

There are several things we can do to ameliorate the impact of vicarious traumatization. These interventions can be grouped into three categories: personal, professional, and organizational. Specific interventions must be tailored to the needs and preferences of the particular therapist. We elaborate these suggestions elsewhere (Pearlman & Saakvitne, in press).

Personal Strategies
The interventions in this category are very similar to things we might suggest to our clients who are survivors of childhood sexual abuse. We list them here because therapists are often much better at caring for others than for themselves.
Identify Disrupted Schemas. Just as trauma therapists help their clients identify disrupted schema areas as a path toward personal change, therapists can benefit from identifying their own salient need and schema areas. Particularly distressing trauma imagery will generally center around themes related to one or more of the five salient need areas identified by CSDT: safety, trust, esteem, intimacy, and con-

trol. If the therapist knows his or her own salient need areas, it is possible to tease out that theme within the trauma stories that are particularly troublesome to the therapist. Once the need area is identified, the difficult imagery generally becomes less intrusive. For example, a therapist may find herself repeatedly thinking about trauma memory a client has related. In considering why that particular memory is intruding into her conscious awareness, she might become aware that the central theme of the memory (for the therapist) is betrayal, related to trust. Her own self-knowledge may tell her that this is a sensitive need area for her, and she may then be able to connect the memory to her own salient themes related to trust. In this way, she can begin to put the memory into context, just as such work with clients helps them to do. At times, the therapist may be able to do this work on her own; at other times, it is better accomplished in a trusting supervisory relationship or in one's own personal psychotherapy.

Maintain a Personal Life. To combat the effects of vicarious traumatization, it is essential to have a fulfilling personal life. Many therapists immerse themselves in clinical or other work; balancing work, play, and rest is essential to healthy functioning.

Use Personal Psychotherapy. For the trauma therapist, personal psychotherapy can be extremely helpful. Among other things, it provides a regular opportunity to focus on oneself, one's own needs, and the origins of one's responses to the work. The explicit acknowledgment of oneself as deserving of care and of one's needs as valid and important is essential. Individual expressive therapy, such as art or movement therapy, can help therapists reclaim their emotional lives.

Group therapy and support groups also can be of great help. Because of the special issues for therapists who themselves are survivors of childhood sexual abuse, we believe a focused incest-survivor group for therapists is an invaluable resource and effective treatment. Such a group provides a safe space both for healing and for exploring the interaction of a therapist's past with his or her current work with survivor clients.

Identify Healing Activities. There are many important ways to engage in restorative self-care at a personal level. Participants in our vicarious-traumatization workshops have contributed to this list, which includes such diverse activities as creating art; enjoying music; spending time with family, friends, and children; keeping a journal; enjoying nature; traveling; taking time off; pursuing hobbies; going to the movies; and simply resting and relaxing. Activities that reconnect the therapist with his or her body are especially useful, such as exercising, dancing, and getting a massage. Other activities, such as performing community service and engaging in political or social activism and nontrauma volunteer work, can provide an outlet for the outrage therapists can feel about child sexual abuse, as well as an antidote to their inability to undo the past harm done to clients. Doing yoga, meditating, and developing a spiritual life are all ways of ameliorating the loss of meaning that is a hallmark of vicarious traumatization. We recommend creating a specific list of healing activities for oneself, updating it every few weeks, and committing oneself to do the activities listed on a regular basis.

Tend to Your Spiritual Needs. The spiritual damage, or the loss of meaning, connection, and hope, that can signal vicarious traumatization is profoundly destructive, and attending to one's spiritual health is critical to survival and growth. Developing a spiritual life means something unique to each individual; it will entail finding a way to restore faith in something larger than oneself, whether by reconnecting with the best of all that is human, with nature, or with a spiritual entity.

Consciously expanding one's frame of reference by taking risks, loving and being loved, and creating and pursuing joy, wonder, and awe addresses the fundamental disruption in meaning created by vicarious traumatization and is a potent antidote to the toxic malevolence childhood sexual abuse therapists can encounter in their work. The cynicism, or overgeneralized negative expectancies (Rotter, 1954), that can develop as a result of trauma work must be actively resisted. It is important to notice and question our cynicism.

There is great restorative value in stepping back from one's work and putting it in perspective. Valuable perspectives include the personal—our work is but one aspect of our lives; the relational—we are working with our clients in a collaborative healing process; the professional—we work within a context of a broad network of people with similar values and goals; the social—as trauma therapists, we are part of an important social movement, activists who are calling attention to a massive hidden social disease; and the historical—our era is simply a snapshot in history.

Professional Strategies

As in the personal realm, there are many things we can do in our professional lives to address our vicarious traumatization.

Arrange Supervision. Regular supervision or consultation with an experienced trauma-therapy supervisor is essential to our self-care, as well as to our ethical commitment to our clients. This work is simply too demanding to do without ongoing, regular professional consultation, regardless of level of experience. In our study of 188 trauma therapists, only 53% (or 100 people) reported that they were receiving trauma-related supervision; of these, 82% said that they found it helpful (74% of the women and 38% of the men in the sample were receiving some kind of supervision [Pearlman & Mac Ian, manuscript in preparation]).

Supervision must afford a place in which to discuss cases and one's responses to the work without shame. It is enormously helpful to have a safe place where one can acknowledge, express, and work through clients' painful material with a supportive colleague. Supervision should include a discussion of therapeutic successes, large and small. Not only can we learn from our successes, but we restore our sense of value and our hope when we observe the efficacy of our work and rejoice in our clients' growth and increased capacity for joy and personal fulfillment.

It is important that the trauma therapist with a personal trauma history have a safe and supportive supervision relationship. In our study of trauma therapists, we found that those who reported a history of trauma had significantly more disrupted schemata than did those who had no trauma history (Pearlman & Mac Ian, submitted for publication). These therapists may find it helpful to talk about the intrusive imagery in their supervision, personal therapy, or elsewhere in order to understand what is particularly disturbing to them about a repetitive intrusive image, as well as possible connections to their own trauma histories. Schatzow and Yassen (1991) have also noted the importance, for the therapist who is a childhood sexual abuse survivor, of having at least one person with whom he or she can acknowledge the abuse and explore its interaction with the trauma work.

Develop Professional Connection. In order to address the sense of disconnection that is a characteristic of vicarious traumatization, we need to reconnect with others in both our personal and professional lives. Building a sense of professional connection can mean attending workshops, using support groups, meeting with colleagues to share coping strategies, and giving supervision. The work is too difficult to do alone. Remaining connected to the community of trauma therapists helps to affirm one's commitment.

Develop a Balanced Work Life. It is important for therapists to try to arrange the various kinds of work they do, over time and within each day, to balance activities and clients (e.g., limit the number of sessions, limit the number of trauma clients, attend to the spacing and sequence of sessions, make time for collegial contact).

Although not always feasible, it is helpful if childhood sexual abuse therapists can consciously modulate their exposure to trauma material. This protection can be achieved in a variety of ways. One way may be to enter empathically into the adult's experience, and to attempt to understand the child's experience without losing oneself in sympathetic or overidentified connection with the suffering child. Some therapists find it helpful to prepare themselves for hearing difficult trauma material by using imagery—by imagining, for example, a protective white light surrounding the therapist and the adult survivor as the survivor begins to recount his or her story. A therapist may be able to limit the ratio and number of survivor clients seen, perhaps by declining to pick up a new trauma case or by setting up extra support for a difficult case. A supervisor may ask supervisees not to share details of their clients' abuse histories at times. Finally, when engaged empathetically with a survivor who is recounting or reexperiencing a childhood abuse memory, it is helpful for the therapist to remain grounded in the present reality, as well as entering into the child's experience.

Outside of the therapy room, we can limit our exposure to traumatic material by not watching violent movies or not reading detailed accounts of gruesome events. We can be selective about what conferences we attend or journal articles we read.

A related professional strategy is to balance one's clinical work with other professional activities. If this option is not immediately available, one can work toward alternative ways of spending one's professional time, for example, in supervision, teaching, research, or writing.

There may be a time when one needs to take a sabbatical from trauma work. If this is to be accomplished in a planned rather than an emergency manner, we must be continuously aware of our feelings, our needs, and our resources. This is another way in which personal psychotherapy and clinical supervision can be helpful.

Remain Aware of Your Goals. Finally, remembering the value, importance, and meaning of our work can be very restorative. Reminding ourselves why we do this work and how it can transform the life of a survivor can renew us.

Organizational Strategies

Therapists who treat adult survivors of child sexual abuse work in a wide range of settings. Some of the strategies that follow will be more appropriate in certain settings than in others. Although these goals represent ideals for our organizations, they are too important to clients and therapists to be dismissed as impossible without serious effort to realize them.

Attend to the Physical Setting. The availability of a safe, private, comfortable therapy space is very important. The therapist's space is part of his or her self-care; it is important that one's office be comfortable, soothing, and grounding. The therapist may want to have personally meaningful items in the office that express his or her identity.

Arrange for Adequate Resources. Organizations should provide opportunities for regular supervision, consultation, and case discussion for clinicians. They should provide resources for and active encouragement of professional development activities such as continuing education. Therapists who work without adequate employee benefits, such as health insurance with provision for mental health care and time off for vacations, are facing strains that make their work even more stressful, and thus endanger the well-being of clients, the therapists, and the organization and profession.

Create an Atmosphere of Respect. A less tangible contribution organizations make to their therapist employees and their clients is an atmosphere of respect for both clients and employees. Client respect, or its absence, is conveyed in a multitude of ways, including the management of telephone calls, intake forms, appointment procedures, and record keeping, and, through all·of this, the observation of client confidentiality. Organizations can aid their therapist employees and clients by helping to arrange financial support when long-term treatment is required. This may mean working to help therapists obtain the training and credentials necessary to make them eligible to have their services reimbursed by third-party payors, working with insurance and managed-care companies to educate them about trauma treatment, establishing "scholarship funds" for clients in need, or working with clients and therapists to develop flexible ways of financing treatment.

Develop Adjunctive Services. Organizations can help by developing resources often needed in the treatment of adult survivors, such as access to experienced medical professionals for medication and physical-health consultation; self-help groups, newsletters, books, and films for survivors; and access to specialized inpatient, partial hospital, and outpatient treatment services (including therapy groups, expressive therapies, and body work). Groups of therapists can share information about resources and opportunities so that each therapist does not have to do it all alone. All of these resources help the therapist do his or her work in a community, again combating the sense of isolation that so readily can befall therapists working with survivors of childhood sexual abuse.

INTERVENTIONS BY HELPING PROFESSIONALS

Here we suggest strategies for professionals working with trauma therapists. These professionals include vicarious-traumatization consultants, clinical supervisors, administrators, graduate-school faculty, trainers, and therapists.

Education and Training

We cannot overemphasize the value of trauma-specific professional education and training. Traumatology is such a new field that very few graduate programs yet provide courses on adult-survivor issues. Because of the prevalence of childhood sexual abuse in the backgrounds of the clinical population, however, such courses should be required in all graduate programs that prepare people to become clinicians. Clinicians who work with adult survivors should obtain as much training as they need to feel comfortable with the wide range of issues these clients bring to treatment. Appropriate training provides theoretical frameworks for understanding and treating adult survivors, which may help to prevent vicarious traumatization (Pearlman & Mac Ian, manuscript in preparation), as well as a thorough theoretical grounding in the principles and techniques of psychotherapy, including the management of boundaries and an understanding of the difference between nurturance and psychotherapy.

In employment and training settings, those who interview applicants, whether for graduate school, internships, postdoctoral fellowships, or staff positions, should inform them of the risks related to doing trauma work. We owe our junior colleagues the respect of informed consent; some may decide not to pursue this work, and those who enter the field must have some idea of the commitment they are making. Those who select candidates must attempt to assess the applicant's resilience. We harm both applicant and client by offering a position to someone who does not have the self capacities, ego resources, and access to support to do this work.

In instances in which individuals do not have a choice about their participation—for example, students who are seeing survivor clients in a practicum setting—our obligation is to provide as much support as possible. This support includes the provision of theoretical frameworks for understanding the work, adequate and appropriate supervision, and preparation regarding the types of histories and needs survivor clients are likely to bring to their new therapists.

As teachers and supervisors, we have a responsibility to educate our students and supervisees about vicarious traumatization. We must help them understand that this is an inevitable part of the work, that it is a natural response. We must validate the difficulty of the work and encourage ongoing discussion of its effects.

We should also attend to symptoms of vicarious traumatization, STS, and other problematic responses in our supervisees and students. When we see our students and colleagues suffering from alienation, numbing, anxiety, shame, or any of a host of related difficulties, we must address them directly in a supportive fashion. Organizations can provide group opportunities to discuss the effects of the work on therapists, thus normalizing and ameliorating these effects.

Finally, teachers and supervisors teach indirectly as well. As they model balance between work and play, limiting caseload and workload, self-awareness, and self-care, their students learn to value balance and self-care as aspects of professionalism.

Clinical Supervision of Trauma Therapies

In many organizations, individuals have multiple roles; it is especially important in supervision to separate these roles, and to create a safe, boundaried space in which a therapist can speak freely about the difficulty of the work. Clinicians need to talk about the strain imposed by their work and about the personal issues it raises. In order to feel safe doing this, they need a place where their disclosures do not affect their performance evaluations.

Trauma-therapy supervision should be a forum in which the therapist can discuss specifics of case material, case management issues, the therapeutic relationship, countertransference responses, and vicarious traumatization. The focus on the therapeutic relationship and the therapy process is essential in trauma therapy, as is the need to remain alert to evidence of vicarious traumatization. Over time, the supervisor and therapist must develop a trusting relationship that can serve as a model for the psychotherapy relationship, with some clear differences. In both therapy and supervisory relationships, both parties are invited to clarify their needs, to speak the truth, and to respect each other. Both relationships require a frame, including a safe, regular, and private meeting place, and confidentiality agreed to by both parties.

Supervision differs from psychotherapy, however. While the therapy supervisor may comment on personal conflicts that may influence the therapist's interpersonal or countertransference responses, he or she does not probe into these conflicts. Rather, the supervisor can respectfully proffer some possibilities based on her or his knowledge of the therapist, and suggest that the therapist explore the issues in her or his own personal psychotherapy. One arena of modeling in supervision is the respectful attention to the boundaries of the relationship. We encourage supervisors to notice when their supervisees are moving into realms that are more appropriately discussed in their own psychotherapy, and to suggest personal therapy to them.

Group supervision is an excellent modality for trauma therapists to meet many of their needs, including those related to vicarious traumatization. As in all groups, it is important to establish norms related to confidentiality, respect for clients, and respect for participants. Supervision groups may come together within an organization, as at staff case conferences or clinical staff meetings. In these groups, it is important to be aware of the multiple roles and relationships therapist participants may have with one another, for example, staff/director, colleague/friend, supervisor/supervisee. These groups can be made safe enough to address issues of vicarious traumatization in part by normalizing these responses to the work and in part by formalizing the discussion of vicarious traumatization and countertransference. It is important that any clinical presentation leave room for the therapist to acknowledge the effect of the work. At our case conferences, we reserve a segment for "feelings" time, to invite us to step back from a more intellectual, theoretical stance and reconnect with our needs, beliefs, emotions, and one another. By building it into each session, the group is saying, "These needs are expectable and meeting them is important."

A second type of trauma-therapy supervision group is organized specifically for this purpose, composed of individuals who may not see one another in any other context or setting. In such groups, it may take the participants longer to develop trust. Issues of competition and esteem are often salient here, as professionals who do not know one another attempt to maintain pride in their work in the face of sometimes overwhelming feelings of helplessness or confusion. This trust can be encouraged by structuring the group, particularly in the beginning, around the presentation of case material, reserving time at the end of each meeting to discuss feelings. The vicarious-traumatization framework can be provided, which helps to normalize therapists' struggles with the work.

Conversely, there may be a greater sense of freedom to be open in a group in which people meet only for the purpose of discussing trauma cases. As therapists reveal their feelings, it is important for the group supervisor (or members, if it is a peer supervision group) to be aware of the potential for them to feel exposed and shamed, and to intervene in a supportive way that normalizes their feelings and restores their connection to themselves and the group.

Vicarious-Traumatization Consultations

A vicarious-traumatization consultation can take a variety of forms; one can consult to an organization, a group, or an individual; the consultation can be a one-time intervention, a short-term intervention, an intermittent or as-needed event, or a regularly scheduled, ongoing consultation. A vicarious-traumatization consultation differs from therapy supervision and individual psychotherapy in that it specifically focuses on the question of how trauma therapy is affecting the therapist. It provides a forum in which the therapist can understand his or her unique responses to survivor clients and the issues they present. In such consultations, we talk more about cases than one would in one's personal psychotherapy, and we talk more about the therapist's personal issues and history than one would in therapy supervision. The survivor therapist may use this as a place in which to discuss how his or her own abuse history interacts with the work. In this forum, the therapist is likely to focus on the effects of his or her abuse history on himself or herself as a therapist rather than to discuss the details of the abuse as he or she might in personal psychotherapy. The consultant will work with the therapist to make the connections with and distinctions between his or her own important trauma themes, strong feelings, and disrupted needs and clients' themes, feelings, and needs.

The consultant provides a framework for helping the therapist understand his or her responses to the work and normalize these responses. He or she will encourage participants to talk about specific disruptions they may be experiencing in frame of reference, cognitive schemata, interpersonal relationships, self capacities, ego resources, and imagery and other sensory memories. Here the consultant works with therapists to sort out the specifics of what is difficult for them, and to connect it to their work and to their concerns and psychological needs.

As we believe one of the most important areas of disruption in vicarious traumatization is in the spiritual realm, an effective consultation must include a spiritual or existential component. We address impairment or changes in the therapist's sense of meaning and hope, connection with something beyond the self, awareness of all aspects of life, including the nonmaterial, and helping him or her to restore these. Helping therapists develop a reasonable ego ideal of themselves as therapists is a very powerful method we have used to assist them in reconnecting with their own resources. This can be done by working with the therapist to identify ways in which he or she finds meaning and what is restorative in her or his own life. This kind of work may draw upon Jungian archetypes for healing as represented in such works as *Women Who Run with the Wolves* (Estes, 1992). Through guided imagery, any individuals are able to connect or communicate with an inner "wise person" or "future self," who is often benevolent, strong, and accepting. This connection has proven to be a valuable asset to therapist clients who have lost track of their priorities, their own value, their sense of strength. Vicarious-traumatization consultations also may contain an expressive component. Therapists who are encouraged to dance, move, draw, or paint are often able to reconnect with their inner resources, including their feelings.

In general, vicarious-traumatization consultations should follow the needs and concerns of the therapist seeking consultation. The consultant needs to listen for areas of disruption, and then, with the therapist, explore reparative approaches in professional, organizational, and personal realms of the therapist's life. This consulting work can lend additional meaning to the consultant's work life, and often helps the consultant to address vicarious-traumatization issues in his or her own life.

CONCLUSION

There is a great need for skilled therapists to treat adult survivors of child sexual abuse. However, we believe that these therapists are at risk of being deeply and profoundly changed by their work and potentially of being permanently harmed. Therapists who work with child sexual abuse survivors need to be protected by actively addressing their vulnerability to vicarious traumatization, and taking preventive and ameliorative measures in the therapist's personal, professional, and organizational realms on a daily basis. Only through regular attention to these issues can child sexual abuse therapists continue to provide much-needed services to their clients.

REFERENCES

American Psychiatric Association. (1994) *Diagnostic and statistical manual of mental disorders.* Washington, D.C.; American Psychiatric Association.

Armsworth, M.W. (1989). Therapy of incest survivors: Abuse or support? *Child Abuse and Neglect, 13,* 546–564.

Brett, E.A., & Ostroff, R. (1985). Imagery and post-traumatic stress disorder: An overview. *American Journal of Psychiatry, 142,* 417–424.

Chessick, R.D. (1978). The sad soul of the psychiatrist. *Bulletin of the Menninger Clinic, 42,* 1–9.

Estes, C.P. (1992). *Women who run with the wolves. Myths and stories of the wild woman archetype.* New York: Ballantine Books.

Follette, V.M., Polusny, M.M., & Milbeck, K. (1994). Mental health and law enforcement professionals: Trauma history, psychological symptoms, and impact of providing services to child sexual abuse survivors. *Professional Psychology: Research and Practice, 25* (3), 275–282.

Friedrich, W.N. (1990). *Psychotherapy of sexually abused children and their families.* New York: Norton.

Fromm-Reichmann, F. (1950). *Principles of intensive psychotherapy.* Chicago: University of Chicago Press.

Gamble, S.J., Pearlman, L.A. & Lucca, A.M., Allen, G.J. (work in progress). Vicarious traumatization and burnout among licensed psychologists: Empirical findings.

Herman, J.L. (1992). *Trauma and recovery.* New York: Basic Books.

Herman, J., Perry, C., & van der Kolk, B.A. (1989). Childhood trauma in borderline personality disorder. *American Journal of Psychiatry, 146*(4), 490–495.

Horowitz, M.J., Wilner, N., & Alvarez, W. (1980). Signs and symptoms of posttraumatic stress disorder. *Archives of General Psychiatry, 37*, 85–92.

Janoff-Bulman, R. (1985). The aftermath of victimization: Rebuilding shattered assumptions. In C.R. Figley (Ed.), *Trauma and its wake: The study and treatment of post-traumatic stress disorder* (pp. 15–25). New York: Brunner/Mazel.

Janoff-Bulman, R. (1989). Assumptive worlds and the stress of traumatic events: Applications of the schema construct. *Social Cognition, 7*(2), 113–136.

Mac Ian, P.S., & Pearlman, L.A. (1992). Development and use of the TSI Life Event Questionnaire. *Treating Abuse Today: The International Newsjournal of Abuse, Survivorship and Therapy, 2*(1), 9–11.

Mahoney, M.J. (1991). *Human change processes: The scientific foundations of psychotherapy.* New York: Basic Books.

McCann, I.L., & Pearlman, L.A. (1990a). Vicarious traumatization: A framework for understanding the psychological effects of working with victims. *Journal of Traumatic Stress, 3*(1), 131–149.

McCann, I.L., & Pearlman, L.A. (1990b, Fall). Vicarious traumatization: The emotional costs of working with survivors. *The Advisor: Newsletter of the American Professional Society on the Abuse of Children, 3*(4), 3–4.

McCann, I.L., & Pearlman, L.A. (1990c). *Psychological trauma and the adult survivor: Theory, therapy, and transformation.* New York: Brunner/Mazel.

McCann, I.L., Sakheim, D.K., & Abrahamson, D.J. (1988). Trauma and victimization: A model of psychological adaptation. *Counseling Psychologist, 16*(4), 531–594.

Neumann, D.A., & Pearlman, L.A. (manuscript in preparation). Toward the development of a psychological language for spirituality.

Pearlman, L.A., Mac Ian, P.S., Johnson, G., & Mas, K. (1992). *Understanding cognitive schemas across groups: Empirical findings and their implications.* Presented at the eighth annual meeting of the International Society for Traumatic Stress Studies, Los Angeles, Calif.

Pearlman, L.A., Dieter, P.J., & Black, A.E. (work in progress). The TSI Feeling Style Inventory: A measure of self capacities.

Pearlman, L.A., & Mac Ian, P.S., (submitted for publication). Vicarious traumatization: An empirical study of the effects of trauma work on trauma therapists.

Pearlman, L.A., & Saakvitne, K.W. (in press). *Trauma and the therapist: Countertransference and vicarious traumatization in psychotherapy with incest survivors.* New York: Norton.

Rotter, J.B. (1954). *Social learning and clinical psychology.* Englewood Cliffs, N.J.: Prentice Hall.

Saakvitne, K.W. (1990, August). Psychoanalytic psychotherapy with incest survivors: Transference and countertransference paradigms. Presented at the annual convention of the American Psychological Association, Boston, Mass.

Saakvitne, K.W. (1991). Countertransference in psychoanalytic psychotherapy with incest survivors: when the therapist was abused. Presented at the 99th annual convention of the American Psychological Association, San Francisco.

Saakvitne, K.W., & Pearlman, L.A. (1993). The impact of internalized misogyny and violence against women on feminine identity. In E.P. Cook (Ed.), *Women, relationships, and power: Implications for counseling* (pp. 247–274). Alexandria, Va.: American Counseling Association.

Schatzow, E., & Yassen, J. (1991). Specialized treatment models for clinicians with a history of trauma. Workshop presentation at the seventh annual convention of the International Society for Traumatic Stress Studies, Washington, D.C.

Schauben, L.J., & Frazier, P.A. (1995). Vicarious trauma: the effects on female counselors of working with sexual violence survivors. *Psychology of Women Quarterly, 19*, 49–64.

Staub, E. (1989). *The roots of evil: The origins of genocide and other group violence.* Cambridge, England: Cambridge University Press.

Straus, M.A., & Gelles, R.J. (1986). Societal change and change in family violence from 1975 to 1985 as revealed by two national surveys. *Journal of Marriage and the Family, 48*, 465–479.

Vaillant, G.E. (1992). The beginning of wisdom is never calling a patient a borderline. *Journal of Psychotherapy Practice and Research, 1*(2), 117–134.
Van der Kolk, B.A. (1989). The compulsion to repeat the trauma: Re-enactment, revictimization, and masochism. *Psychiatric Clinics of North America, 12*(2), 389–411.
Vissing, Y.M., Straus, M.A., Gelles, R.J., & Harrop, J.W. (1991). Verbal aggression by parents and psychosocial problems of children. *Child Abuse and Neglect, 15*, 223–238.
Westen, D., Ludolph, P., Misle, B., Ruffins, S., & Block, J. (1990). Physical and sexual abuse in adolescent girls with borderline personality disorder. *American Journal of Orthopsychiatry, 60*(1), 55–66.

9

Preventing Secondary Traumatic Stress Disorder

JANET YASSEN

In order to prevent Secondary Traumatic Stress Disorder (STSD) we must first understand what Secondary Traumatic Stress (STS) is and second, what prevention is. Other chapters in this volume describe the impact of traumatic experiences on individuals who have provided care for survivors of medical emergencies, disasters, the Holocaust of World War II, torture, political repression, rape, incest, physical violence, and war. The understanding of this impact is the foundation underlying the development of a model for prevention of STSD.

This chapter presents an understanding of the concept of prevention and offers an ecological model as a framework for planning for the impact of STS. It is based on the premise that STS in itself cannot be prevented since it is a normal and universal response to abnormal (violence induced) or unusual events (disasters). The enduring or negative effects of this response, however, can be prevented from developing into a disorder (STSD). This chapter emphasizes the various components of a

---

Editor's Note: This chapter focuses on the prevention of secondary traumatic stress disorder (STSD). In conceptualizing prevention and prevention planning, Yassen introduces an ecological perspective to assist professionals in developing treatment plans that include recognition of the secondary impact of traumatic stressors. Tables and illustrations assist the reader in understanding and appreciating the many factors associated with preventing STS from developing into a disorder.

comprehensive prevention program including the individual and environmental aspects of self-care. It assumes that unless we prepare, plan, or attend to the effects of STS, we can cause harm to ourselves, to those who are close to us, or to those who are in our professional care.

The second section of this chapter discusses implementation of a prevention plan. It identifies factors that influence successful prevention planning and makes suggestions for combatting resistance to prevention planning. It is through the creation of an ecological model that stresses the interaction of the personal and environmental influences of prevention that human healing and growth in the face of trauma in enhanced. It is only in this context that the prevention of the deleterious effects of STS can be assured.

Although the primary focus of this chapter is on professional caregivers (including those who provide care in a volunteer capacity), the information provided is also relevant to those who have been indirectly affected by victimization in their personal lives through the victimization of friends, neighbors, community members, significant others, and so on.

Overall, the management of STS and preventing it from developing into disorder means acknowledging its existence and preparing for it. Simply put, the management of STS is developing a lifestyle and skills that will provide a foundation for dealing with the various levels of impact. This foundation will provide the optimum conditions for the prevention of STSD.

UNDERSTANDING PREVENTION

Conceptualization

The concept of prevention in mental health is drawn from the fields of public health and medicine. The public health field studies entire populations and identifies the spread of disease symptoms and the conditions that promote the disease. The medical model of illness focuses on individual symptoms, diagnosis, and treatment. The integration of these two models forms the basis for a mental health prevention model, which assumes that the psychological and social diseases involve both the individual and society, and that the prevention of the deleterious effects and the spread of the diseases must be addressed at various levels (Heller & Monahan, 1977).

Davis and Brody (1979) categorize prevention as: primary, secondary, or tertiary. Broadly stated, primary prevention deals with the underlying social causes of a problem, secondary prevention emphasizes activities that could reduce the risk of violence or provide preparation to face its impact should it occur, and tertiary prevention focuses on intervention in the aftermath of violence in the form of crisis intervention. Figure 1 illustrates this multidimensional view and the expected results of primary, secondary, and tertiary prevention. This multifaceted approach to prevention of mental health problems has also been described as an ecological approach (Harvey, 1995). It is this ecological approach that is offered here as a practical guide for preventing individual secondary traumatic stress (STS).

The Ecological Approach

Prevention in mental health combines the understanding of the psychological and social impact of disease with the concepts pf primary, secondary, and tertiary prevention. An ecological model draws its view from science concerning the interrelationship of organisms and their environment. This approach is the basis upon which the fields of social work and community psychology are founded. Community psycholo-

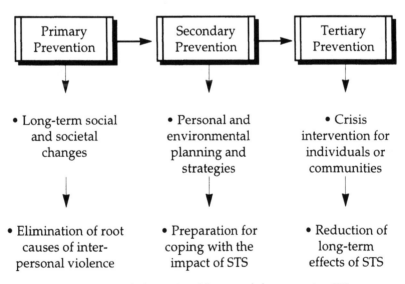

Figure 1. Multidimensional framework for preventing STS

(Based on Davis, L. & E. Brody in *Rape and Older Women*, U.S. Dept. of Health, Education, & Welfare, NIMH, 1979, p. 46. Figure 2: Prevention of Rape—Overview of Simultaneous Activities)

gist James Kelly (1977) stresses the interdependence of persons and social settings. This model is based on three assumptions:

1. Physical, social, and psychological environments affect personal behavior.
2. Personal adaptations to environmental conditions facilitate growth and development.
3. Community health is determined by energy flow and the cycling of resources.

There is evidence that while individual adaptation is important (Figley, Mackey, & Meshad, 1991; Flannery, 1990; Lazarus & Folkman, 1984; Medeiros & Prochaska, 1988; O'Rear, 1992), individual coping strategies alone do not alleviate the strain caused by job stress (Shinn, Rosario, Morch, & Chestnut, 1984; Pearlin & Schooler, 1978; Cherniss, 1980). Furthermore, individual adaptation has an important social component that serves as a buffer against disease and stress, and is also a mediator of healing and recovery from the effects of STS (Caplan, 1972; Etzion, 1984; Flannery, Fulton, Tausch, & DeLoffi, 1991; Koss & Harvey, 1991; McCann & Pearlman, 1990). Harvey (1995) applies an ecological perspective to recovery in the aftermath of sexual trauma. She reports that community values and resources have a direct correlation with positive recovery outcome. The application of an ecological approach to the prevention of STS that combines individual and environmental interventions is consistent with these findings.

Several programs are already in existence that address some of the effects of STS on individuals. They include psychodrama groups (Thacker, 1984); models for debriefing debriefers (Armstrong, O'Callahan, & Marmar, 1991; Mitchell, 1983; Talbot, 1990; Talbot, Manton, & Dunn, 1992; U.S. Department of Health and Human Services, 1988); and opportunities to share clinical material (Herman, 1992; McCann & Pearlman, 1990; O'Rear, 1992). They concur with Flannery's four-step approach to stress reduction (1987, 1990), which includes personal control, task involvement, lifestyle choices, and social supports. However, many of these programs do not always explicitly incorporate an ecological approach and thus are limited in preventing long-term effects of STS.

One model that meets all of the criteria of the Kelly approach to ecological prevention is the Community Crisis Response Team (CCRT) of the Cambridge (Mass.) Hospital Victims of Violence Program. The CCRT integrates the prevention of STS in personal providers, as well as in professional caregivers. It is unique because the team itself parallels

the services that it provides for others. Composed of three part-time staff
members and a group of volunteers representing more than 40 agencies
and various professional disciplines, the CCRT offers crisis intervention
to communities that are affected by violence—including schools, church
groups, cohorts of friends, staffs, and neighborhoods. Team members
can furnish a range of services, from workshops and consultations to
debriefing meetings. The CCRT is based on a community empowerment
model that stresses Kelly's interdependence of person and environment.
Through its group debriefing meetings, it models the importance of
social support as the basis of healing in the aftermath of violence, and it
provides information to direct victims, as well as to secondary victims,
regarding the impact of trauma and effective strategies to cope with it. It
serves as a resource for referrals for people who may need additional
individual counseling support, either from a resource in their own community or through services at the Victims of Violence Program. The
CCRT is an active participant in city and state wide violence-prevention
initiatives. Its services are free, and thus it is a resource that is accessible
to all.

For the pairs of volunteers who participate in the community interventions, there are planning meetings, as well as debriefing meetings
after the interventions. This allows the facilitators of an intervention to
plan for as well as process the STS that they may experience as a result
of the crisis response. There are also monthly meetings of the entire
team, which can include a further sharing of STS responses or may
involve learning a new skill, sharing resources, or developing team
cohesiveness. The significance of the CCRT model also lies in the way it
models for itself the ecological approach to the prevention of STS in its
focus on the physical, social, and psychological aspects of the individuals and communities that it assists.

The CCRT illustrates incorporation of the primary, secondary, and
tertiary prevention paradigm as illustrated in Figure 1. Specifically, it
incorporates the following prevention concepts.

1. Primary prevention. Workshops, antiviolence campaigns, coalition-
building, and community involvement address the root causes of violence.

2. Secondary prevention. Debriefing meetings and educational activities assist participants in preparing and planning for the potential
impact of trauma.

3. Tertiary prevention. Community crisis interventions (debriefings)
and identification and referral of individuals who need additional support alleviate the recurrence of emotional distress (Koss & Harvey, 1991).

The following components reflect an ecological view of planning for

STS for providers in order to prevent deliterious effects. This view is dynamic, competency-based, and proactive.

COMPONENTS OF PREVENTION OF INDIVIDUAL STS

Several researchers have developed guidelines for stress reduction, burnout, and prevention that apply to caregivers of trauma survivors (Hamberger & Stone, 1985; Edelwich & Brodsky, 1980; Yassen, 1983; Lazarus & Folkman, 1984; Pines & Kafry, 1981; Freudenberger, 1974; Maslach, 1982; Cherniss, 1980; Holt, Fine, & Tollefson, 1987; Fischman, 1991; Smith & Steindler, 1983; Newman & Beehr, 1979; Medeiros & Prochaska, 1988; Flannery, 1987, 1990; O'Rear, 1992; Raphael, 1986; Mitchell, 1983). The recurring themes include the importance of active planning and involvement and a holistic, multidimensional approach that combines knowledge, strategies, and techniques. These interventions are secondary prevention if they build a foundation for individuals before a traumatic event or tertiary prevention if they are activated in the aftermath of trauma.

Personal

While many of these personal components may be common knowledge, it is important to make them explicit and to offer readers the opportunity to review their current status in these categories. They address the prevention of the deleterious effects of STS as outlined in Table 1, including its physical, psychological, cognitive, interpersonal, behavioral, and spiritual components.

Physical

Body Work. Body work means maintaining the health of our bodies. Having a well-paced life, as well as incorporating all of the other self-care components, will increase body self-care and decrease wear and tear.

The importance of vigorous exercise in stress reduction has been documented in the stress-management literature (Flannery, 1990; Sinyan, Schwartz, & Peronnet, 1982). However, for some, fitting exercise into their lives becomes an additional stressor. One colleague's solution was to exercise at work by walking up and down the stairs. It is recommended that one choose a form of exercise that fits one's lifestyle, and that may meet some other needs (e.g., desire to have time alone or, conversely, to spend some time with a friend, or to be competitive through team sports). Whatever form of exercise is selected, it is clear that doing it regularly increases one's overall strength, endurance, cognitive clarity, and sense of well-being.

TABLE 1
The Personal Impact of Secondary Traumatic Stress

Cognitive	Emotional	Behavioral	Spiritual	Interpersonal	Physical
• Diminished concentration	• Powerlessness	• Clingy	• Questioning the meaning of life	• Withdrawn	• Shock
• Confusion	• Anxiety	• Impatient	• Loss of purpose	• Decreased interest in intimacy or sex	• Sweating
• Spaciness	• Guilt	• Irritable	• Lack of self-satisfaction	• Mistrust	• Rapid heartbeat
• Loss of meaning	• Anger/rage	• Withdrawn	• Pervasive hopelessness	• Isolation from friends	• Breathing difficulties
• Decreased self-esteem	• Survivor guilt	• Moody	• Ennui	• Impact on parenting (protectivness, concern about aggression)	• Somatic reactions
• Preoccupation with trauma	• Shutdown	• Regression	• Anger at God	• Projection of anger or blame	• Aches and pains
• Trauma imagery	• Numbness	• Sleep disturbances	• Questioning of prior religious beliefs	• Intolerance	• Dizziness
• Apathy	• Fear	• Appetite changes		• Loneliness	• Impaired immune system
• Rigidity	• Helplessness	• Nightmares			
• Disorientation	• Sadness	• Hypervigilance			
• Whirling thoughts	• Depression	• Elevated startle response			
• Thoughts of self-harm or harm toward others	• Hypersensitivity	• Use of negative coping (smoking; alcohol or other substance misuse)			
• Self-doubt	• Emotional roller coaster	• Accident proneness			
• Perfectionism	• Overwhelmed	• Losing things			
• Minimization	• Depleted	• Self-harm behaviors			

Some trauma-treatment specialists emphasize the importance of additional nurturance. This can include massages, warm baths, therapeutic body work, wearing clothes that feel good, and buying household/office furniture and accessories that are pleasant to look at and are comfortable to live with.

In general, it is important to listen to one's body. It often will communicate what it needs, and is sometimes the first to know. Since it is important to keep it well tuned, regular physical examinations are suggested.

Adequate Sleep. From the wisdom of cartoonist Ashleigh Brilliant, (1974): "What I need is a well-deserved rest, but I haven't deserved it yet." Not everyone has this attitude, but it is commonly expressed in the trauma-treatment community. Thus a recent event or one's work may interfere with sleep.

Adequate sleep is essential to well-being. Those who have undergone sleep deprivation can testify to its debilitating effects, including impaired cognitive and neurological functioning and irritability. Be aware of how much sleep you need to function well. In experiencing specific kinds of sleep disturbances (e.g., inability to fall asleep, early rising, waking in the middle of the night, regular nightmares), be sure to address these problems before they become a pattern.

Nutrition. Eating good, nutritious meals is a vital part of human functioning. Unless we keep our bodies well fueled, we will not have enough energy to live our lives properly. Many of us not only do not eat correctly (i.e., balanced meals at regular intervals with selections from the four basic food groups), but may have developed poor eating habits as a result of our hurried, full lives—such as eating in our cars, having meetings during lunch, not taking a lunch break, or eating too quickly to permit proper digestion. Flannery (1990) maintains that stress can be exacerbated by the intake of refined white sugar, caffeine, or nicotine, and points to studies that tie the modification of the use of these substances to stress reduction. One caregiver relates that when she is under stress, it is not exercise that is the first to go, it is vegetables. In war or poverty affected areas, food supplies may be inadequate to meet nutritional needs.

Appetite also can be affected by stress. Some people tend to overeat, some to undereat, and others to substitute eating for having feelings. In understanding our relationship to food and nutrition, we first must become aware of what our eating patterns are now compared with what they were in the past, keeping in mind what, when, how, and why one eats. Then we must decide if changes are desired or needed. Changes in our eating habits are one of the hardest to make, so don't be too hard on yourself in the process.

Psychological

  Life Balance. In Flannery's approach to stress reduction (1990), the first step is to reduce somatic arousal. This reflects the view that it is important to maintain a life that is marked by a diversity of activities as well as a moderate pace. It does not mean that there will not be periods in your life that are more stressful than others. Rather, it emphasizes the value of striving for an overall balance of work, outside interests, social contacts, personal time, and recreation. Life balance includes a commitment to life and life-enhancing activities.

  Relaxation. As cartoonist Ashleigh Brilliant (1974) puts it, "Please don't make me relax, it's my tension that's holding me together." Those involved in trauma work find it difficult to relax because of the nature of this work, and because they may feel a mission to absolve the world of violence (certainly an important goal). Nevertheless, relaxation must be incorporated on a daily basis, as well as at more extended intervals (i. e., vacations). Relaxation can take the form of fun. Daily relaxation, sometimes called "downtime," can be short in duration, so long as it is regular.

  Contact with Nature. With our absorption in the realm of human interactions, it is easy to forget that we live on Planet Earth. Once, while I was experiencing some major life transitions, a wise consultant suggested that I start a garden. She contended that the changes, the cycle of the seasons—the planting, the harvesting—would offer an important perspective on life, and literally would be "grounding" and an antidote to stress.

  Contact with nature can give us a larger view of the world and our place in it. Even short trips to the park, a spontaneous canoe trip, watching the night sky, or a plunge into the ocean can be rejuvenating. Some clinicians may need longer stretches with nature, such as mountain climbing, snorkeling, hiking, camping, earthkeeper missions, skiing, or rafting. Caring for pets or plants can also be restorative, and animals can be a source of comfort as well.

  Creative Expression. As our brains become more and more involved in the intellectual work of our professions or in trying to manage personal scheduling, we need to make a concentrated effort to engage the more creative parts of our minds. This can include, but is not limited to, writing, drama, photography, cooking, drawing, painting, dancing, handicrafts, utilizing one's sense of humor, or playing a musical instrument. Through creative expression, we become more expansive, and also may find new modalities for handling STS.

  Skill Development. There are some skills that help to enhance the prevention of STS. These include:

- Assertiveness training. Learn and practice the skills associated with having the belief and self-confidence to stand up for oneself or to say "No" when necessary.

- Stress reduction. Learn comprehensive techniques that have proven effective in reducing the physical and mental effects of stress.
- Interpersonal communication. Learn about your personal communication style and how interpersonal interactions can be improved to enhance social or colleagial support.
- Cognitive restructuring. Evaluate how you view your situation and the world and learn more effective problem-solving strategies.
- Community organizing. Learn how to be an effective organizer in order to be more successful and satisfied in social action.
- Time management. Learn techniques to effectively set priorities and organize your time in a productive manner.

Meditation/Spiritual Practice. Meditation can be healing to the body and the spirit. Flannery (1990), Borysenko (1988), Kabat-Zinn (1990), Benson (1976), and others document how meditation can effect the well-being of the body. Blood pressure is lowered, breathing becomes more regular and efficient, and muscles are more relaxed.

Such practice does not change the reality of the external traumatic events, but it does minimize the wear and tear on the body, and assists in developing healthy coping strategies. The practice of meditation does not have to involve fancy techniques, following a certain guru, or many years of study. At its most basic level, it means paying attention to one's breathing and approaching life with an attitude of mindfulness.

Another dimension relates to spirituality, which may or may not entail connection with an organized religion. As mentioned before, the impact of trauma can be such as to shatter or impel one to reevaluate one's spiritual belief system. For some, this means a questioning of previously held beliefs: for others, it means turning for comfort and community to religious groups; and for still others, it means expanding their beliefs in new ways. Flannery (1990) reports that, in his study, those people who had a spiritual outlet underwent less stress.

We need to confront our spiritual beliefs and learn how to derive meaning from what we have personally experienced or to which we are bearing witness. We need to acknowledge the resiliency of the human spirit. This process will enable us to maintain a sense of hope and vision.

Self-Awareness. Prevention of STS is partially determined by the character of the individual. Therefore, an assessment of oneself is an important component of prevention. Lazarus and Folkman (1984) suggest evaluating one's health and energy, existential beliefs, problem-solving skills, social skills, social supports, and material resources. In providing trauma treatment, Medeiros and Prochaska (1988) stress the importance of self-evaluation in maintaining optimistic perseverence, seeking inner peace, and instituting contigency control. It is important to understand which work or client situations may be particularly difficult for you. Evaluate whether you are really able or want to be objective in this situation.

This self-evaluation should be conducted with an openess toward acknowledging personal resources and identifying areas in which one would like to, and is willing to, change. It also means exploring who we are not. For instance, as a white person, one can never truly know what it is like to be an African American. Fischman and Ross (1990) remind us of the importance of a cultural–social–political anaylsis of ourselves and of this self-awareness in providing care.

Self-awareness denotes a nonjudgmental and compassionate attitude toward oneself, an understanding of one's current life circumstances, and a level of maturity that enables one to accept oneself. It involves a willingness adduce personal meaning from traumatic experiences, and to incorporate these lessons into a self view. It also means accepting the small ways in which one can take control in the face of powerlessness. A police officer noted how much satisfaction he was beginning to take in finishing his paperwork. It was a small way in which he could feel productive—by completing a manageable task.

Finally, self-awareness means knowing when outside help is needed.

Humor. Maintaining a sense of humor and using humor as a coping strategy are vital prevention techniques. Humor is increasingly adding a special dimension to our lives, as evidenced by the proliferation of comedy clubs and the publication of Norman Cousins' (1979) popular book, *Anatomy of an Illness*, which describes his use of humor in the face of his terminal illness. Humor can reduce stress, release tensions, and allow us to keep an emotional distance. Socially, humor can create group cohesion, or it can afford a vehicle for social criticism (Dyergrov & Mitchell, 1992; Flannery, 1987, 1990; Kelly, 1977). But there is clearly a difference between using humor at the expense of others and having the "ability to laugh at oneself and to see lightness in everyday joyful and tragic events" (Kelly, 1977).

Social/Interpersonal

Social Supports. Since trauma from abuse results in the breach of attachments with others, for survivors of abuse, connections with other people are restorative. This is true for caregivers as well.

Social supports are a central component of the prevention of personal and professional STSD, and it is important to expand one's interventions beyond a focus on the individual to a focus on one's social network. This involves evaluating the quality of the network. An analysis might question your supports' understanding of and belief systems concerning trauma; their availability, resourcefulness, and ability to give and receive feedback; and their receptivity to change. Once this analysis is complete, one may decide to make changes by either adding to or subtracting from current sources of supports.

In addition to evaluating or changing one's support system, there may also be the task of educating social supports about one's needs and experiences. This education process may include the challenge of changing the attitudes and the skills of those whom one cares about. It is crucial to build in regular time with loved ones, friends, and acquaintances in order to nurture our connections with others. If it is a loved one who has been traumatized, time away and support from others can be useful. This time out may feel like an additional burden, but it is one of the vital forces militating against isolation and the stress of secondary victimization. Included should be time with children, if at all possible. Children bring a fresh view of life and demand that one be in the moment with them. They offer feelings of hope, joy, beauty, and playfulness to conteract the more heinous aspects of human nature to which we are exposed in our work.

Getting Help. Getting help is not something for which people generally plan. However, if a foundation is laid, help can be more accessible and more effective. Accepting and accessing help in a timely manner has been associated with preventing the long-term effects of post-traumatic stress. Establishing a plan of help includes developing the attitude that getting help is a sign of personal strength, identifying specific people in one's personal and professional life who are viewed as helpful, and becoming familiar with professional resources should one choose to use them.

Social Activism. Another way to maintain a sense of hope and purpose in doing trauma work is to be involved in social activism. This has the effect of combating the feeling of powerlessness that results from STS, as well as of providing a sense of shared mission with others, which can mitigate social isolation. There is wisdom in the saying, "There is power in numbers." Holmes (1981) describes the importance of class advocacy combined with case advocacy for enhancing one's self-worth, as well as for improving services. Comas-Diaz and Padilla (1990) suggest that a sense of social responsibility helps to contain horror.

Social activisim may or may not be related to the trauma. For one person, working on an antiviolence public education campaign can be valuable, whereas someone else may find meaning in working for the establishment of a new neighborhood playground. Members of the Victims of Violence Program of Cambridge Hospital engaged in social activism as a team by having a public statement in support of Anita Hill, a law profes-

sor who came forward to report sexual harassment by their Supreme
Court nominee, Clarence Thomas, read at the 1991 annual meeting of
the International Society of Traumatic Stress Studies.

Social activism can also be an outlet for frustration. Letting the public
know your views, beliefs, and ideals can be an antidote to the secretive
and silencing nature of trauma. What may seem like small acts of
activism can also combat powerlessness. For example, residents and
workers in a refugee camp organizing bus service to take them to town
twice a week. Social activism offers the opportunity to change the present and the future, while the past can only be confronted and, learned
from, but not changed.

Professional

While Table 2 delineates the ways in which STS can affect professional functioning, the following guidelines are suggested for the prevention
of professional STS.

Balance

Balance is important in several ways. One issue is how much work to
do—the number of work hours per week and the proportion of the work
that relates to direct trauma treatment. It is important to have diversity
in one's work life. For example, if working on the hotline in a battered
women's shelter, or acclimating new residents to the shelter, it may also
be important to have the opportunity to work on public education, do
administrative tasks, or become involved in other professional activities.
In other words, to have balance in the quantity and quality of tasks in
one's work life is crucial.

Another aspect of balance is pacing. This means paying daily attention to the effects that your work is having on you and creating a pace
that will maximize your emotional and physical health. Pacing includes
taking regular breaks, making time for meals, and taking vacations.

Boundaries/Limit Setting

Setting good boundaries is important for self-care, as well as for providing a model for those to whom care is provided. Boundaries have
several components.

Time Boundaries. These include being on time for appointments and
being careful not to go over the specified time. Although going beyond the
time limit can be seen as a sign of caring, it can also be perceived as a broken contract or create fear of the unknown. These are particularly sensitive
areas for trauma survivors. It is also important that we guard our own time
boundaries so that there is the opportunity to have a balanced life.

TABLE 2
Impact of Secondary Traumatic Stress on Professional Functioning

Performance of Job Tasks	Morale	Interpersonal	Behavorial
• Decrease in quality	• Decrease in confidence	• Withdrawal from colleagues	• Absenteeism
• Decrease in quantity	• Loss of interest	• Impatience	• Exhaustion
• Low motivation	• Dissatisfaction	• Decrease in quality	• Faulty judgment
• Avoidance of job tasks	• Negative attitude	of relationship	• Irritability
• Increase in mistakes	• Apathy	• Poor communication	• Tardiness
• Setting perfectionist	• Demoralization	• Subsume own needs	• Irresponsibility
standards	• Lack of appreciation	• Staff conflicts	• Overwork
• Obsession about details	• Detachment		• Frequent job changes
	• Feelings of incompleteness		

Overworking. This includes taking on too many responsibilities, working overtime on a regular basis, constantly bringing work home or taking calls at home, and being unable to separate from the work emotionally. In the extreme, this can mean actually taking clients home. Even excessive reading can be a form of taking clients home, and can be an attempt to overcome feelings of inadequacy, incompetency, or helplessness.

Therapeutic/Professional Boundaries. Since the core of abuse is the violation of boundaries, it is important that the care provider and the client have an understanding of the nature and the process of the helping relationship, and of therapy itself. When one is in the care of others in the aftermath of trauma, this can bring up feelings on the part of the client that are not always understood. Some of the feelings of rage, helplessness, and so on, might be projected onto the caregiver. It may be hard not to take these feelings personally. Understanding the nature of the therapeutic or helping relationship can help to depersonalize possible abuses by those receiving care. Explaining the reasons for particular interventions can defuse the situation.

Personal Boundaries. It is important to resolve how much of oneself to disclose to clients and under what circumstances. An example of this dilemma is the therapist who is pregnant and is treating survivors of childhood sexual abuse. How does she respect the possible jealousy, as well as natural curiousity, of her clients while balancing her desire to maintain her privacy and her joy about the upcoming birth of a child? What does she do with her own resentment? Or consider the clergy member who has lost a child to gang violence. When is it appropriate to disclose his experience to those in his care?

Human service workers who live and work in refugee camps or other ongoing traumatized communities may have to be extremely creative in creating boundaries for themselves. One worker whom I met in Croatia, decided that she would have a schedule for when residents could come to see her and that she would only see a certain number of people a day. The basic structure and intervention offered her hope of creating some boundaries between herself and the onslaught of urgent needs and requests that her fellow refugees brought to her.

Service providers must understand the importance and implications of physical touch for trauma survivors. This affects their own as well as their clients' personal boundaries. It can have different meanings, depending on the kind of trauma. Different work settings may also have different standards concerning touch. Nurses and doctors regularly use touch in the course of their work. In addition, there seems to be more of a norm for physical contact in bereavement groups in the aftermath of murder than in groups dealing with the aftermath of chilhood sexual abuse. Service providers who are therapists must decide what role physical touch should play in their clinical practices.

Dealing with Multiple Roles. Clinicians may be undergoing their own healing processes and thus may meet their clients in other environments (e.g., Al-Anon, Alcoholics Anonymous, or other mutual-help groups). They should be prepared to handle these situations. It is usually the case that human service workers will have to limit their own activities and find resources that will feel comfortable for their healing, and they may sometimes feel as though their own support system is being compromised. This is not always an easy task. Sometimes there is a scarcity of resources and sometimes you are living and working in the same communities so multiple roles are more a part of your daily lives.

Realism. Knowing our limits in doing this work is important as well as humbling. We cannot be the parents that our clients never had, we cannot erase the Vietnam conflict or the Holocaust, we do not have the power to eliminate interpersonal violence. No amount of work or self-sacrifice can ever achieve such goals. Pines (1986) reminds us that we have to accept the limitations of insight in the face of massive traumatization. It is important to take the time to appreciate what we actually are doing and the contributions that we are making to help the world become a better place. Sometimes, when we are in the midst of the work, we do not see its effects, or if a client does not improve, we focus on our failings. We also may not have the opportunity to witness the full recovery process. For example, if we have only provided crisis intervention services, we may not be able to observe over the long term how a family eventually adapted to the murder of a loved one. If you are working with people who are continuing to be in ongoing danger, you may help them face the realities of their situation or provide them with some temporary relief, but you may not be a part of their lives to help them pick up the pieces when the violence has ceased. Or, you may be working with children or teenagers who do not have developmental maturity to integrate some of the meaning of the trauma that they have experienced, so you may feel good about the tools you have taught them, but may not see them as they integrate the meaning of their pasts into their adult lives. Take the time now to appreciate the efforts of your work.

Getting Support/Help

Etzion and Pines (1986) and others (Himle, Jayaratne, & Thyness, 1991) have documented the importance of social support in moderating the negative consequences of stressful life events. The key element in developing a support structure is that it be emotionally safe to be able to talk honestly about the impact of one's work on one's own life. The timing of support is also important. Some caregivers prefer immediate support, whereas in other situations, as Dyregrov and Mitchell (1992) point out, they may still be functioning in an emotionally distant mode and could benefit better from support after a delay. The development of trusting professional relationships ensures that there will be those who will notice that one is having difficulties, and will be available for support or to make recommendations. Various kinds of support are available.

Peer Support. Peer support means that one has the opportunity to receive from and give support to colleagues who are involved in similar work tasks. This support should be in addition to or in conjunction with clinical support, and can take place on or off one's work site. In their classic article on vicarious traumatization, McCann and Pearlman (1990) describe a weekly case conference meeting in which their staff members spend the first hour discussing and conceptualizing difficult cases and the second hour as "feelings" time in which to process their own reactions. Off-site groups have the advantage of including a variety of people from different settings, and, therefore, can offer varying perspectives. Peer support may also come more informally as speaking with a co-worker.

The benefits of peer support include nurturing colleagiality, as well as relieving isolation. It is important for caregivers to have a variety of peer support resources to allow easy access to the immediate, uncensored ventilation of feelings, and to be able to share with others the burden of bearing witness to traumatic events. Isolation can also be reduced by such strategies as setting up coleadership of groups, teaching, or responding to crises in pairs, which help as well to reduce feelings of helplessness and powerlessness.

Peer support can help with finding an equilibrium and can assist with the elimination of STS symptoms. Peer groups offer a sense of continuity over time (Kaplan, 1992). As members get to know and trust each other, they can help one another to recognize their professional "blind spots," as well as to develop professional challenges.

Supervision/Consultation/Therapy. No matter how experienced we are, it is important to build in supervision or consultation on a regular basis. It is crucial to get an outside perspective from someone trusted or to receive guidance in facing a new challenge. Supervision provides the opportunity to have someone listen solely to us, as we have had to do with our clients. If this is not available at work, outside arrangements should be made.

Consulting with an expert can be particularly helpful and reassuring. For example, one colleague began an evaluation with a woman who revealed that her estranged husband had been following her. After consulting with an expert on battered women, the clinician decided that it did not make sense to continue to provide services to this woman in the context of private practice, as it might not be safe for either of them. She recommended a group at a battered women's shelter, together with continuation of the evaluation at a hospital-based outpatient treatment facility that could assure security for both client and practitioner.

Outside consultation can also be an important resource for staffs to evaluate the ways that their group as a whole may be manifesting symptoms of STS. When one realizes that personal and/or professional functioning become inpaired, it is important to seek out therapeutic resources to supplement professional ones.

Role Models/Mentors. Finding other professionals whose work, style, writing, ability, or the like, one admires can be a source of inspiration and professional growth.

Plans for Coping

With full understanding of the impact of trauma work, it is important for caregivers to develop their own self-care plans for their workdays. These plans should include the various components outlined in the section on personal prevention. In addition, caregivers should plan for the periods before, during, and after client meetings, and for emergency situations (e.g., a client suddenly reports suicidal or homicidal thoughts, or is threatening). Trauma-survivor caregivers should be prepared in the event that new memories or flashbacks occur during meetings. Another particularly vulnerable situation that may need additional coping strategies comes from work with children. Helpers may find that their usual coping strategies are inadequate in caring for two children who have been traumatized since children are unable to protect themselves (Dyregrov & Mitchell, 1994). If children have been killed or who have lost parents, this may evoke particularly strong feelings and call for particularly active coping plans.

Emergency workers (e.g., police officers, ambulance attendants, healthcare providers) need to develop personal guidelines that incorporate regular coping strategies. Dyregrov & Mitchell (1992) found that emergency personnel developed certain on-scene coping mechanisms, such as using activity to restrict reflection, consciously suppressing emotions while in the moment, actively avoiding thinking about the ramifications of the event, preparing themselves mentally, regulating the amount of exposure to stressors, focusing on some task or distraction, or finding a purpose in performing the task. Coping strategies should also include contact with colleagues on a regular basis. Again, this breaks the isolation and sets up a climate in which workers are encouraged and expected to exercise self-care. Plans for coping should include cognitive and mental preparation, with possible role plays of potentially difficult situations.

Evaluation of One's Own Healing.

For clinicians who are also trauma survivors, it is important to remember that survivors have something unique to offer this field (Kaplan, 1983; Shrum, 1989; Scurfield, 1985; Yassen & Schatzow, 1991; Yassen, 1993). It is the survivors themselves who have taught caregivers about the nature of the recovery process. However, as an individual, there needs to be a self-evaluation by the clinician of the personal motivations for doing this work and of where he or she is at in the recovery process. In early recovery, there are risks of overidentifying with clients or confusing personal healing with clients' healing. It may be tempting to work on one's own healing by helping others work through theirs. This should not be done. Survivors need their own space and time and some distance from the process to be able to achieve a balance in life. Also, having experienced a traumatic event does not mean that one is qualified to help other survivors. One must ascertain what in one's own experience may be useful to others, and what skills and training are needed in order to help them. For some survivors, helping others may be a defense against their own pain, or something they do because they feel as though they "should" in order to keep the memory alive.

If one has been in recovery for a while and suddenly recovers new memories or goes through a life transition that initiates another healing cycle, one may begin to question one's own skills and competency as a caregiver. Healing, however, is a lifelong process. At some points, it may be important to take breaks for self-care. This should not be confused with professional incompetence. And this is true for any caregiver and for any issue that may have personal relevance for clinicians (e.g., working with cancer patients as a cancer survivor, working in adoption having experienced infertility).

Healing takes place on a continuum, and survivors who are also healers must continually evaluate and reevaluate what their own needs are in this process. It is crucial that a setting be provided in which survivors who are also caregivers can talk openly and candidly about the interface between their own experiences, countertransference, and vicarious traumatization. In the Boston area, treatment interventions are available specifically for female therapists and human-service professionals with a history of sexual abuse (Yassen & Schatzow, 1991). Two models that have been developed are a daylong workshop focusing on issues of self-care and a 12-week, time-limited group model. These interventions have been effective in reducing isolation and increasing participants' coping skills.

Recently, I participated in a U.S. government–supported project that provided workshops for human service providers in Croatia and Bosnia to learn about the various levels of impact that the war is having on them and to develop action plans to address the issues of STS. This demonstrated worldwide acknowledgment of the importance of the mental health of human service providers.

For nonsurvivors, as well as survivors, doing this work may trigger memories of prior losses, even if they were not trauma related. These need to be attended to in order to prevent their interference with work and/or emotional well-being. One caregiver revealed, "I thought that I had finished grieving my mother's death until someone was referred to me whose mother had been murdered. I realized that in fact I had avoided dealing with my own mother's death by immediately going back to work. I was surprised that even though she had died 10 years ago, hearing about this murder caused flashbacks to my own mother. I went to a bereavement group, and not only do I feel much better, I really believe that I am a better therapist."

Professional Training

It is essential to access the adequecy of one's training in preparation to do trauma treatment. In the past, professional training schools of social work, psychiatry, and psychology perpetuated societal denial of the prevalence and impact of violence on human lives. Newberry (1985) contends that many clinicians believe that PTSD symptoms can only occur with people who are predisposed characterologically. This assumption perpetuates professional denial that human disasters can strongly affect well-adjusted people. Herman (1992) suggests that this denial *in mental health professions* leads to professional isolation of those professionals who work primarily in the field of trauma. These theoretical differences can lead to conflicts with colleagues as well as to the subtle stigmatizing of trauma survivors. Our professional identies can be used as a defense against feeling the pain that exists from trauma. This can result in a victim blaming, distancing, or devaluing. Many survivors who are professionals feel unable to speak openly about their histories for fear of being judged by others and objectified and having their motivations questioned.

Fortunately, there has been a proliferation of conferences, workshop, and professional organizations that offer the opportunity to supplement existing skills and to reevaluate prior values and assumptions. Seeking out new and different sources of training (e.g., collaboration of veterans groups and rape crisis centers) enriches one's knowledge base and combats misinformation that still exists in some settings. Kelly (1970) reminds us again about the importance of interdisciplinary interaction and learning.

In certain professions, there seems to be a reluctance to new and varied sources of learning. Colao and Hunt (1983) report that professionals who received degrees from institutions of higher education found it difficult to assume the role of students in trainings provided by rape crisis center staff, despite the reality that was the rape crisis movement that first brought the issue of rape to public awareness and developed the first models of rape crisis counseling.

The values that are sometimes taught in professional training also need to be challenged. One such value is the "neutral stance." Herman (1992) describes the process of neutrality as the therapist (caregiver) refraining from advancing her/his personal agenda. However, it has come to mean that therapists appear blank. Herman makes an important distinction between "maintaining technical neutrality" and taking a stance against human-induced violence while maintaining a neutral environment in which a client is free to explore the many responses to his/her victimization (including fantasies of graphic revenge or ambivalence towards a batterer). This is often difficult to do and professional training inadequately addresses these issues.

Another important contribution training can make is to provide a theoretical framework that not only informs the kind of interventions to be made, and also offers intellectual containment in the face of violence and the powerlessness/helplessness it can engender. Theoretical understanding through training or reading professional literature can be a preparation for what may be encountered in the aftermath of trauma. It can provide structure and emotional distance. As a caregiver, this preparation can provide an anchor to assist with feelings or affect and being more present for the people in one's care.

Professional training and identity can be enhanced through participation in professional organizations. Professional activism offers the potential to make changes in training curriculum and can also help to change professional attitudes towards trauma survivors, treatment, and the impact of STS on caregivers. Affiliations with national and international organizations can combat overwhelming feelings of the isolation that results from facing violence and its aftermath on a regular basis.

Kelly (1970) also contends that training can lead to an attitude of arrogance. One antidote he offers for arrogance in training psychologists (and probably all professionals) is for them to become participants in local community activities and events. This keeps helpers in touch with the reality in peoples' lives and contributes to the broadening of the definition of competent helpers.

Another important component of professional training and identity is participation in professional organizations. Professional activism offers the potential to make changes in training curricula, as well as in professional attitudes toward trauma survivors, treatment, and the impact of STS on caregivers.

Job Commitment

We all need to evaluate regularly our commitment to the work we do. Is this the right setting? Is this the right content area for me? Do I need additional training? Am I stuck here? What are my short- and long-term professional goals?

Fogelman & Savran (1980) note the importance of analyzing our personal motivations for doing trauma treatment at all, and suggest such possible motivations as the desire to acheive social and political goals, survivor guilt, or the ability to empathize with people who come from similar situations. Thus it is necessary to consider exactly why one is doing this type of work. Perhaps, too, the intensity of doing trauma work can become a reinforcer in itself.

Many caregivers report job satisfaction because they consider trauma work meaningful. They describe a growing compassion for others; an ability to tolerate a larger range of feelings, both within themselves and in others; and a feeling that they have gained wisdom from the people whom they have met. Whatever one's motives, one must make conscious decisions about one's commitment and devise ways to include optimism. Although not everyone has choices or can control the work situation, with reflection, one will be able to do better trauma work and can make better plans for preventing STS.

Replenishment

Those who have chosen human services as a profession are involved in giving care to others. We, too, are a mini "ecosystem." We must be sensitive to our own needs for professional, as well as personal, replenishment. Sometimes the two can be combined. For instance, one can travel to a conference in an unfamilar city, or attend a local workshop with a colleague whom one would like to know better. There is a natural human desire to learn and to grow. In fact, Penn, Romano, and Foat (1988) report that the opportunity for professional development is the one consistent factor differentiating those who are satisfied with their jobs from those who are not. There needs to be continual professional opportunities to challenge oneself, to be exposed to other points of view. Updating ourselves with new information also ensures that we are offering the people in our care the most up-to-date skills available.

Replenishment also means participating in other work-related activities that are challenging and different (e.g., research, education, training). It may also mean making contributions to the field so that others may learn from one's ideas and experience. Replenishment keeps the ecosystem of our lives nourished and functioning well.

COMPONENTS OF ENVIRONMENTAL-STS PREVENTION

As mentioned before, individual prevention is only one component of STSD prevention. Environmental prevention interventions are another. Prevention of environmental STSD mainly rests on secondary and tertiary prevention activities, since they entail planning, preparation, and larger societal issues (see Figure 1). It is possible, however, that the catalyst for implementing some of these interventions may have resulted from experiencing STS or crisis intervention, and, therefore, arose from a tertiary prevention activity (Figure 1). The three areas of management of environmental STS addressed are social, societal, and work settings.

Social Setting

Another part of one's environment is society at large, which may be evidencing denial, misinformation, or prejudices. Societal actions include:

- Educational interventions—utilizing activities aimed at changing attitudes or providing information
- Coalition building
- Building alliances with various groups in order to exert a greater influence
- Legislative reform—using the legal system to enforce rights
- Social activism—planning actions that include public activities to draw attention to a problem, usually, but not consistently, through the law
- Mass media education and global communications

Work Setting

Just as the work setting can impact STS and STS can impact the work setting, interventions directed toward the work setting can influence job satisfaction, self-care, and prevention of STSD. Thus one needs to assess the environment in which one is working (Quick & Quick, 1984). On a physical level, this includes such things as having an office, as well as, lighting, noise level, accessibility, furnishings, privacy, environmental safety, security, employee amenities (e.g., access to coffee, lunch, office supplies, secretarial assistance, places in which to take breaks), and availability of colleagues.

Other aspects of the work environment are less tangible, and relate to the values, expectations, and culture characterizing the setting. Having a clear philosophical value base has been identified by Harvey (1985) as a key element in comparing rape crisis centers. Other values may go unstated, but clearly have an effect on work settings. For instance, in some settings, it may be assumed that if employees do not work over-time, they are not committed to their work, or that clinicians who do not take vacations are more committed to their work than are others.

Workers need to understand the explicit as well as implicit demands of their work environments. Self-care can best be achieved if manage-ment's policies are made clear to employees. Some important aspects to clarify are as follows:

- Value system
- Tasks: job descriptions, philosophy, realistic expectations, task variety, adequacy of supervision, in-service and career opportunities, training and orientation that prepare the employee for the job, job security, job overload, pay
- Managerial: lines of authority, accessibility of leaders who are open to feedback, role models, accountability, ability to motivate/build morale
- Interpersonal: personnel guidelines, respect for differences, value of social support/mutual aid, trust among staff (cooperation vs. competiton), sensitivity to the needs of individuals (e.g., personal days, stress management training)

IMPLEMENTATION OF A PREVENTION PLAN

Transforming ideas for prevention planning into action is often diffi-cult. Kelly (1977) offers important principles to help in designing an eco-logical prevention plan. A primary consideration is that prevention changes over time. Prevention planning requires honesty about commit-ting time and developing long-range plans that can be adapted to new personal and environmental resources. Besides maintaining this overall "attitude," it is important to remember that each personal and social set-ting is unique, and so will require its own prevention plan developed to meet its own culture. However, Kelly reminds us that more than one set of ideas is always needed. Others have associated being active in creating prevention planning as a significant factor in reducing stress and burnout (Koss & Harvey, 1991; Lazarus & Folkman, 1984).

From the Author's Experience

With these principles in mind, I will use some of my own experience to illustrate STSD prevention planning over a span of 20 years. The prevention strategies are identified in parentheses.

I began my career in antiviolence work in 1972 as a cofounder of the Boston Area Rape Crisis Center, or BARCC (social activism, facing societal myths, community involvement, learning new skills, social support). Surviving my continuing involvement with BARCC, I have answered the 24-hour hotline, provided individual and group counseling, trained and supervised volunteers, served on countless committees, remained with the group as it became transformed from a feminist collective to a feminist hierarchy, testified before local and national legislators regarding legislative reform, furnished training and education to hundreds of community and professional participants and the media, and participated in statewide planning efforts to address the issue of sexual assault (diversity of tasks and audiences, social action, articulated value system).

From 1973 to 1975, I attended graduate school, where I completed my master's degree in social work, participated in my first consciousness-raising group, and fought with professors about the relevancy of the impact of sexual assault (training, replenishment, colleagial support, facing professional denial). After graduate school, I continued my affiliation with BARCC, and worked full time planning and providing services for developmentally disabled offenders and victims (more diversity). At the time, I was also teaching Sunday school (spiritual connections and involvement with children). To survive the collective group process of the rape crisis center, I learned to knit (creative expression, humor).

My career continued as I added two new components (reaffirmation of job commitment). One was integrating into it an international aspect of antiviolence work by providing training in other countries and consulting with international programs (worldwide social activism, expanded social supports, teaching, replenishment, multicultural diversity, recreation, nature and beauty). The second was becoming affiliated with the Victims of Violence Program at Cambridge Hospital. This affiliation has given me the opportunity to work with colleagues whom I respect, to be involved with developing a team that tries to put into practice the principles that it is trying to teach, and to participate in an academic environment that values teaching and research. Through my work with our CCRT, I am able to apply my skills to community situations and to maintain a realistic perspective while changing my skills and adapting them in a changing world (community context, multicultural diversity). We also have a program that offers graduate- and postgraduate-level training in a variety of disciplines (colleagial support, replenishment, task diversity, balance of job tasks, environmental-change agent, work-setting challenges, role models, teaching opportunities). I continue my connection with the "real world" through BARCC, and take part in as many demonstrations as I can (diversity of ideas, social change). I am associated with several citywide and statewide coalitions to implement educational programs and to respond to issues as they present themselves on an ad hoc basis (social activism, multidisciplinary affiliations).

Through the years, I have faced many political and emotional challenges. One that stands out is maintaining my involvement in both grassroots organizations and professional groups, which often do not understand each other's perspectives and what each has to offer.

Another challenge has been to face my own blind spots and, vulnerabilities, regarding multicultural diversity. The Boston area is a community that not only is routinely segregated according to ethnic group, but also reacts to the same historical influences that result in racist attitudes in society at large. I have made a personal committment to combat racism, classism, heterosexism, sexism, and the various other "isms," and the self evaluation that entails. This evaluation has led me to assess that kinds of services that are provided, and their accessibility, value base, and assumptions about the people who are served. It is easy to avoid such issues and focus instead on service delivery, not only because of the emotions they evoke, but also because there are institutional and societal resistances to meeting the challenge.

As my life has progressed professionally, so it has personally. I have needed to explore over the years my motivations for continued involvement in this work (self-awareness). I have done this through personal psychotherapy, as well as through professional support groups, especially one peer group that I have been in for 10 years (colleagial support). I have two children and a number of close friends, all of whom tolerate my mood swings (social supports, children, humor), life balance, and who can offer me different life perspectives.

I have also learned some new skills that I have added to my self-care tool kit. The main one is meditation. The passage of time has been helpful as well. I now have a broader perspective, and sometimes more patience. I am able to see that everything does not happen at once, and that self-care and prevention of STSD can take place in different cycles. This perspective has afforded me understanding of the process, as well as hope

for achieving the prevention of the deleterious effects of STSD. Making
mistakes is also inevitable, and an important part of the process, which I
need to become more tolerant of. I have learned about the importance of
reaching out and accepting help. One thing that I would still like to
change is that sometimes I seek help only after I have passed my break-
ing point. In writing this chapter, I have needed help in countless ways
(emotional, technical, professional, spiritual), and have found new ways
of getting it, which I have now included in my "getting help" repertoire.

While my case is illustrative of just one person's experience, the
guidelines are applicable to caregivers in general, whether street workers, therapists, relief workers, emergency workers, significant others,
clergy, law enforcement personnel, or any professionals furnishing
human services. In general, the successful implementation of a prevention plan involves an understanding of the personal characteristics of the
individual, the social and cultural atmosphere in which he or she was
raised, and the contemporary work and social context in which he or she
currently lives. Personal and environmental obstacles need to be
assessed in order to develop a realistic prevention plan. As the descrip-
tio of the ecological framework points out, it is important to select goals
from both the individual and environmental components of prevention
planning. Figure 2 provides a summary of the ecological framework of
STS prevention. The following guidelines are offered to assist in developing a prevention plan.

1. Review current self-care and prevention functioning.
2. Select one goal from each category (individual and
   environmental, Figure 2).
3. Analyze the resources for and resistances to achieving this goal.
4. Discuss goals and implementation plan with support person(s).
5. Activate plan.
6. Evaluate the plan weekly, monthly, and yearly with support
   persons.
7. Notice and appreciate the changes.
8. Repeat step 1.

CONCLUSION

The impact of affording care to those traumatized by violence can be
all pervasive. Secondary traumatic stress is a natural consequence of giving this care. This chapter provides an understanding of the various levels of prevention, and offers an ecological model for individual and envi-

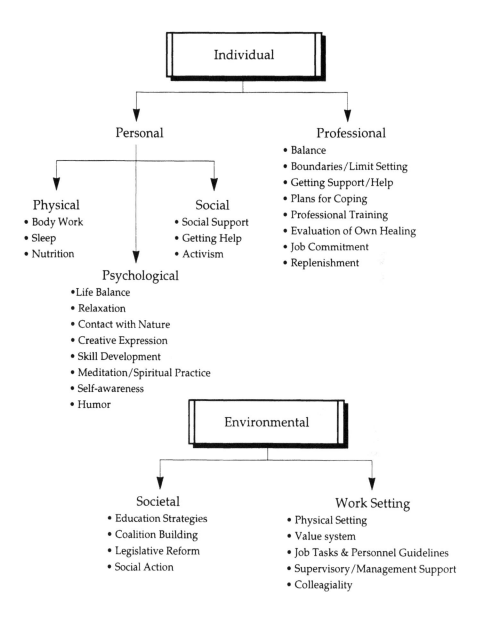

Figure 2. Ecological model for the prevention of STSD.

ronmental prevention. Although the focus is on the prevention of STSD in individuals, it is important to stress that it is not the individual's sole responsibility to prevent individual STSD. Primary prevention activities require long-term planning, and sometimes are more difficult to implement. However, it is the joint responsibility of policy makers, administrators, educators, and professional caregivers, as well as individuals, to ensure comprehensive prevention planning that includes primary in addition to secondary and tertiary interventions. Some of these settings are addressed elsewhere in this book. There are other areas that this chapter was not able to cover that need to be further explored, such as gender issues, multicultural influences, developmental issues, a more in-depth understanding of the physiological affects of stress, and the prolonged effects of STS.

The plans suggested here are designed to prevent the potential negative effects of secondary traumatic stress. Such prevention can be implemented through awareness, planning, and action. This chapter, it is hoped, has provided guidelines for all three.

REFERENCES

Armstrong, K., O'Callahan, W., & Marmar, C.R. (1991). Debriefing Red Cross personnel: The multiple stressor debriefing model. *Journal of Traumatic Stress, 4*(4), 581–593.

Benson, H. (1976). *The relaxation response,* New York: Avon Books.

Borysenko, J. (1988). *Minding the body, mending the mind.* New York: Bantam Books.

Brilliant, A. (1974). *Pot-shots.* Santa Barbara Calif.: Brilliant Enterprises.

Caplan, G. (1972). Support systems. Keynote address to Conference of Department of Psychiatry, Rutgers Medical School and New Jersey Mental Health Association, Newark, N.J.

Cherniss, C. (1980). *Professional burnout in human service organization.* New York: Praeger.

Comas-Diaz, L.,& Padilla, A. (1990). Countertransference in working with victims of political repression. *American Journal of Orthopsychiatry, 60*(1), 125–134.

Cousins, N. (1979). *Anatomy of an illness.* New York: Norton.

Davis, L.J., & Brody, E.W. (1979). Rape and older women: *A guide to preventional protection.* U.S. Department of Health and Welfare, National Institute of Mental Health, DHHS Publication No. ADM 78–734.

Dyregrov, A., & Mitchell, J. (1992). Work with traumatized children: Psychological effects and coping strategies. *Journal of Traumatic Stress, 5*(1), 5–19.

Edelwich, J., & Brodsky, A. (1980). *Burnout: Stages of disillusionment in the helping professions.* New York: Human Sciences Press.

Etzion, D. (1984). The moderating effect of social support on the relationship of stress and burnout. *Journal of Applied Psychology, 69*(4), 615–622.

Etzion, D., & Pines, A.M. (1986). Sex and culture in burnout and coping among human service professionals. *Journal of Cross Cultural Psychology, 17*(2), 191–209.

Figley, C., Mackey, D., & Meshad, S. (1991). Helping the helper: Theoretical model and program of intervention and prevention. Symposium at seventh annual meeting of the International Society for Traumatic Stress Studies, Washington, D.C.

Fischman, Y. (1991). Interacting with trauma: Clinicians' responses to treating psychological aftereffects of political repression. *American Journal of Orthopsychiatry, 61*(1), 35–42.

Fischman, Y., & Ross, J. (1990). Group treatment of exiled survivors of torture. *American Journal of Orthopsychiatry, 50*(10), 96–108.

Flannery, R.B., Jr. (1987). Towards stress-resistant persons: A stress management approach to the treatment of anxiety. *American Journal of Preventive Medicine, 3*(1), 25–30.

Flannery, R.B., Jr. (1990). *Becoming stress resistant*, New York: Continuum.

Flannery, R.B., Jr., Fulton, P., Tausch, J., & DeLoffi, A. (1991). A program to help staff cope with psychological sequelae of assaults by patients. *Hospital and Community Psychiatry, 42*(9), 925–938.

Fogelman, E., & Savran, B. (1980). Brief group therapy with offspring of Holocaust survivors: Leaders' reactions. *American Journal of Orthopsychiatry, 50*(1), 96–108.

Freudenberger, H.J. (1974). Staff burnout. *Journal of Social Issues, 30*, 159–165.

Hamberger, K., & Stone, G.B. (1985). Burnout prevention for human service professionals: Proposal for a systematic approach. *Journal of Holistic Medicine, 5*(2), 149–162.

Harvey, M.R. (1985). Exemplary rape crisis centers: A cross-site analysis and case studies. For National Institute of Mental Health, U.S. Department of Health and Human Services, Rockville, Md.

Harvey, M.R. (forthcoming, 1995). An ecological view of psychological trauma and trauma recovery. *International Journal of Traumatic Stress.*

Heller, K., & Monahan, J. (1977). Psychology and community change. Homewood, Ill.: Dorsey Press.

Herman, J. (1992). *Trauma and recovery.* New York: Basic Books.

Himle, D., Jayaratne, S., & Thyness, P. (1991). Buffering effects of four social suppport types on burnout among social workers. *Social Work Research and Abstracts, 27*(1), 22–27.

Holmes, K. (1981). Services for victims of rape: A dualistic practice model. *Social Casework: Journal of Contemporary Social Work, 62*, 30–39.

Holt, P., Fine, M., & Tollefson, N. (1987). Mediating stress: Survival of the hardy. *Psychology in the Schools, 24*, 51—58.

Kabat-Zinn, J. (1990). *Full catastrophe living: Using the wisdom of your body and mind to face stress, pain, and illness.* New York: Dekta Books.

Kaplan, B. (1983). A survivor's story. *Boston Globe Magazine, 8*, 57–63.

Kaplan, B. (1992). Coping strategies for therapists who provide trauma treatment. Boston, MA: Personal interview.

Kelly, J.G. (1970). Antidotes for arrogance: Training for community psychology. *American Psychology, 25*, 524–542.

Kelly, J.G. (1977). The ecology of social support systems: Footnotes to a therapy. Presented at the symposium "Toward an Understanding of Natural Helping Systems," at the 85th annual meeting of the American Psychological Association, San Francisco.

Koss,M., & Harvey, M. (1991). *The rape victim: Clinical and community interventions.* Newbury Park, Calif.: Sage Publications.

Lazarus, R., & Folkman, S. (1984). *Stress appraisal and coping.* New York: Springer.

Maslach, C. (1992). *Burnout: The cost of caring.* Englewood Cliffs, N.J.: Prentice Hall.

McCann, L., & Pearlman, L. (1990). Vicarious traumatization: A framework for understanding the psychological effects of working with victims. *Journal of Traumatic Stress Studies, 3*(1), 131–149.

Medeiros, M.E., & Prochaska, J.O (1988). Coping strategies that psychotherapists use in working with stressful clients. *Professional Psychology: Research and Practice, 1*, 112–114.

Mitchell, J.T. (1983). When disaster strikes: The critical incident debriefing process. *American Journal of Emergency Services*, pp. 105–118.

Newman, J.E., & Beehr, T.A. (1979). Personal and organizational strategies for handling job stress: A review of research and opinion. *Personal Psychology, 32.*

O'Rear, J. (1992). Post-traumatic stress disorder: When the rescuer becomes victim. *Journal of Emergency Medical Services*, pp. 7–12.

Pearlin, L.I., & Schooler, C. (1978). The structure of coping. *Journal of Health & Social Behavior, 19*, 2–21.

208 *Preventing Secondary Traumatic Stress Disorder*

Penn, M., Romano, J., & Foat, D. (1988). The relationship between job satisfaction and burnout: A study of human service professionals. *Administration in Mental Health, 15*(3), 159–165.

Pines, A., & Kafry, D. (1981). Coping with burnout. In J.W. Jones (Ed.), *The burnout syndrome* (pp. 139–150). Park Ridge, N.J.: London House Management Press.

Pines, D. (1986). Working with women survivors of the Holocaust: Affective experiences in transference and countertransference. *International Journal of Psychoanalysis, 67*, 295–307.

Quick, J.C., & Quick, J.D. (1984). *Organizational stress and preventive management*. New York: McGraw-Hill.

Raphael, B. (1986). *When disaster strikes: How individuals and communities cope with catastrophe.* New York: Basic Books.

Scurfield, R. (1985). Post-trauma stress assessment and treatment: Overview and formulations. In C.R. Figley (Ed.), *Trauma and its wake: The study and treatment of post-traumatic stress disorder* (pp. 219–256). New York: Brunner Mazel.

Shinn, M., Rosario, M., Morch, H., & Chestnut, D. (1984) Coping with job stress and burnout in the human services. *Journal of Personality and Social Psychology, 46*(4), 864–876.

Shrum, R. (1989). *The psychotherapy of adult women with incest histories: Therapists' affective responses.* Unpublished doctoral dissertation, University of Massachusetts.

Sinyan, D., Schwartz, S.D., & Peronnet, F. (1982). Aerobic fitness level and reactivity to psychological stress: Physiological, biological, and subjective measures. *Psychosomatic Medicine*, pp. 391–404.

Smith, R., & Steindler, E. (1983). The impact of difficult patients upon treaters. *Bulletin of the Menninger Clinic, 47*(2), 107–116.

Talbot, A. (1990). The importance of parallel process in debriefing crisis counselors. *Journal of Traumatic Stress, 3*(2), 265–270.

Talbot, A., Manton, M., & Dunn, P. "Debriefing the debriefers." An intervention strategy to assist psychologists after a crisis. *Journal of Traumatic Stress, 5*(1), 45–63.

Thacker, J.K. (1984). Using psychodrama to reduce burnout in the helping professions, *Journal of Group Psychotherapy, Psychodrama and Sociometry*, pp. 14-25.

U.S. Department of Health & Human Services. (1988). *Prevention and control of stress among emergency workers: A pamphlet for team managers* (DHHS Publication No.ADM 88–1496). Washington, D.C.: U.S. Government Printing Office.

Yassen, J. (1983). Reflections from a loyalist: 10 years of survival in the anti-rape movement. *Equal Times, 8*(159), 3.

Yassen, J. (1993). Group work with clinicians who have a history of trauma. *Clinical Newsletter*. National Center for Post-traumatic Stress Disorder, VA Medical Center, Palo Alto, Calif.

Yassen, J., & Schatzow, E. (1991). Specialized treatment models for clinicians with a history of trauma. Presented at 7th annual meeting of the International Society of Traumatic Stress Studies, Washington, D.C.

10

Preventing Compassion Fatigue: A Team Treatment Model

JAMES F. MUNROE, JONATHAN SHAY,
LISA FISHER, CHRISTINE MAKARY,
KATHRYN RAPPERPORT, and
ROSE ZIMERING

Social support has been identified as a source of significant psychological benefit for trauma survivors (Keane, Scott, Chavoya, Lamparski,
& Fairbanks, 1985), and a team approach can provide similar support
for mental health professionals working with these clients. More important, a team also can provide, on a regular basis, active intervention in
the prevention of secondary traumatization. The ideas presented here
are derived primarily from work with Vietnam combat veterans, but
our experience suggests that the concepts and practices have applicability to therapists working with other survivor populations. For therapists who do not have a team available, attention is paid to building
preventive alliances.

Editor's Note: There are a number of outpatient treatment teams that work with traumatized people. In this chapter, such a team describes some important methods it has perfect-
ed for teams to work together to identify, prevent, and treat secondary traumatic stress
disorder among team members and other colleagues. Similar to the other chapters in this
volume, the authors suggest that secondary trauma in therapists parallels that of primary
trauma, and the intensity and duration of their exposure to traumatized clients are seen as
predictive of responses.

THE EXISTENCE OF SECONDARY TRAUMA

As the field of trauma has grown, it has become increasingly apparent that the effects of traumatic events go beyond those who directly experience them. Secondary trauma refers to effects in people who care for, or are involved with, those who have been directly traumatized. Solomon (1990) found that wives of Israeli veterans with post-traumatic stress disorder (PTSD) suffered from increased psychiatric symptomatology, somatic complaints, and loneliness. Others (Eth & Pynoos, 1985; Pynoos & Nader, 1988) noted that the symptoms that appear in traumatized children are contagious to nontraumatized children who play with them. Figley (1988) wrote about the "deleterious effects on family members exposed to a traumatized member," identifying them as "families of catastrophe," and Van der Ploeg and Kleijn (1989) identified the families of hostage victims as additional "victims in need of professional care." Utterback and Caldwell (1989) found that "debilitating symptoms may be seen in some friends, family members, or bystanders who did not experience the trauma per se." The effects of secondary trauma also have been described in family members who had not yet been born when the events occurred (Danieli, 1985; Figley, 1988; Milgram, 1990; Nagata, 1990).

The literature provides evidence that working with trauma survivors has debilitating effects on therapists. Some have described these effects as burnout (Doyle & Bauer, 1989), many have applied the concept of countertransference (Haley, 1974; Schwartz, 1984), and others have described the work as exhausting (Egendorf, Kadusin, Laufer, Rothbert, & Sloan, 1981) or challenging to the therapist's affect tolerance (Herman, 1988). McFarland (1986) notes that the emotional impact of disaster on research workers could interfere with their objectivity, and that these workers experienced a feeling of threat that "had little to do with their actual experience." Danieli (1984) notes that therapists dealing with Holocaust survivors reported "sharing the nightmares of the survivors they were treating." Langer (1987) identifies his experience of nightmares similar to those of his prisoner-of-war clients as "a kind of derivative neurosis." Herman (1988, 1992a) suggests that PTSD could be viewed as contagious, requiring precautions for the protection of therapists. Mollica (1988) states that therapists become infected with their clients' hopelessness, and McCann and Pearlman (1990) say that, through vicarious traumatization, "therapists may find themselves experiencing PTSD symptoms."

One of the best predictors of symptom development in traumatized individuals is the intensity and duration of exposure (Gleser, Green, &

Winget, 1981; Hartsough, 1988; Kolb, 1988), and several authors have posited a cumulative effect of traumatic experiences (Abse, 1984; Kolb, 1988; Scurfield, 1985). It seems reasonable to assume that these factors will be related to secondary trauma as well. Munroe (1991) studied therapists and found responses of intrusiveness and withdrawal that were significantly related to their exposure to combat PTSD clients. Therapists were not protected by age or experience. This study also demonstrated that these responses were distinct from burnout, as suggested by McCann and Pearlman (1990).

These findings imply that therapists dealing with PTSD are at risk with regard to secondary trauma, and this evidence further suggests an ethical duty to warn and prepare clinicians for what can be considered an occupational hazard. The question as to the level at which secondary trauma becomes an impairing therapist condition that compromises the quality of services to clients also must be raised. The ethical codes of all professional mental health workers require that corrective action be taken if a worker is impaired. Determining appropriate actions for preventing secondary trauma requires an understanding of how the therapist is traumatized.

THE NATURE OF SECONDARY TRAUMA

It seems reasonable to assume that the process of secondary trauma is similar to that of primary trauma, and that existing theoretical models can shed light on that process. Erikson (1963, 1967) has described the capacity for basic trust as the human's first developmental achievement in the social world, the foundation upon which all subsequent developmental accomplishments rest. He describes the child as receiving from the parents "a firm sense of personal trustworthiness within the trusted framework of their community's lifestyle." The parents also communicate "a deep, almost somatic conviction that there is meaning to what they are doing," and a belief in "Fate's store of good intentions." Traumatic events that shatter trust can be seen in key concepts related to trauma, such as shattered assumptions (Janoff-Bulman, 1992), disrupted schemas (McCann & Pearlman, 1991), a lost sense of invulnerability (Lifton, 1979), and loss of community (Erikson, 1976; Lifton, 1979).

An event can be defined as traumatic to the degree to which it violates the sense of basic trust. Behavior is then altered to be functional in a world that is based on an expectation of exploitation rather than a sense of basic trust (Munroe, 1991; Munroe, Fisher, Shay, Wattenberg,

Makary, Keefe, Cooks, & Rapperport, 1990a). In clinical work, secondary trauma involves a violation of the therapist's sense of basic trust, where the therapist's assumptions are undermined or shattered. As assumptions are undermined, the behavior of the therapist is likely to be altered as well. Secondary trauma occurs not only by being exposed to the clients' trauma material (McCann & Pearlman, 1990), but also by being engaged to participate in reenactments of the themes and relationships inherent in the clients' trauma.

THE PREVENTION MODEL

Like direct trauma, then, secondary trauma violates trust, severs connections to community, and destroys meaning. Thus a treatment team can serve as a community to prevent secondary trauma in therapists. The primary function of the team is to identify and alter trauma engagement patterns. The therapist who is engaged is often not aware that he or she is being engaged. But even the therapist who is aware of being engaged may find it extremely difficult to find a way out. Like the survivor whose world view has been narrowed by trauma, the therapist's perception becomes narrowed by secondary trauma. The therapist who is engaged behaves within the patterns generated by the client, and sees few options for relating in other ways. The team supplies those other options through discussion with the therapist or direct involvement in the case. The treatment team that expects secondary trauma on a regular basis is in a unique position to recognize emotional and behavioral responses of therapists that signal engagement. The team can support or confront the engaged therapist as necessary.

As a therapist is being engaged in client reenactments, the team also maintains relationship patterns that provide support and promote trust. These nonexploitative relationships serve as a counterpart to the isolating effects of secondary trauma. A trusting community, or team, also values its members and attends to their well-being, which is a direct challenge to the trauma world view.

Although therapists may belong to communities outside their workplaces, the most effective place for a preventive community is the work site where secondary traumatization takes place. The greater the exposure to trauma clients, the greater will be the need for a treatment team. The program described here illustrates the functioning of such a team. The concepts and practices of the team, however, can be applied to other client populations and treatment situations where teams are not readily available.

THE VETERANS' IMPROVEMENT PROGRAM

The Veterans' Improvement Program (VIP) offers long-term intensive outpatient treatment, centered on group therapy within a milieu and supported by a behavioral point system to maintain good standing in the therapeutic community. Veterans participate in several group therapies a week, and most engage in pharmacotherapy and individual psychotherapy. There is also an emphasis on family involvement, including family therapy. Additional therapy modalities and special events are employed as the opportunity arises. Each veteran has therapeutic relationships with various members of the team, and efforts are made to consolidate all therapy within the program.

The Client Population

The program provides treatment for Vietnam combat veterans diagnosed with PTSD. Most have severe trauma histories, such as multiple combat tours, and many have additional trauma histories from both before and after their military service. A smaller section of the program directly addresses childhood physical and sexual abuse. Herman (1992a, 1992b) argues that the current diagnosis of PTSD is derived from a single circumscribed traumatic event, and describes a complex form of PTSD that involves prolonged, repeated trauma under conditions of captivity. These veterans fit Herman's description well in that they suffer from the severe, disabling, and often life-threatening sequelae of prolonged, repeated trauma under conditions from which escape was impossible. This is further complicated because the role of combat veteran includes being a perpetrator as well as a victim of violence. Veterans referred to the program are severely disabled in most aspects of their daily lives and are frequently seen as poor treatment candidates who are disruptive to programs. Working with such a population presents a high risk of secondary trauma.

The Treatment Team

The team consists of six primary members who devote varying degrees of their time to the program. Members include a full-time clinical director from the psychology service, a half-time psychiatry resident, a quarter-time psychiatrist, a quarter-time clinical psychologist, and a three-quarter-time master's-level counselor. The assistant chief of the psychology service is also an active team member, but with limited time. Each team member has professional contacts with other survivor populations in addition to those in the program. The team members have different levels and types of training, as well as different ideas about and approaches to the treatment of trauma. Team members also have differing roles within the power structures and hierarchies of the institutional setting. At any given time, three to six psychology interns or trainees also are part of the team. Over the past 11 years, we have developed the team model in response to the treatment needs of the population and the psychological survival needs of the staff. We hold three tenets regarding the team's functioning and secondary trauma.

The first tenet is the acceptance of the reality of secondary trauma, including an understanding and expectation that each team member will be affected by the work we do with traumatized veterans on an ongoing basis. This is not an issue that is ever resolved, and no team member is assumed to have any immunity or special status with regard to being affected. It is assumed that on any given day or with any given case, each team member will vary in the degree to which he or she is affected.

The second tenet is that these therapist responses be regarded as a natural and valuable process rather than as a deficiency on the part of team members. Such responses of team members to any given client or situation are assumed to be significant clinical information. This is especially true where therapist responses are different or contradictory. It is also assumed that therapist responses such as vague feelings or dreams are personally valid and clinically relevant.

The third tenet of team functioning is the assumption that each team member can be an accurate observer of how other team members are personally responding to secondary trauma, and how such responses influence treatment interventions. Team members not only have permission to verbalize these observations, but also have the responsibility to do so. This assumption means that the observations or opinions of any team member concerning any other team member have validity regardless of differences in training, discipline, power, or institutional role. Team members must learn to trust and listen to one another.

Therapist Background

It is not necessary to assume any prior unresolved conflicts in the personality of the therapist for him or her to be affected by the processes of secondary traumatization. The therapist, like the client, however, does not exist in a vacuum. He or she may have conflicts that are amplified by the work, or may have a trauma history of his or her own. A trauma history is not be seen as a detriment to the therapist's ability to function or as a susceptibility to secondary trauma. A therapist who has worked through his or her own healing process has a distinct advantage in understanding the client and being able to model healing. If there is an unacknowledged trauma history, however, it appears that the processes of secondary traumatization exacerbate responses. Trauma therapists require an ongoing process of monitoring their responses. The question of why the therapist chooses to do trauma work is pertinent because the therapist is a participant and always has patterns of his or her own.

COMMUNITY AS PREVENTION OF SECONDARY TRAUMA

Erikson's concept of basic trust is employed above to understand the effects of trauma, but it is also useful for conceptualizing a prevention model. Healing from trauma, or, in this case, preventing secondary trauma, involves strengthening social networks. The team functions as a social network for the therapist and provides a community in which the secondary trauma experience can be worked through. This is accomplished through validation of feelings and provision of valued relationships.

A community absorbs the traumatic experience of an individual by diffusing its effects among many people and demonstrating that the survivor's feelings are understood. Absorbing can be seen at a wake, where people come together to mourn the loss of someone cared for and to support those closest to the deceased. The wake validates the feelings of those directly traumatized, through others who express or demonstrate similar feelings. The survivors are also actively included in the social network of those who attend. Similarly, the team can validate the feelings of the therapist as he or she is exposed to trauma material or reenactments.

The community that validates the survivor and continues to include him or her as a valued member provides roles and relationship patterns that are not repetitions of the trauma. A team that validates the therapist's responses to secondary trauma can continue to include that therapist in professional healing relationships. A community that organizes and rebuilds after a disaster provides valued roles for its members. Such efforts can strengthen community trust and reaffirm for the traumatized individual "a deep, an almost somatic conviction that there is a meaning to what they are doing" (Erikson, 1967). The team provides a complementary function that enables the therapist to maintain the valued role of a healer.

FAMILY FUNCTIONS OF THE TEAM

The therapist's role as a healer caring for a client is in some ways similar to the role of a parent caring for a child. When one parent is a primary caregiver, the other plays a complementary role. For the therapist who is a primary caregiver for a client, the team can fulfill the complementary role. In his book on raising a psychologically healthy child, Winnicott (1964) identified three different ways in which the complement to the primary caregiver is valuable:

1. Helping the primary caregiver feel well cared for and providing a sense of social security and hope for the future.
2. Supporting the authority of the primary caregiver while allowing for splits that do not destroy anyone concerned.
3. Enriching the life of the one receiving care through the personal qualities, ideals, knowledge, and liveliness of the other.

Each of these benefits can also be gained from a supportive team. The dependence of the primary caregiver on others for their personal qualities not only provides a great deal of support for the therapist, but also models and invites a variety of healthy patterns of engagement. The sense that others will provide additional enrichment relieves the primary caregiver of the pressure to be more than is humanly possible, expands his or her role options, and allows him or her to be more comfortable with "not knowing."

In *A Good Enough Parent*, Bettleheim (1988) emphasizes the importance of a team approach, as well as the importance of just being good enough. He discourages efforts to become perfect, along with expectations that others be perfect. "Perfection is not within the grasp of ordinary human beings. Efforts to attain it typically interfere with that lenient response to the imperfections of others...which alone makes good human relations possible." Bettleheim focuses on the benefits to the one receiving care, but he also recognizes the difficulty of providing care in an environment in which caregivers are not supported, and are often blamed for any bad outcome associated with their work. When working with a population that tends to act out, the lack of support for therapists can be especially devastating. The complementary and supportive functions of the team become increasingly important as the engagement pressures of secondary trauma accumulate.

SPLITTING

Splitting is probably familiar to anyone who has worked with severely traumatized clients, although it is usually identified as symptomatic of borderlines (Kernberg, 1975). Gabbard (1989) summarized numerous views on splitting and described both intrapsychic and interpersonal splitting in borderlines. The interpersonal component includes projective identification in which the staff members treating a client unconsciously identify with the client's issues and begin to feel or behave accordingly (Ogden, 1979). Stanton and Schwartz (1954) describe the intensity of staff and client involvement in splits as pathological excitement. Splitting is directly relevant to secondary trauma in that splits involve interactive situations in which engagement patterns are acted out. Splits are important to the trauma therapist because of the intense personal involvement generated. Staff members become direct participants in engagement patterns as the splits unfold.

A split is the presence of an unacknowledged disagreement, negative emotion, or adverse value judgment among staff members that is amplified by clients. These often occur along lines of existing staff tensions, such as differences in theoretical orientation, discipline, experience, age, sex, race, or power. Any staff team will have conflicts that are accidently discovered or actively exploited by clients. If sufficient conflict does not exist, trauma clients may attempt to engineer them because splits are functional to survival in at least two ways.

The primary function of a split for the survivor is that it tests the trustworthiness of the community—or, in this case, the treatment team. Because trauma survivors do not trust, by definition, they will not accept a community without convincing evidence of trustworthiness. (They may sometimes blindly overtrust in a test that is bound to fail and prove untrustworthiness.) Survivors can generate splits by giving conflicting information to different staff members or by singling out certain staff members as good or bad. Staff members can become enmeshed in these splits, and amplify and stimulate them as well. Splits generate a parallel process of mistrust that can be initiated or exacerbated from either side. Splits also test the trustworthiness of the community of clients and staff by involving those outside, such as clinic administrators or family members of the clients.

The secondary function of a split is that if the tested community proves to be untrustworthy as expected, the survivor can exploit the side in the split that is most functional to serving his or her own immediate needs. When the world is perceived as hostile and untrustworthy, attending to one's own basic needs becomes necessary for survival.

Exploiting a split to meet one's needs is a survival tactic that people who have been traumatized seem to learn well.

Splits generated or amplified by clients are based on the patterns of relating that embody their trauma experience and world view. Splits become a stage for the reenactment of the themes of the trauma. A disagreement between an administrator and a therapist may replicate for a veteran the experience of a rear-echelon command to a field officer who has more knowledge of the immediate combat conditions. Does the field commander trust the wisdom of the higher command? Does the higher command listen to the field officer's input? Will the soldier live or die as a result of how authorities handle the situation? For a veteran, a split within the team may replicate the indecision of leaders during a firefight that resulted in comrades' being killed or wounded. Splits can be terrifying threats to the very existence of survivors, and their responses can generate intense countertransference in therapists. Community decisions may be more influenced by conflicts between individuals or subgroups than by the well-being of community members. Survivors are keenly aware of splits because their own well-being depends on how splits influence decisions. A split on a treatment team may be perceived by a survivor who depends on that team as a direct threat to his or her existence. The most dangerous characteristic of a split is its covert or unacknowledged nature, because it cannot be directly addressed or resolved. A split that is overt loses a great deal of its destructive power in that it can be openly discussed, and its influence on decisions can be minimized. The survivors' amplification approach serves either to speed the process to a disastrous conclusion or to force it into the open.

Attempted split amplification by survivors will frequently take the form of overt challenges to treatment plans, rules, or authority of any kind. The competence or integrity of a staff member may be challenged. These provocations can easily disrupt the treatment team's ability to attend to the business of prevention or treatment. Such behaviors by clients, frequently seen as symptoms or acting out, may be viewed as tests of the trustworthiness of a community.

Therapists who are involved in splits are being secondarily traumatized by being actively engaged as participants in reenactments of the survivors' traumatic experiences. Their sense of trust in the professional community is being undermined in the process. Therapists end up more isolated and their collective resources are depleted. The prevention of secondary trauma associated with splits lies in the ability to acknowledge them and deal openly with them. This requires a good deal of trust and communication among treatment team members. The goal in prevention is not to avoid or resolve splits completely, but to be able to struggle with them openly. The effectiveness of a team in struggling through splits is that those members who are less engaged can identify the splits and recognize how treatment decisions are influenced by them. Team members diffuse splits by taking on involved roles in which they do not take sides in the conflict.

The ability to acknowledge and deal with splits also allows survivors to begin to trust the community. If splits or attempted splits can be seen as tests of trust, a unique opportunity is available to work directly on influencing the survivors' world view. Working through splits requires that team members relate in cooperative rather than exploitative ways, and therefore model trusting relationships for survivors. The prevention of secondary trauma from splits coincides with the effective treatment of survivors.

PATTERNS OF TRAUMA ENGAGEMENT

Splits, reenactments, challenges, parallel processes, transference, and countertransference all relate to the patterns of engagement that embody the trauma experience. Each individual's patterns of engagement will be unique to his or her traumatic experience. Recognizing the client's patterns can be an avenue to identifying the specific aspects of trauma that need to be addressed in treatment. More important, with regard to secondary trauma, the therapist can recognize and use the patterns to determine how he or she is being engaged to reenact the trauma theme. Awareness can help minimize the effects of secondary trauma by affording the therapist more control and insight into the process.

Exploiter/Exploited

Perhaps the most basic pattern in trauma perpetrated by humans is the theme of exploiter and exploited, which is also experienced as perpetrator and victim. The therapist is frequently accused of being "just like all the others" who abused the survivor, or an intern is accused of "only wanting to learn from us." Efforts to help the client talk about traumatic events in a session may be interpreted as the therapist's attempt to retraumatize the client. If the therapist changes approaches, the client may then accuse him or her of denying the reality of the client's experience. The client may also put the therapist in the position of the exploited by missing or rescheduling appointments or by demanding letters to avert some crisis. The client may call at night or during weekends and vacations, or save highly charged material for the last five minutes of a session. He or she may try

to get the therapist to intervene in situations that are outside the boundaries of therapy, such as talking to a landlord to whom the client owes
back rent. In either role, exploiter or exploited, the therapist has confirmed
the theme that relationships are based on exploitation.

Allies/Enemies

Another, closely related pattern that is common among combat veterans is that of allies and enemies. In this pattern, the veteran essentially
forces the therapist to choose between these roles. The veteran will usually communicate some variation of the idea that if the therapist is not
completely with him, then he or she must be completely against him.
These are the only options. Therapists are not usually comfortable in the
position of enemy when they are trying to help a client. Discomfort with
the enemy role can result in the therapist's not challenging or disagree-
ing with the client, even when he or she should, to avoid being identified as an enemy. A therapist can just as easily be derailed by being cast
as an ally. The ally is in the position of the idealized therapist in which
the therapist is the only one who understands. The idealized therapist is
on a pedestal, and it is tempting to dilute the difficulties of therapy in
order to stay on the pedestal. The enemy position clearly replicates the
combat situation, but the ally position does the same, since the alliance is
against some enemy. The war goes on.

Aggressor/Aggressee

Closely related is the aggressor and aggressee pattern. This pattern is
prominent in those who have experienced a world based on violence
and intimidation. They attempt to influence the therapist through direct
intimidation or threats, although actual physical violence may be rare. It
is more significant that everyday transactions are framed in the context
of threats, either overt or veiled. We would hope that it is even more
rare that the therapist takes a role involving physical violence and intimidation, but it is easy to become accustomed to the survivor's style and
therapists might fail to challenge clients' threats to themselves or others.
For example, a veteran who reports getting his way in a store by threatening a clerk and notices that this elicits a chuckle from the therapist,
will draw the conclusion that the therapist agrees that the world is a
hostile environment in which violence is necessary. The survivor may
frequently present the therapist with "what if" situations and ask how
the therapist would handle things. These are usually violent situations
that reflect experiences of the client. They are designed to get the thera-

pist to agree that the situation calls for violence, and any answer to the forced situation will probably result in the therapist's getting caught in one of those uncomfortable dilemmas.

Rescuer/Rescuee

A most important, and potentially dangerous, pattern is that of rescuer and rescuee. Therapists are particularly prone to becoming caught in this pattern because of their desire to help. Relationships with clients are often begun as a result of some crisis or emergency, and the therapist is immediately cast in the role of rescuer. The danger is that crisis may become the only basis of the relationship. The client who shows up only in crisis, then disengages from treatment, has established a pattern that will negate any therapeutic change. The need to be rescued and the related behavior of the rescuer confirm each time that the world is a hostile place. The role of rescuee is particularly dangerous because of the need of escalating emergencies to mobilize rescuers. It can lead to risky and suicidal behavior. The rescue pattern replicates many of the situations of combat, and the relationships surrounding rescues become a substitute for intimacy. The intensity of a rescue creates a strong bond between the parties, but it is one that fades as soon as the crisis passes. Many survivors have established families or relationships that are crisis-bound, in that they need a crisis for them to pull together, and then they drift apart until the next crisis. Such relationships are based on a contract of, "If you love me, you will rescue me, and I will prove I love you by rescuing you." The therapist who is engaged in a pattern of rescue is subverting the establishment of relationships based on trust. The client may quickly respond to any situation in which a rescue operation can be performed for a therapist. Such opportunities may arise out of splits when the client tries to come to the therapist's aid. Being rescued, of course, replicates the rescue theme, and the therapist should realize that it is time to address this openly.

An important variation of the rescue theme is the Lone Ranger pattern. This is seen in therapists and is a parallel of the John Wayne pattern for combat veterans. The Lone Ranger therapist is enlisted to fight the bad guys, single-handedly, for the good of the client. This is an attractive image in our culture, but it should be noted that the Lone Ranger is fighting a hostile world, and that he is not part of a community, but is alone. The Lone Ranger therapist may be verbalizing appropriate therapy, but he or she is modeling a traumatized world view. (The legend of the Lone Ranger is significant in that he was the sole survivor of company of rangers who were massacred. It is not surprising that a traumatized world view is modeled.) Being part of a team is a very useful protection against becoming a lone ranger, but the attraction of the role is powerful. Any therapist who works alone, or frequently feels alone in therapy, may be easily engaged in this pattern. Any therapist who thinks that he or she can recognize and respond to engagements without the input of others is at risk of being a lone ranger.

There are many variations on these patterns, and probably many others that need to be identified. Although engaging in these patterns may challenge the therapist's sense of trust, on some level, this may be the only way to begin a relationship with someone who has been traumatized to the point that he or she has no other basis on which to relate.

PATTERNS OF COOPERATION AND TRUST

For the therapist who is engaged in having his or her world view challenged and trust undermined, the effects of secondary trauma may soon follow. Engagement in the patterns will also produce an increasing amount of affect in the therapist, with alternate periods of numbing and withdrawal. The primary functions of the team in addressing secondary trauma are (1) validating the affect, (2) identifying the trauma patterns, and (3) proposing healthy alternative patterns that restore trust.

The generation of healthy alternative patterns will be specific to the situation, but some general approaches can be identified. The therapist must be keenly sensitive to ensuring that relationships with clients are cooperative, not exploitative. Nonexploitative relationships should involve looking out for the best interests of both parties and including others in the work. It is not unusual for therapists to allow themselves to be abused in small ways for some perceived good of the client. These situations can be openly identified so that either party has an option to refuse his or her role. Ally and enemy roles are most easily defused by direct and open communication. When a client identifies an enemy to a therapist, the therapist can suggest that they both talk to the enemy. Even if the client declines, the therapist can go ahead with establishing a cooperative relationship with the identified enemy in full view of the client.

Aggressive relationships are best diffused by including others in the community who are not directly threatened. Rescue relationships are replaced by prediction and planning as a regular and ongoing part of treatment. Crisis defusing is an approach in which the team works with the client to anticipate and plan for the crisis cycle so that rescues are minimized. Using the input of the team is the best overall way to identify healthy patterns that do not replicate the trauma.

It is important to note that clients are aware of the process of secondary traumatization. They will screen the amount of material they bring to the session to protect the therapist from becoming disabled (Munroe, Makary, & Rappaport, 1990). The team not only provides a healing environment for the therapists, but relieves the client of the burden of protecting the therapist. It is not uncommon for clients to ask the therapist if he or she is enlisting the support of the team when the content of sessions becomes intense. If a survivor knows that the therapist has support, he or she can attend to therapy rather than concentrate on being the therapist's rescuer.

Clients may be much less aware of the patterns since these embody basic assumptions that have been established through the experience of trauma. For them, this is simply the way the world is. The team addresses patterns in two ways. It can assist any team member to realize what patterns are operating, and it can offer suggestions to alter the therapist's responses. The team can also directly involve other therapists who have varying relationships with the client. Multiple therapists offer multiple patterns that provide alternative world views to the client. Even if the client resists all of these, the therapist has modeled a pattern of trust in a community by enlisting the team while disengaging from the client's pattern. Enlisting the team not only helps the therapist, but is a powerful intervention to demonstrate trust to the client. The power of such a move by the therapist may lie in the action taken. Trauma clients attend to what therapists do, not necessarily to what they say.

Survivors often have been exploited by words as a part of their trauma, and though words are a comfortable medium for therapists, clients may respond more to their behaviors. The therapist who uses the team as a trusted community when faced with secondary trauma behaviorally demonstrates a coping process. The team is a preventive environment for therapists, who can generate a parallel process for the clients.

EXAMPLES

The following examples illustrate some of the processes of secondary traumatization. Each involves patterns of engagement in clinical work. Several patterns may be operating simultaneously, and the reader is invited to note patterns in addition to those identified. Any one of the patterns exemplified could be disruptive for a therapist, but the accumulation of such exposure increases the likelihood that the therapist will begin to show the effects of secondary trauma.

The Rescuer

Therapist A had been client X's individual therapist for several years. They had established close ties and client X had said that he really trusted and counted on this therapist. Increasingly over the past several years, client X had called therapist A when on drinking binges. At these times, he threatened suicide. These were not idle threats, as he had made several serious suicide attempts.

The most recent call came one morning before a staff meeting. The therapist asked another team member to cover a group because he had to go out and find client X, who had told him that he had a gun and that life was no longer worth living. Therapist A left before the team member could respond.

When therapist A returned to a team meeting that afternoon, he was confronted by the team about his rescue mission. He angrily replied, "I was out saving a man's life. What were you doing?" The team then asked him to describe more of his feelings. He said he felt alone and responsible for this client. The team pointed out that the therapist's feelings and behaviors mirrored some of the client's experience in Vietnam, and that he was reinforcing rather than changing the client's behavior. The team was then able to work out emergency plans. Other team members took on increased responsibility for the client. A plan in which the police and the hospital would be notified was drawn up. Finally, the client was asked to meet with the team and was informed of the new procedures and of how the team would respond.

When the client, intoxicated and suicidal, again called the therapist, the new plan was carried out. The call was a test of the rescue role and the new plan. The team then joined the hospital in insisting on inpatient alcohol treatment. The drinking, and suicide–rescue pattern, eventually stopped. The therapist reported feelings of relief, support, and empowerment.

Allies and Enemies

When the program was threatened with cutbacks that made effective operation very difficult, the veterans were furious that the government was treating them unfairly again. Several team members reacted by becoming angry at and suspicious of all authority. They felt that no one outside the team could be trusted, and several plans for the team members to join with the veterans to fight the system were suggested. Some of the team members, however, began to express concern about this suspiciousness and identification. It was pointed out that the team was behaving as if the administration were an enemy. The team reevaluated its position. When the team returned to a more therapeutic stance, the veterans took the lead and successfully and peacefully advocated for the program's continuation.

Therapist Response to Trauma Material

Therapist B, a female clinician in a mental health clinic, found that her caseload increasingly included women who had been traumatized by rape or domestic battering. Over time, she began to feel uneasy when walking in unattended parking lots or in her neighborhood at dusk. She became jittery when alone at night in her apartment. After several weeks of being nervous, she accepted a new female client, who reported the details of a recent brutal rape by an acquaintance.

Afterwards, therapist B began to withdraw from friends, skipped late-afternoon meetings in order to avoid going home after dark, and had difficulty sleeping, which resulted in occasional tardiness at work. When the team questioned her meeting attendance, she denied any problems.

Soon, therapist B consistently refused to accept new male clients, and the team recognized her behavior as indicative of a problem. The team members asked her if she were getting enough support for her work and encouraged her to talk about her feelings as associated with trauma work. One team member discussed his own experience of nightmares following sessions with a client. Through these discussions, necessary adjustments were made to her caseload, matters surrounding her own physical safety were discussed, and her reaction prompted a series of discussions about support for the effects of trauma work for all team members. Therapist B now feels less isolated and participates more in staff meetings.

A Split

Therapist C, a female team member, was the target of a sarcastic comment by one of the veterans in the program in the presence of other veterans. She interpreted the comment seriously and felt that the veteran was trying to intimidate her. When she brought her concerns before the team, a clear difference of opinion emerged. Two team members held the position that "you have to be tough to work with tough clients" and nonchalantly dismissed the issue. Other team members felt that this was a serious issue, which also had been raised by interns, who saw several veterans as being aggressive. One team member suggested that the team needed to examine how intimidation was endorsed and supported in the community's culture. The issue was still unresolved by the end of the meeting.

Therapist C felt that the two team members had challenged her competence to do trauma work because she was not tough enough. She was fearful of her safety with the client who had threatened her, but she said nothing because she did not want to risk further embarrassment. Therapist C felt very angry at the team members who dismissed the issue. (Fortunately, this split did not divide along lines of gender, professional discipline, race, or experience.)

Several days later, two team members from opposite sides of the issue were coleading a group. Friction was increasing in the group, and threatening remarks were directed toward the team member who had spoken against intimidation by patients in the program. After the group session, this team member became angry and berated the coleader for not trying to defuse the situation. The team explored this issue and recognized that toleration of the aggressiveness of combat veterans could be seen as promoting the behavior. The "get tough" attitude of some team members was identified as an engagement in a survivor pattern. One member connected the threat in the group to the comment made to therapist C, to which the team had not responded. Therapist C was able to express her feeling of being victimized by the other two team members, as well as by the veteran.

The team met with the veterans who had been threatening and identified their behavior as an inappropriate way of getting needs met. The team also took responsibility for any behavior or lack of behavior that may have condoned intimidation. The question of how both staff members and clients condone aggressiveness was then discussed openly in all of the group meetings. Intimidating behavior decreased, and both staff members and veterans expressed feelings of increased safety.

TEAM LIMITATIONS

The potential benefits that team participation can afford to therapists in preventing secondary trauma are numerous. These benefits promote strong feelings of loyalty to the team and solidarity among its members. These same positive forces, however, may become limitations, and, on occasion, have resulted in negative consequences. Team cohesiveness may lead to an unspoken desire for unanimity. The term *groupthink* has been used in social psychology's study of small-group behavior to illustrate the deterioration of function that may arise from in-group pressures (Janis, 1972). The team is susceptible to in-group pressure as the nature and intensity of the work fluctuate. Dangers include the development of stereotyped views of other groups, self-censorship of deviations from group consensus, and the exclusion of information or persons not in accord with the group consensus.

The stereotypic response may be seen in a view that administration is insensitive or unresponsive to requests from the team. This can set up an "us against them" mentality that precludes accepting administrative behavior that goes against the stereotype. (This mentality provides a foundation in cultivating a split.)

An example of self-censorship on our team was noted when one member found herself surprised when she could not justify to a colleague outside of the team why she chose to continue seeing a patient despite his repeated no-shows and her own clinical guideline of three no-shows resulting in referral to another clinician. She was influenced by an unspoken team consensus that the veteran deserved another chance.

Team discussions of treatment interventions or solutions to problems frequently may be generated by alternatives that have worked previously. Persons with minority opinions or special knowledge may be discounted because of a subtle threat to group conformity. Although a team may outwardly value and ask for alternative opinions, there may exist a subtle and covert pressure to maintain unanimity. We have sometimes tested new members of the team in a pattern similar to how veterans test us, and we took very seriously a reference to the team as a cult. It is possible for an entire team to be engaged in a trauma pattern.

Team decisions may be slower and more cumbersome to reach than those made by an individual, but they are more effective in that they are less likely to be sabotaged or miscommunicated. There are times, however, when decisions may be made without the full team. This can easily lead to difficulties if the information is not adequately communicated and discussed as soon as possible.

PREVENTIVE TEAM PRACTICES

The ideas and concepts presented in this chapter are not specific to the program in which they were developed. The prevention of secondary trauma is dependent on the practices of the treatment team rather than the treatment setting, the program model, or the theoretical orientation. The practices described below rest on three primary assumptions: (1) no therapist is immune to the effects of secondary trauma, (2) prevention of secondary trauma lies in membership on a team, and (3) the higher the intensity of exposure to trauma work, the greater is the need for a team. Some basic structure is necessary for the team to enact the practices.

The existence of a community requires a minimum of three people so that alliances can be made, broken, and reformed within the ongoing unit. A team requires the minimum addition of a third party to the therapist–client dyad. The third party is another therapist who can observe and intervene in the engagements that occur. An optimal size might be five to eight team members, but the minimum requirement is that all members are in regular communication.

Our team meetings take two and a half hours a week to cover all administrative and clinical issues, including treatment planning with clients present at the team meeting. Our program is structured around the time when team meetings can take place, but the number or lengths of meetings are not of primary importance. Team meetings need to be regular, and all members must be able to attend. If this is taken seriously, part-time and temporary team members can be accommodated. The functioning of a team does not depend on the content of the program, the style of therapy, the treatment modalities, or the theoretical approach of the staff.

The practices are not considered rules that must be followed, but ideals to keep striving to meet. The goal is continually to keep the struggle of maintaining a functioning team alive, rather than to arrive at some fixed way of operating. The reader is encouraged to integrate the practices that follow into his or her own prevention plan.

Team members regularly pose questions about secondary traumatization that include: (1) How are team members being engaged? (2) How do they feel about it? (3) What will we do about it?

Therapist self-care is expected, and the team reminds members of this if they neglect this responsibility. Chapter 9 in this volume provides excellent information to enable therapists to meet this obligation. The team is not expected to fulfill all the supervisory and preventive needs of the therapist. Overwork is discouraged.

The feelings of team members are considered important. These include countertransference feeling around trauma material, feelings toward clients, and feelings aroused among team members. The last are essential to uncovering splits.

Team members give each other permission to, and accept the responsibility to, comment on behaviors and decisions that are relevant to treatment and secondary trauma. It is expected that this process will become extremely uncomfortable at times. Identifying engagements may require confrontation and courage. Splits contain highly emotional issues that must be faced when the nature of the split is acknowledged. The team must provide a safe environment in which to do this.

Each team member is respected in that all members are willing to be influenced by other members. It is assumed that any member's suggestions have merit unless proved otherwise. Members can also bring up their own dreams and hunches as relevant. This respect is extended to other treatment providers as well. Other treatment providers can be included on the team temporarily, or their team can be joined in any given client situation.

The team does not grant privileges to some members to speak and others to be silent. Members with different degrees, training, or power are encouraged to struggle with each other. The weight of ideas is not determined by who presents them. Inequalities in speaking privileges allow splits to go unacknowledged.

Information on treatment or secondary trauma is shared, and confidentiality is seen as resting within the team. The therapeutic alliance is to the team rather than to an individual. More than one team member is always actively working with a client, and cotherapists are used whenever possible. Functional roles among team members are intentionally blurred and traded from time to time. Authority is considered to reside in the team rather than in any single individual, and the team as a whole operates as openly as possible. These practices maximize the possibility of a third party's being able to recognize a pattern of engagement.

Unique skills and abilities of members are recognized and utilized. Members are expected and encouraged to have outside interests and commitments. These promote regular disengagement from trauma patterns.

Diversity of thought is valued, and the team does not require agreement with regard to theories, models, techniques, or schools of thought. Different approaches may provide different ways to establish healthy relationship patterns.

Working with trauma can be an intensely disturbing experience. A sense of humor and playfulness are considered useful coping mechanisms for the team as a whole.

CONCLUSIONS

These practices identify approaches for the prevention of secondary trauma. Many of these practices can be viewed as simply good communication, but they become necessities when trying to identify and alter engagement patterns. Not all therapists will be comfortable operating in these ways, and some will be very difficult to reach when they are engaged in trauma patterns. Implementation of these practices may be met with resistance and denial; however, if no one is immune to secondary trauma, then active prevention should be the concern of all therapists working with survivors. A team that can continually refocus itself on prevention can produce more effective and longer lasting therapists.

REFERENCES

Abse, D. W. (1984). Brief historical overview of the concept of war neurosis and of associated treatment methods. In J. H. Schwartz (Ed.), *Psychotherapy of the combat veteran* (pp. 1–22). New York: Medical & Scientific Books.
Bettleheim, B. (1988). *A good enough parent.* New York: Knopf.
Danieli, Y. (1984). Psychotherapists' participation in the conspiracy of silence about the Holocaust. *Psychoanalytic Psychology, 1*(1), 23–42.
Danieli, Y. (1985). The treatment and prevention of long-term effects and intergenerational transmission of victimization: A lesson from Holocaust survivors and their children. In C. R. Figley (Ed.), *Trauma and its wake* (pp. 295–313). New York: Brunner/Mazel.
Doyle, J. S., & Bauer, S. K. (1989). Post-traumatic stress disorder in children: Its identification and treatment in a residential setting for emotionally disturbed youth. *Journal of Traumatic Stress, 2*(3), 275–288.
Egendorf, A., Kadusin, C., Laufer, R. S., Rothbert, G., & Sloan, L. (1981). *Legacies of Vietnam: Comparative adjustment of veterans and their peers, a study conducted for the Veterans Administration.* Washington, D.C.: House Committee Print No. 14, 97th Congress, 1st Session.
Erikson, E. H. (1963). *Childhood and society.* New York: Norton.
Erikson, E. H. (1967). Identity and the life cycle. *Psychological Issues, 1.*
Erikson, K. T. (1976). *Everything in its path: Destruction of community in the Buffalo Creek flood.* New York: Simon & Schuster.
Eth, S., & Pynoos, R. S. (1985). Developmental perspective on psychic trauma in childhood. In C. R. Figley (Ed.), *Trauma and its wake* (pp. 36–52). New York: Brunner/Mazel.
Figley, C. R. (1988). A five-phase treatment of post-traumatic-stress disorder in families. *Journal of Traumatic Stress, 1*(1), 127–141.
Gabbard, G. O. (1989). Splitting in hospital treatment. *American Journal of Psychiatry, 146*(4), 444–451.
Gleser, G. C., Green, B. L., & Winget, C. (1981). *Prolonged psychological effects of disaster: A study of Buffalo Creek.* New York: Academic Press.
Haley, S. A. (1974). When the patient reports atrocities. *Archives of General Psychiatry, 30,* 191–196.
Haley, S. A. (1985). Some of my best friends are dead: Treatment of the PTSD patient and his family. In W. D. Kelley (Ed.), *Post-traumatic stress disorder and the war veteran patient.* New York: Brunner/Mazel.
Hartsough, D. M. (1988). Traumatic stress as an area for research. *Journal of Traumatic Stress, 1*(2), 145–154.
Herman, J. L. (1988). Father–daughter incest. In F. M. Ochberg (Ed.), *Post-traumatic therapy and victims of violence* (pp. 175–195). New York: Brunner/Mazel.
Herman, J. L. (1992a). *Trauma and recovery.* New York: Basic Books.
Herman, J. L. (1992b). Complex PTSD: A syndrome in survivors of prolonged and repeated trauma. *Journal of Traumatic Stress, 5*(3), 377–392.
Janis, I. L. (1972). *Victims of groupthink.* Boston: Houghton-Mifflin.
Janoff-Bulman, R. (1992). *Shattered assumptions: Towards a new psychology of trauma.* New York: Free Press.
Keane, T. M., Scott, W. O., Chavoya, G. A., Lamparski, D. M., & Fairbank, J. A. (1985). Social support in Vietnam veterans with post-traumatic-stress disorder: A comparative analysis. *Journal of Consulting and Clinical Psychology, 53*(1), 95–102.
Kernberg, O. (1975). *Borderline conditions and pathological narcissism.* New York: Jason Aronson.
Kolb, L. C. (1988). A critical survey of hypotheses regarding post-traumatic stress disorders in light of recent research findings. *Journal of Traumatic Stress, 1*(3), 291–304.
Langer, R. (1987), Post-traumatic stress disorder in former POW. In T. Williams (Ed.), *Post-traumatic stress disorders: A handbook for clinicians* (pp. 35–50). Cincinnati, Ohio: Disabled American Veterans.
Lifton, R. J. (1979). *The broken connection.* New York: Simon & Schuster.

McCann, I. L., & Pearlman, L. A. (1990). Vicarious traumatization: A framework for understanding the psychological effects of working with victims. *Journal of Traumatic Stress*, 3(1), 131–150.

McCann, I. L., & Pearlman, L. A. (1991). *Psychological trauma and the adult survivor: Theory, therapy, and transformation*. New York: Brunner/Mazel.

McFarland, A. C. (1986). Post-traumatic morbidity of a disaster: A study of cases presenting for psychiatric treatment. *Journal of Nervous and Mental Diseases*, 174(1), 4–14.

Milgram, N. (1990, October). Secondary victims of traumatic stress: Their plight and public safety. Presented at the sixth annual meeting of the Society for Traumatic Stress Studies, New Orleans, La.

Mollica, R. F. (1988). The trauma story: The psychiatric care of refugee survivors of violence and torture. In F. M. Ochberg (Ed.), *Post-traumatic therapy and victims of violence* (pp. 295–314). New York: Brunner/Mazel.

Munroe, J. F. (1991). Therapist traumatization from exposure to clients with combat related post-traumatic stress disorder: Implications for administration and supervision. Unpublished doctoral dissertation, Northeastern University. Available from Dissertation Abstracts, Ann Arbor, Mich.

Munroe, J., Fisher, L., Shay, J., Wattenberg, M., Makary, C., Keefe, E., Cook, J., & Rapperport, K. (1990a). Trust and team techniques in treating Vietnam combat veterans. Workshop presented at the sixth annual meeting of the Society for Traumatic Stress Studies, New Orleans, La.

Munroe, J., Makary, C., & Rapperport, K. (1990b). PTSD and twenty years of treatment: Vietnam combat veterans speak. Videotape presentation at the sixth annual meeting of the Society for Traumatic Stress Studies, New Orleans, La.

Nagata, D. K. (1990). The Japanese American internment: Exploring the transgenerational consequences of traumatic stress. *Journal of Traumatic Stress*, 3(1), 47–70.

Ogden, T. H. (1979). On projective identification. *International Journal of Psycho-Analysis*, 60, 357–373.

Pynoos, R. S., & Nader, K. (1988). Psychological first aid and treatment approach to children exposed to community violence: Research implications. *Journal of Traumatic Stress*, 1(4), 445–474.

Schwartz, H. J. (Ed.). (1984). *Psychotherapy of the combat veterans*. New York: Medical & Scientific Books.

Scurfield, R. M. (1985). Post-trauma stress assessment and treatment: Overview and formulations. In C. R. Figley (Ed.), *Trauma and its wake* (pp. 219–256). New York: Brunner/Mazel.

Solomon, Z. (1990, October). From front line to home front: Wives of PTSD veterans. Presented at the sixth annual meeting of the Society for Traumatic Stress Studies, New Orleans, La.

Stanton, A. H., & Schwartz, M. S. (1954). *The mental hospital: A study of institutional participation in psychiatric illness and treatment*. New York: Basic Books.

Utterback, J., & Caldwell, J. (1989). Proactive and reactive approaches to PTSD in the aftermath of campus violence: Forming a traumatic stress react team. *Journal of Traumatic Stress*, 2(2), 171–184.

Van der Ploeg, H. M., & Kleijn, W. C. (1989). Being held hostage in the Netherlands: A study of long-term aftereffects. *Journal of Traumatic Stress*, 2(2), 153–169.

Winnicott, D. W. (1964). *The child, the family, and the outside world*. Reading, Mass.: Addison Wesley.

11

Preventing Institutional Secondary Traumatic Stress Disorder

DON R. CATHERALL

Institutions that deal with trauma or with trauma survivors will inevitably encounter secondary traumatic stress (STS). This includes institutions that deal directly with trauma—such as police departments, fire departments, and emergency medical technician teams—as well as those that must deal with trauma survivors—such as hospitals, mental health clinics, and employee-assistance programs. In the case of institutions that deal with physical dangers, such as police departments, their members can be traumatized both directly and indirectly; that is, they can be exposed to both primary stressors and secondary stressors. All institutions that are exposed to STS will find that it exacts a toll on the functioning of the staff, unless deliberate steps are taken to prevent, or at least limit, its pernicious effects.

Editor's Note: This final chapter is devoted to systemic traumatization: how institutions struggle to deal with trauma as a result of one or more employees' dying or being traumatized. The author outlines an approach, based on the literature reviewed in previous chapters in this book, that helps institutions recover and, more important, prepare for future upheavals. Much of the approach is education of management and workers about the predictable nature of traumatic stress, including secondary traumatic stress and secondary traumatic stress disorder, and methods of engendering solidarity and cohesion to overcome the effects once it happens.

The focus of this chapter is on how institutions can prevent or limit the harmful effects of STS. The first rule is that preventive mechanisms should be in operation *before* incidents actually occur. Those preventive mechanisms include (1) psychoeducation, (2) preparedness, and (3) planning. Exposure to STS cannot always be avoided, but institutions can ensure that (1) the stress is recognized and (2) the exposed members have the best possible opportunity to process their stressful experiences in a supportive environment.

INSTITUTIONAL STS AND ITS PREVENTION

Implementing an STS-prevention program involves a number of requirements. The need for prevention must be identified, the effects of STS must be understood and communicated to the staff, appropriate responses and contingencies must be planned, and an ongoing state of preparedness must be maintained. Each staff member must understand his or her unique role in the overall enterprise. For an operation of this magnitude to be effective, there needs to be a high degree of cohesion and morale—that is, team spirit—among the institutional personnel. There are several questions that should be considered with regard to institutions and STS.

How do institutions differ with regard to exposure?
The first step in preparing for institutional STS is identifying the potential for its occurrence and estimating the degree and frequency of exposure. As noted above, institutions vary in their members' exposure to primary and secondary stressors. If any personnel are exposed to primary stressors, then all other personnel are in danger of secondary stress. Some institutions, such as emergency rooms and trauma institutes, regularly expose staff members to STS, whereas others, such as some community mental health centers, may expose the staff less frequently.

Who is responsible for prevention?
Prevention is the responsibility of everyone, but every institutional role has its associated responsibilities. Those roles include those of policy makers, administrators, trauma workers, and ancillary personnel. Policy makers are responsible for identifying the need and initiating all programmatic efforts. Administrators are responsible for planning and implementing psychoeducational activities and all other planned activities, and for maintaining preparedness. Trauma workers are responsible for maintaining preparedness, implementing plans, and providing feed-

back to administrators and policy makers regarding the suitability and relevance of plans and psychoeducational efforts. Finally, all members of the institution are responsible for employing the skills and attitudes that acknowledge STS and facilitate healthy processing by exposed personnel.

How do institutions differ with regard to their ability to facilitate a healing experience for members?

Institutions vary along the same dimensions as do families with regard to their ability to facilitate a healing experience for traumatized members. Figley (1989) has identified the importance of a number of variables in providing a healing environment for family members who have been affected by traumatic stress. All of those variables apply equally well to the environment of an institutional "family." The following describes the institutional environment that is most facilitative for the recovery of traumatized personnel.

1. The stressors are accepted as real and legitimate.
2. The problem is viewed as an institutional problem and not as a problem that is limited to the individual.
3. The general approach to the problem is to seek solutions, not to assign blame.
4. There is a high level of tolerance for individual disturbance.
5. Support is expressed clearly, directly, and abundantly in the form of praise, commitment, and affection.
6. Communication is open and effective; there are few sanctions against what can be said. The quality of communication is good; messages are clear and direct.
7. There is a high degree of cohesion.
8. There is considerable flexibility of roles; individuals are not rigidly restricted to particular roles.
9. Resources—material, social, and institutional—are utilized efficiently.
10. There is no subculture of violence (emotional outbursts are not a form of violence).
11. There is no substance abuse.

What are the underlying assumptions in healthy institutions that facilitate the effective prevention of STS?

Ochberg (1991) has identified three principles that underlie effective post-traumatic therapy. These principles—in concert with Figley's healthy-family characteristics outlined above—form the foundation of a set of assumptions that must be a part of the institutional milieu if STS is to be effectively processed. Ochberg's principles refer to (1) individuality, (2) normalization, and (3) empowerment.

1. The individuality principle stresses that every individual has a unique pathway to recovery after traumatic stress. The institution must respect each member's unique needs and approach to recovery.
2. The normalization principle balances the emphasis on the uniqueness of the individual's recovery. It identifies a general pattern of post-traumatic adjustment and emphasizes the essential normality of the disturbing thoughts and feelings that make up this pattern.
3. The empowering principle emphasizes the need for the trauma survivor to be included as an active agent in his or her own recovery so that he or she can recover dignity and a sense of power and control.

What are the manifestations of effective support by other institutional personnel?
   Social support has been shown to be an effective moderator of both general stress (Cobb, 1976) and traumatic stress (Flannery, 1990). Social support has been empirically divided into (1) emotional support, (2) information, (3) social companionship, and (4) instrumental support (Flannery, 1990). All of these aspects of support apply in institutional settings; in addition, the literature on functional coping by families can serve as a model for effective social supportiveness in an institutional setting. The utility of family support in the management of stress has been widely demonstrated (Cobb, 1976; Dean & Lin, 1977; Hirsch, 1980; Solomon, Mikulincer, & Hobfoll, 1987). The general concept of social supportiveness in families has been found to include emotional support, encouragement, advice, companionship, and tangible aid (Burge & Figley, 1982; Figley, 1983). Figley (1989) identifies skills common to families that effectively support traumatized members. These include tangible assistance in the form of (1) providing resources, as well as specific social supportiveness skills in the form of (2) clarifying insights, (3) correcting distortions, and (4) supporting reframes. To these, I would add empathic attunement.

1. Institutional personnel can be supportive by providing resources. Resources refer to such tangible aid as financial aid, increased flexibility in the work schedule or time off from the job, changes in duty assignments, and generally staying abreast of the needs of traumatized workers.

2. Other personnel can help a worker who has been traumatized as a result of exposure to STS. They can help the traumatized worker clarify his or her insights by listening carefully and nonjudgmentally, by getting the facts straight, and by accepting all the feelings that the traumatized worker is experiencing.

3. Other personnel also provide support by listening to the traumatized worker and correcting distortions in the worker's assessment of his or her behavior and responsibility with regard to the trauma. This is particularly relevant when the worker feels guilty. Informed listeners can help him or her assign blame and credit more objectively. Since other institutional personnel often have an intimate understanding of the worker's role in dealing with the secondary stressor—such as the actual trauma survivor—they can offer an invaluable perspective on the realities of the worker's situation.

4. The perspective that co-workers can offer the traumatized worker will often constitute a reframe of the trauma. They can support more generous or accurate perspectives on the impairing stress reactions. This can lead the traumatized worker to develop a different cognitive appraisal of his or her role in dealing with the original trauma survivor.

5. Co-workers provide support by being empathically attuned to the worker traumatized by STS. They do this by recognizing and responding to the emotional experience of the affected worker, and by maintaining the empathic link even when the worker is experiencing strongly dysphoric emotions (Rowe & MacIsaac, 1989). The state of empathic attunement underlies the listening skills and provides the opportunity to offer a different perspective.

STS ISSUES SPECIFIC TO INSTITUTIONAL SETTINGS

There are a number of issues related to STS that are unique to certain aspects of institutional settings, including the institutions' hierarchical structure, their often impersonal nature, and their institutional mission, as well as the general nature of group dynamics.

Issues Related to the Hierarchical Structure of Institutions

Institutions are generally structured in a hierarchical fashion. This can be less true in smaller institutions, but becomes an inevitable aspect of the institutional structure as the size of the institution increases. Hierarchical structuring allows large groups of people to function together for common purposes. One aspect of the hierarchical structure is that decision-making power is distributed unequally; individuals who are higher in the hierarchy have greater power. This allows for a more efficacious use of time, but it also can create a social structure that unequally distributes status. Individuals who are lower in the hierarchy usually do not have easy access to those who are higher up. The time of individuals with "higher" status tends to be viewed as more valuable than does the time of individuals with "lower" status.

The hierarchical structure thus can contribute to the appearance that (1) some people are more important than others, (2) some people cannot be expected to spend much time responding to others, and (3) some people are more replaceable than others. These misleading implications of hierarchies not only are destructive to the self-esteem of members, but can significantly interfere with the ability of personnel to deal with STS among themselves.

Hierarchical relationships can impede the "leveling" experience that is an important aspect of normalization, whether in the treatment of a survivor with post-traumatic stress disorder (PTSD) or the supervision of a worker with secondary traumatic stress disorder (STSD). People who are at different status levels are constrained from being able to respond to one another in a normal fashion. Thus the elements of supportiveness are more difficult to implement in a hierarchically structured environment.

In order to overcome the obstacles posed by the hierarchical structure, the personnel at its higher levels must endorse and actively foster an environment that emphasizes the value of all personnel, regardless of their standing in the institutional hierarchy. The notion that some people are less important or more replaceable must be constantly repudiated, and the actions of policy makers, administrators, and managers must convey their respect for the dignity of every employee under their authority.

Issues Related to the Impersonal Nature of Many Bureaucracies

Some institutions are overly routinized and rule driven, a phenomenon that is generally restricted to large institutions that must deal with very large numbers of clients. Over time, those dealings can become too narrowly focused, giving the institutional personnel less autonomy and decision-making authority to make exceptions or to exercise discretionary power. This kind of bureaucratic environment creates an internal climate that impedes workers' feelings of empowerment. Outsiders often encounter this feeling of disempowerment when they run into red tape and bureaucrats who proclaim that they can do nothing because policy prevents them.

A bureaucratic, impersonal, disempowering environment is in direct opposition to the empowerment principle. Institutions with such environments contribute to the individual's experience of being a victim, someone who is acted upon and has no control over his or her fate. Institutions that expose workers to secondary traumatization need to foster an environment that empowers the individual, regardless of his or her role in the institution. This means that administrators must maintain a more personal management style, and that policies (and policy makers) should remain flexible and leave latitude for employees to exercise their discretion. An institution that cannot be flexible and make allowances for the personal needs and proclivities of individual workers is a poor environment for people working with trauma.

Issues Related to the Mission of the Institution

The perceived missions of some institutions can fit less well with the vulnerability and emotional processing that underlie successful coping with exposure to traumatic stress. For example, the mission of a mental health clinic is to enhance and preserve the mental health of its constituency. Consequently, the values associated with effective coping are more likely to be manifest in such an institution than they might be in a police department, where the mission is to enhance and preserve the physical safety of its constituency. In the police department, it would be reasonable to expect that considerable attention would be paid to the safety of workers, but not necessarily to their mental health needs. In effect, the mission of the institution influences the extent to which effective coping strategies are supported.

It is thus important for policy makers clearly to define the mission of the institution. If that mission will require workers to be exposed to STS, then STS can be more effectively anticipated and prevention efforts implemented. But if exposure to traumatic stress is not inherent in the institution's mission statement, then the institution is not likely to prepare adequately. The mission of any institution that must deal with STS should include an acknowledgment of its effects on workers—either in the mission statement or in the strategies that support the mission statement. This should be in the form of a written policy statement that identifies the primary mission of the institution, the actions for accomplishing that mission, and the actions for dealing with the expected effects of STS.

This is an example of a mission statement for a police department: "The mission of the institution shall be to enforce the law and preserve the safety of the citizens of this community." And here is an example of a strategy that addresses STS: "A high level of employee functioning and a low burnout rate will be pursued by maintaining policies that are respectful of individual differences and responsive to the traumatizing effects of this work on staff."

Issues Related to Group Dynamics

The intense primitive emotions precipitated by traumatization and experienced empathically in secondary traumatization can be very disruptive in groups. Such intense emotional states influence the group dynamics and can polarize group members (Gabbard, 1989). The experience of the trauma survivor, who feels alienated and misunderstood, is likely to be enacted in the dynamics of the group unless this phenomenon is specifically anticipated and steps taken to prevent it. This untoward event is usually made manifest by a distancing reaction; the traumatized member is viewed as not functioning well because there is something wrong *with* him or her, rather than because something happened *to* him or her. Viewing the secondary traumatization as indicative of something wrong with the individual allows other members to disown their own vulnerability to traumatic stress and protects them from identifying with the traumatized member's disturbing affect, a mechanism that has long been recognized in group processes (Jaques, 1955).

This experience is common to both primary and secondary traumatization, but it is exacerbated in a group setting. Groups establish consensual perceptions of reality. Once several members of a group believe something to be so, that belief takes on considerable power. Since relating to the reality of traumatization threatens members' fundamental assumptions and the consequent stability of their world views and feelings of security (Janoff-Bulman, 1992), it does not take much for them to accept a view that protects them from recognizing their common link with the traumatized individual. That individual is then left feeling alienated, vulnerable, and personally damaged. This social cutoff exacerbates the original stress response in primary traumatization and has been referred to as a secondary trauma (Catherall, 1989) or a "second injury" to victims (Symonds, 1980).

From the perspective of group dynamics, the affected member is carrying the vulnerable feelings for the entire group when the other members disown their common link with him or her (Yalom, 1970). If he or she can be pushed out of the group, either physically or psychologically, then the other members of the group can maintain the illusion that they are free from the threat of traumatization.

The implications of this group phenomenon are especially relevant to institutions that expose workers to STS. Unless institutional leaders take specific steps to anticipate the group reaction to traumatized workers, it is likely that those workers will be psychologically ostracized by at least some members of the group. That, of course, will only exacerbate the deleterious effects of the traumatization. Institutional leaders can take the following steps to ensure that traumatized workers are not ostracized.

1. Leaders must recognize the group that exists—either formally, such as in the form of an adminstrative section, or informally— and they must recognize that the group will have an emotional reaction to the traumatized worker.
2. Leaders must create regular opportunities for the group to meet and talk about their exposure to traumatic stress. A primary goal of such meetings is to normalize the experience of feeling affected by secondary exposure. These ongoing meetings are not likely to take place unless someone in a position of leadership takes responsibility for seeing that they do.
3. Leaders must actively respond when individual workers have been affected by traumatic stress, by bringing the issue to the group and encouraging group members to share their reactions. The leader discourages the process of ostracism by defining and approaching the issue as a group problem, not as an individual problem.

These steps may sound a lot like conducting group therapy and so may not appeal to some institutions. But it is not really group therapy. The leaders do not need to have advanced training in group dynamics, and the members need not be expected to bare their souls. The recommended discussions can occur in general staff meetings, and the leaders simply have to indicate the need for the discussion and their assumption that it is a group problem. This may not fully resolve the issues, but it does establish a general framework for keeping the traumatized worker connected to the group.

IMPLEMENTING AN INSTITUTIONAL STS PREVENTION PROGRAM

Now that we have discussed some of the factors involved in the prevention of institutional STS, let us consider what the institution needs to do in order to implement a program of prevention. The prevention program can be broken down into five steps: (1) projection of exposure, (2) development of plans, (3) psychoeducation of staff, (4) implementation of preparedness structure, and (5) evaluation of the program.

Projecting Exposure to STS

The first step is for the policy makers and administrators to assess the likelihood of exposure to STS and identify the likely avenues of exposure. This action assumes a certain level of awareness on their part. If the policy makers and administrators are naive in the area of traumatic stress, then they should first obtain education and consultation from qualified sources. Assuming they have an adequate level of awareness, their task then focuses on examining and thinking through the ways in which their staff can conceivably be exposed. Which staff members are in positions that will expose them to traumatic stressors? What is the nature of the traumatic stressors that are likely to be encountered? What are the likely frequency and intensity of exposure? Are some staff members in positions in which they are more likely to be exposed than would be other staff members? What staff members are in positions that will insulate them from exposure, and how much do they interact with the staff members who will be exposed?

It can help to draw up an organizational chart that identifies levels of exposure among staff. This can give administrators a visual picture of how the institution can be affected, and may result in their choosing to make structural changes if the patterns suggest that some staff members are in overexposed positions or are too cut off from sources of support.

Developing Plans

The development of plans is a complex process that involves many levels of the institution. It is the responsibility of policy makers and administrators actually to develop the prevention plans, but they cannot accomplish that task without the input of trauma workers and supervisors. The planning process may involve multiple revisions as the plans develop and are refined according to the feedback from the supervisors and trauma workers. Once the plans are completed, they should address the following.

The *process* (and time frame) for enacting prevention should be clearly outlined. At what point in a new worker's orientation should he or she be educated about STS? How often should the subject be discussed among staff members? What meetings are appropriate for such discussions? What steps are to be taken when a worker has been exposed to and affected by traumatic stress?

The *responsibilities* of each individual should be outlined. Who will teach the psychoeducational classes? Who is responsible for notifying whom when a worker has been exposed? Who is responsible for tracking the individual worker and assessing whether the worker is reacting to secondary (or primary) traumatic stress? These responsibilities need not be particularly complicated; they just need to be clear. For example, in some institutions, the worker himself or herself may be responsible for assessing whether he or she is traumatized, and if so, is supposed to notify a supervisor.

Educating Staff Members

The psychoeducation of staff members must include the opportunity for feedback and response. As in the development of plans, the staff members need to have input into the nature of the psychoeducational material. They need to be educated about the prevention process and the responsibilities of institutional staff. But most important, they need to be educated about the nature of traumatic stress and secondary traumatization. The education ideally should be presented to groups so that the process of intragroup communication of trauma-related feelings and attitudes can be initiated and facilitated. This is not a topic that can be presented in a dry lecture format without the opportunity for people to express their reactions. Education in this area is *psycho*educational, a form of teaching that goes far beyond simply passing on facts.

The content of the psychoeducational programs will vary according to specific aspects of the setting, the amount and kind of exposure, and the mission of the institution. For example, the personnel in a police department are exposed to both primary and secondary traumatization. Because of this regular exposure to primary and secondary stressors, there is often a high level of numbing-type defenses. Psychoeducational efforts may have to penetrate such defenses as denial, minimization, and rationalization in order for workers even to acknowledge the effects of traumatic stress. Secondary stressors are particularly likely to be minimized in settings that include exposure to primary stressors.

The group plays an indispensable role in these institutional settings. Processing their exposure to secondary stressors within the group can allow workers to (1) normalize their reactions, (2) better understand their reactions, and (3) have a safe environment in which to share and work through their reactions (McCann & Pearlman, 1990). Psychoeducational efforts must consider the prevailing group culture and address all avoidance behaviors that are supported by the group, since there is an interaction between individual and social factors in coping with major stressors (Bartone & Wright, 1990). Some groups work together as a large team, such as medical personnel in an emergency room; others work in small groups, such as the partners in a police squad car. Existing groups should be recognized and kept intact in the psychoeducational process. Partners should not be split up and sent to classes separately. A central goal of psychoeducation is to influence the group norms, to create patterns of communication that facilitate the processing of traumatic stress.

Other settings—such as a community clinic providing individual therapy—may not have a discrete work group. This is a disadvantage to workers exposed to traumatic stress. The effectiveness of psychoeducational interventions is enhanced by a group process that is expressive and accepting. Thus a goal of the psychoeducation would be to identify and strengthen the informal groups that already exist in such settings.

Initiating a Preparedness Stucture

When an institution initiates a structured program of preparedness for dealing with STS, it should be written up and distributed to all staff members. The presentation should include the institution's general philosophy of prevention, as well as specific plans. This is a basic first step in attempting to alter any group norms that would interfere with acknowledging and supporting the exposed individuals. The preparedness program should include both regular ongoing structures, such as group meetings, as well as response structures, such as critical-incident stress debriefings (Mitchell, 1983). Those structured activities that necessarily occur only infrequently probably will need to be practiced.

Concurrent with mechanisms for handling extreme stress, the institution should facilitate healthy mechanisms for coping with stress in general. Activities for general stress relief, such as diet classes and exercise programs, are an important adjunct to the mechanisms for verbal and emotional processing of traumatic stress (Ochberg, 1991). Preparedness should be viewed as a full-time attitude toward the effects of stress, both normal and traumatic.

Evaluating the Effectiveness of the Program

The development of an institutional program for handling traumatic stress is incomplete without a mechanism for evaluating the program's effectiveness. The evaluation should include some form of statistical tabulation of indices that are normally studied in assessing burnout. These would include such items as use of sick days, turnover rate, and job satisfaction. Ideally, this data should start being collected before the prevention program is implemented so that the effects of the program can be assessed. Additionally, the evaluation should address the subjective experience of the workers. This can mean self-report measures, but should definitely include face-to-face feedback from the personnel most affected by the program. Again, the group format is an excellent vehicle for obtaining this information.

Finally, the evaluation of the program should not be confined to assessing the difference between no program and some kind of program. A program may be implemented with initial enthusiasm, but deteriorate into the same old situation. The effective evaluation of an institutional program for handling traumatic stress must be an ongoing process, just as the attitude toward processing stress reactions must be an ongoing attitude. Administrators responsible for evaluating these programs must institute both initial follow-up mechanisms for the implementation and fine-tuning of the program, as well as ongoing mechanisms for determining the program's continued viability.

EXAMPLE

Here is one institution's approach to handling secondary stressors and preventing, or at least controlling, secondary traumatization. The setting is a mental health institute that specializes in treating people who have been traumatized. The institute was formed recently, and thus the administration had some awareness of the need for dealing with secondary stressors. Also, there was an opportunity to address the group culture during the formation period. Finally, the institutional staff was composed of a sophisticated group of clinicians, a number of whom had had considerable experience in dealing with secondary stressors. Nevertheless, many of the usual difficulties with processing traumatic stress were encountered. Though trained clinicians may have certain advantages in coping with secondary traumatization, they also may have special needs with regard to its understanding and integration (Talbot, Manton, & Dunn, 1992). One of the first lessons was that experience and sophistication do not safeguard a group from enacting defenses against acknowledging and effectively processing STS.

Psychoeducational efforts consisted of classes conducted with the entire institutional staff, including administrative/clerical personnel. Reading materials on post-traumatic stress and principles of recovery were distributed to all staff members. After an initial period of education for the entire staff, a weekly group was begun for those staff members who were most involved in the trauma work. The first several months consisted of more didactic presentations and group discussions. A concerted effort was made to establish the group as a safe place where individuals could be free to express a full range of feelings. Group members were encouraged to discuss their subjective reactions to this kind of work.

Eventually, a highly unusual intervention was employed. A therapist from the local community who had recently been traumatized by a violent crime was brought in for several sessions to discuss his experience. He did not come in as a patient, but as a peer who both could teach something to the group and obtain some support. His feelings about his trauma were extremely intense and provoked a remarkable amount of anxiety among the group members. The anxiety was expressed through the usual group mechanisms, such as talking outside of group (there was a confidentiality rule), ambivalence about membership, and challenges to the leadership of the group. Perhaps most telling was the attempt by several group members to prevent the return of the traumatized therapist, and an effort to redefine the traumatized therapist as a "patient," and not as a peer.

To the credit of the clinicians in the group, everyone continued to attend, and the anxieties and other feelings were brought into the group and discussed openly. The visiting therapist was particularly helpful in sharing his experiences of being ostracized in the community and his understanding of what was going on in the group. The result was that the group members had a firsthand experience of the power of traumatic affect and STS on group processes. After this experience, the group approached clinical problems with a greater sensitivity to the feelings of all the members. Discussions of the clinical work were more emotional and presented in a less intellectual fashion. The difference was similar to Bugental's (1987) distinction between "experience-distant" and "experience-near" styles of therapy. Individuals were more able to bring their subjective reactions to their work into the group with a feeling of safety and of greater understanding by all the group members. The group eventually evolved into an ongoing case-conference format.

CONCLUSION

The issue of secondary traumatization on an institutional level is more relevant than ever. We have increasing numbers of institutions whose mission it is to deal with trauma and with the victims of trauma. Research evidence is building that the personnel in these institutions are being affected by their exposure (Genest, Levine, Ramsden, & Swanson, 1990; Horowitz, 1985; McCammon, Durham, Allison, & Williamson, 1988). But we are only beginning to build a base of knowledge about the effects of secondary traumatization on co-workers (Bartone & Wright, 1990; McCann & Pearlman, 1990). Certainly, more research is needed on the subject of secondary traumatization, including that among people who are linked through work relationships. We already know that secondary stressors can be as powerful as primary stressors. We need to know more about the processes of transmission and how those processes are made manifest in institutional settings. In the meantime, it behooves administrators in exposed institutions to learn more about STS, and to begin implementing programs of preparedness and prevention.

REFERENCES

Bartone, P.T., & Wright, K.M. (1990). Grief and group recovery following a military air disaster. *Journal of Traumatic Stress, 3*(4), 523–539.

Bugental, J.F.T. (1987). *The art of the psychotherapist*. New York: Norton.

Burge, S., & Figley, C.R. (1982). The social support scale. Unpublished manuscript, Purdue University, Lafayette, Ind.

Catherall, D.R. (1989). Differentiating intervention strategies for primary and secondary trauma in post-traumatic stress disorder: The example of Vietnam veterans. *Journal of Traumatic Stress, 2*(3), 289–304.

Cobb, S. (1976). Social support as a moderator of life stress. *Psychosomatic Medicine, 38*, 300–314.

Dean, A., & Lin, N. (1977). The stress-buffering role of social support. *Journal of Nervous and Mental Disease, 165*, 403-417.

Figley, C.R. (1983). Catastrophes: An overview of family reactions. In C.R. Figley & H.I. McCubbin (Eds.), *Stress and the family: Vol. 2. Coping with catastrophe* (pp. 3–20). New York: Brunner/Mazel.

Figley, C.R. (1989). *Helping traumatized families*. San Francisco: Jossey-Bass.

Flannery, R.B. (1990). Social support and psychological trauma: A methodological review. *Journal of Traumatic Stress, 3*(4), 593–611.

Gabbard, G.O. (1989). Splitting in hospital treatment. *American Journal of Psychiatry, 146*, 444–451.

Genest, M., Levine, J., Ramsden, V., & Swanson, R. (1990). The impact of providing help: Emergency workers and cardiopulmonary resuscitation attempts. *Journal of Traumatic Stress, 3*(2), 305–313.

Hirsch, B.J. (1980). Natural support systems and coping with major life changes. *American Journal of Community Psychology, 8*, 159–171.

Horowitz, M.J. (1985). Disasters and psychological responses to stress. *Psychiatric Annuals, 15*, 161–167.

Janoff-Bulman, R. (1992). *Shattered assumptions: Towards a new psychology of trauma*. New York: Free Press.

Jaques, E. (1955). Social systems as defence against persecutory and depressive anxiety. In M. Klein (Ed.), *New directions in psychoanalysis* (pp. 478–497). New York: Basic Books.

McCammon, S., Durham, T.W., Allison, E.J., & Williamson, J.E. (1988). Emergency workers: Cognitive appraisal and coping with traumatic events. *Journal of Traumatic Stress, 1*, 353–372.

McCann, I.L., & Pearlman, L.A. (1990). Vicarious traumatization: A framework for understanding the psychological effects of working with victims. *Journal of Traumatic Stress,* 3(1), 131–149.

Mitchell, J. (1983). When disaster strikes: The critical incident stress debriefing process. *Journal of Emergency Medical Services,* 8(1), 36–39.

Ochberg, F.M. (1991). Post-traumatic therapy. *Psychotherapy, 28*(1), 5–15.

Rowe, C.E., & Mac Isaac, D.S. (1989). *Empathic attunement: The "technique" of psychoanalytic self psychology.* Northvale, N.J.: Jason Aronson.

Solomon, Z., Mikulincer, M., & Hobfoll, S.E. (1987). Objective versus subjective measurement of stress and social support: Combat-related reactions. *Journal of Consulting and Clinical Psychology, 55*(4), 577–583.

Symonds, M. (1980). The "second injury" to victims. *Evaluation and Change,* Special Issue, pp. 36–38.

Talbot, A., Manton, M., & Dunn, P.J. (1992). Debriefing the debriefers: An intervention strategy to assist psychologists after a crisis. *Journal of Traumatic Stress, 5*(1), 45–62.

Yalom, I.D. (1970). *The theory and practice of group psychotherapy.* New York: Basic Books.

Epilogue:
The Transmission of Trauma

CHARLES R. FIGLEY

As a final discussion of compassion stress and fatigue, it is important to consider once again the fourfold purpose of the book and the fundamental questions answered throughout. The first purpose of this book was to discuss the results of a systematic reevaluation of the field in general, and of post-traumatic stress disorder (PTSD) in particular, after more than a decade of use. The introduction and Chapter 1 suggested that the emerging field of traumatology has inadvertently ignored a large segment of traumatized people—individuals traumatized as a result of their compassion for those in harm's way. Moreover, it was noted early in the book that the field lacked a comprehensive model that could account for the great variety of traumatic stressors, stress reactions, and methods of coping in widely varying contexts that was sensitive simultaneously to biological, psychological, and social indicators.

This was connected to the second goal of the book: to introduce a reconceptualization of trauma, traumatic events, traumatic stress, and traumatic stress disorders that appreciates the varying degrees of impact of traumatic events on individuals and interpersonal relationships or systems, depending upon the proximity to harm. Such a model was presented by Valent, in his "survival strategies model" in Chapter 2. Moreover, less pervasive, but no less innovative, were the models offered throughout the book. These included Beaton and Murphy's "theoretical systems model of secondary traumatization," in Chapter 3; Harris' "etiology of integration of secondary traumatic stress" model, in Chapter 5; and Yassen's "multidimensional framework for preventing STS" and her "ecological model for the prevention of STS" both presented in Chapter 9. Each attempts both to organize the current understanding about secondary traumatic stress (STS) reactions and, thereby, to account for why some professionals succumb to compassion stress and fatigue, while others do not.

The third and fourth goals of the book were to review the scholarly and clinical literature vis-à-vis this new conceptualization, and to propose new approaches to conceptualizing, researching, and treating traumatic stress, built upon the new conceptualization. Each author was responsible for reaching these last two goals, drawing on his or her own conceptualization, or those of others, as it applies to the particular professionals of concern. The early chapters primarily reviewed the research that suggested axioms relevant to treatment. The middle chapters focused on innovative ways of assessing and treating professionals who are especially vulnerable to compassion stress and fatigue. And the final group of chapters focused on preventing compassion stress and fatigue.

THE TRAUMA TRANSMISSION CONUNDRUM

Although we now know much more than ever about the least-known traumatic stress, STS and secondary traumatic stress disorder (STSD), the most fundamental question remains a conundrum. How is it that the traumatic stress first found in one person, call that person a "victim," is also found among those who attend to the victim, call them supporters or helpers? Scholars and clinicians require a conceptualization that accurately describes the indices of traumatic stress for *both* those "in harm's way" and those who care for them and become impaired in the process, and the models noted above provide this. But how did the traumatic material get there and how can it be removed?

The trauma transmission model, depicted in Figures 1 and 2, suggests that members of systems, in an effort to generate an understanding of the victimized member, require identification with the victim and his or her suffering. They attempt to answer for themselves the five victim questions: What happened? Why did it happen? Why did I act as I did then? Why have I acted as I have since? If it happens again, will I be able to cope? (Figley, 1982, 1989). These supporters try to answer these

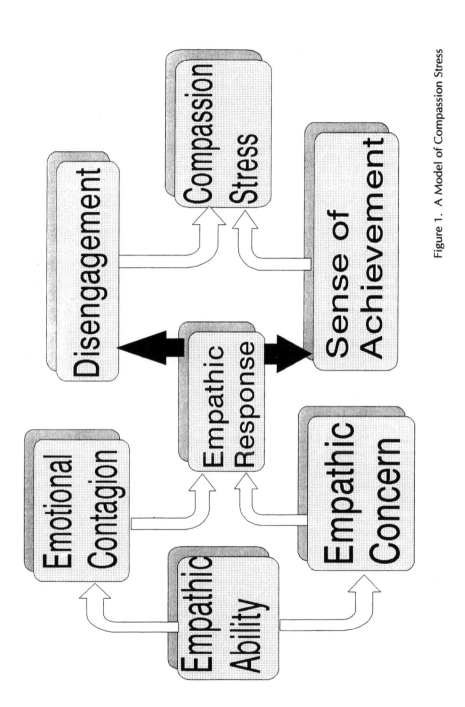

Figure 1. A Model of Compassion Stress

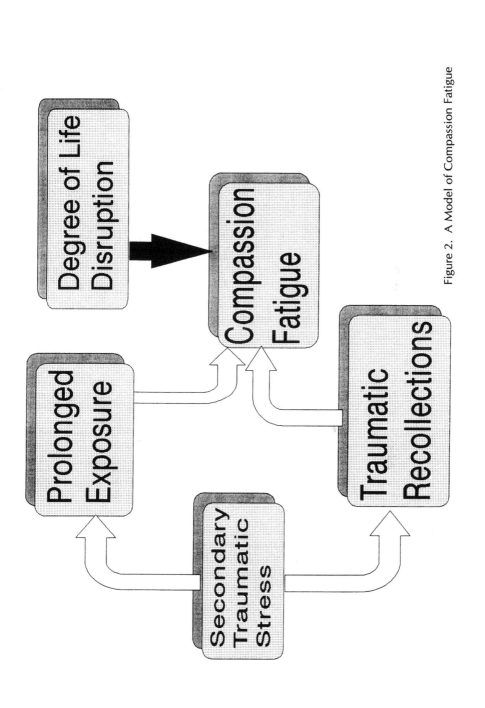

Figure 2. A Model of Compassion Fatigue

questions *for* the victim in order to change their own behavior accordingly. Yet, in the process of generating new information the system member *experiences* emotions that are strikingly similar to those of the victim. This includes visual images (e.g., flashbacks), sleeping problems, depression, and other symptoms that are a direct result of visualizing the victim's traumatic experiences, or of being exposed to the symptoms of the victim, or both. The terms most relevant to this process include cognizance, discernment, sensitivity, understanding, comfort, identify with, understand, approve, endorse, sanction, embrace, receive, welcome, abide, bear, endure, suffer, tolerate, accept, commiseration, pity, compassion, and sympathy. This model draws from all of the important research and theoretical literatures that have contributed to understanding both traumatic stress, interpersonal relationships (e.g., empathy studies), and worker burnout (especially Miller, Stiff, & Ellis, 1988). The model suggests that the burnout of STS is due, in part, to one's empathic ability, actions toward the sufferer and the inability to find relief from one's actions through depersonalization, and a sense of satisfaction for helping to relieve suffering.

This component of the model (see Figure 1) illustrates how compassion stress is a function of six interacting variables. Compassion stress is defined as the stress connected with exposure to a sufferer. Empathic ability is defined as the ability to notice the pain of others. It is frequently the characteristic that leads people to choose the role of helper, especially as a social worker, counselor, or other type of professional helper. This ability is, in turn, linked to one's susceptibility to emotional contagion, defined as experiencing the feelings of the sufferer as a function of exposure to the sufferer. This is similar to the feeling of being "swept up" in the emotion of the victim(s), and is the very essence of the feeling of compassion for another. Much of this is associated, in turn, with identifying with the victim(s), having the feeling of "but for the grace of God, there go I." It is one of the reasons why emergency medical, rescue, and law enforcement professionals become so upset when exposed to victimized children (e.g., those hurt in an automobile accident, or as the result of domestic violence). Empathic ability is also linked to empathic concern, the motivation to act. Without the motivation to respond to the victim, the helper does nothing—irrespective of the helper's ability to respond and the extent to which the helper is exposed to the suffering of the victim. Both empathic ability and emotional contagion account for the extent to which the person makes an effort to reduce the suffering of the sufferer. The effort is the empathic response. Efforts to help relieve the suffering of the victim take many forms and are entirely a subjective assessment on the part of the helper. For psychotherapists, it is bearing witness to the pain of the victim, reassurance, providing hope of recovery. For Red Cross workers and others working in crisis situations, it is providing these in addition to food, clothing, shelter, protection, and other basic needs. The extent to which the helper is satisfied with his or her efforts (sense of achievement), and the extent to which the helper can distance himself or herself from the ongoing misery of the victim(s), accounts for how much the helper experiences compassion stress. Those who experience very little compassion stress and yet are exposed to enormous emotional contagion and have considerable empathic ability and empathic concern find a sense of satisfaction in their empathic response because they believe that they relieved suffering and thus have a sense of achievement or because they are able to avoid identifying with or they become obsessed with the difficulties of the victim(s), and thus are effective at distancing themselves psychologically from the sufferer. A sense of achievement is satisfaction in reducing the suffering. Depersonalization is separating the self from the sufferer.

This second component of the trauma transmission model (see Figure 2) illustrates how compassion fatigue is a function of four interacting variables. Compassion fatigue is defined as a state of exhaustion and disfunction—biologically, psychologically, and socially—as a result of prolonged exposure to compassion stress and all that it evokes. Prolonged exposure means an ongoing sense of responsibility for the care of the sufferer and the suffering, over a protracted period of time. The sense of prolonged exposure is associated with a lack of relief from the burdens of responsibility, the inability to reduce the compassion stress. Moreover, traumatic recollections are provoked by compassion stress and prolonged exposure. These recollections are of traumatic memories that stimulate the symptoms of PTSD and associated reactions, such as depression and generalized anxiety. Compassion fatigue is inevitable if, added to these three factors, the helper experiences an inordinate amount of life disruption as a function of illness or a change in lifestyle, social status, or professional or personal responsibilities.

FINAL NOTE

The work of helping traumatized people is gratifying. Helpers discover early in their careers that those who are traumatized can be relieved by a caring professional who understands and respects their pain, can engender hope in recovering from it, and can go about the task with confidence and succeed quickly. By understanding compassion stress and compassion fatigue, the natural, predictable, treatable, and pre-

ventable consequences of trauma work, we can keep these caring professionals at work and satisfied with it.

Yet many professionals, mainly those who have had little experience,
training in, or commitment to working with traumatized people do
great harm to them. And these failures often cause additional pain for
the traumatized. But it should be noted that, in general, these professionals did not intend to cause such pain; many were experiencing pain
themselves as a result of their exposure to the traumatized, for all the
reasons noted in this book. We now know, finally, that something can be
done to help these ineffective professionals to recognize their shortcom-
ings and their special vulnerability to compassion stress and fatigue, and
to help them cope more effectively with the cost of caring.

There is no doubt that traumatic events will continue to take place
and affect hundreds of thousands of people each year. These traumatized people require the services of professionals who are well prepared
to help them, and, in turn, to help themselves.

REFERENCES

Figley, C. R. (1982). Traumatization and comfort: Close relationships may be hazardous to
    your health. Keynote presentation at a conference, "Families and Close Relationships:
    Individuals in Social Interaction," Texas Tech University, Lubbock, Texas.
Figley, C. R. (1989). *Helping traumatized families*. San Francisco: Jossey-Bass.
Miller, K. I., Stiff, J. B., & Ellis, B. H. (1988). Communication and empathy as precursors to
    burnout among human service workers. *Communication Monographs, 55*, 9.

Name Index

Abarbanel, G., 135
Abrahamson, D., 138
Abramowitz, S., 95, 96
Abramson, L., 35
Abse, D., 211
Ader, R., 23
Albano, A., 3
Alexander, D., 58
Alexander, F., 23
Allen, D., 133
Allison, E., 52, 57, 115–129, 246
Alvarez, W., 57
Andrews, G., 23
Andur, M., 5
Antonovsky, A., 94
Appels, A., 36, 39
Armstrong, K., 54, 73, 125, 126, 181
Arons, J., 135
Aronson, E., 11

Baade, E., 35
Bard, M., 57
Barglow, P., 36
Barr, D., 12
Bartemeier, L., 22, 35
Bartone, P., 243, 246
Bartrop, R., 36
Bassuk, E., 136
Bauer, S., 210
Bean, N., 34
Beard, P., 131
Beaton, R., 51–77, 115
Beebe, G., 22
Beehr, T., 183
Bennet, G., 22
Benson, H., 187
Berah, E., 25, 35
Besner, H., 62
Bettleheim, B., 216
Blake, D., 3
Blanchard, D., 26, 37

Blanchard, E., 61
Blanchard, R., 26, 37
Bliss, E., 142
Booth, A., 39
Borysenko, J., 187
Boulanger, G., 64
Bowlby, J., 26
Boylin, W., 85, 87, 97
Bradbury, L., 53
Bradshaw, S., 135
Brain, P., 26
Bray, G., 51, 57, 64, 66, 70, 75, 76, 77, 118, 119, 120, 121, 123, 124
Brende, J., 135
Brenman, M., 143
Breuer, J., 24, 143
Briggie, C., 85, 87, 97
Brill, A., 5
Brill, N., 24
Brodsky, A., 84, 87, 97, 183
Brody, E., 179
Brown, L., 96
Brutus, M., 26
Buchele, B., 142
Budd, F., 84
Bugental, J., 245
Burge, S., 57, 235
Burgess, A., 68
Burke, R., 71
Burno, A., 52
Buskirk, J., 144

Calabrese, J., 36
Caldwell, J., 210
Campbell, D., 57, 66
Cannon, W., 26, 37
Capitano, J., 33, 34
Caplan, G., 181
Carnera, A., 33
Catherall, D., 136, 232–246
Cerney, M., 1, 144
Chavoya, G., 209

Cherniss, C., 11, 181, 183
Chestnut, D., 181
Claiborn, J., 61
Clark, D., 108
Clevenger, S., 22
Clifft, M., 131
Clipp, E., 63
Close, J., 52
Cobb, S., 235
Coe, C., 34, 36
Coffman, S., 9
Colao, F., 135, 142, 198
Colligan, M., 65
Comas-Diaz, L., 189
Cooley, E., 97
Corey, G., 9
Corneil, W., 65, 70
Courage, M., 11
Courtois, C., 83, 84, 85, 86, 87
Cousins, N., 188
Cross, H., 61
Cummings, E., 33, 39

Dahl, B., 9
Daleva, M., 61
D'Amato, F., 33
Danieli, Y., 9, 87, 92, 210
Daniels, M., 26
Darling, R., 106
Darwin, C., 25, 37
Davis, L., 179
Dean, A., 235
de Jong, J., 61
DeLoffi, A., 181
Deutsch, C., 96, 139
Diemer, R., 10
Dienstbier, R., 35
Dixon, A., 38
Domingo, G., 58
Doyle, J., 210
Drabek, T., 25, 72
Dubos, R., 22

255

Weiss, D., 66
Weiss, J., 35
Weissberg, M., 33
Wells, A., 58
White, J., 106
Wiggers, T., 139
Wilkinson, C., 64, 66, 72, 73
Williams, D., 11
Williams, J., 83

Williamson, J., 52, 128, 246
Wilner, N., 57
Wilson, E., 26, 33, 39
Wilson, J., 7, 137
Winget, C., 211
Winnicott, D., 133, 216
Wissler, A., 97
Wite, P., 9
Wolff, C., 36

Wright, K., 243, 246

Yalom, I., 239
Yassen, J., 178–206
Yorke, C., 131
Youniss, J., 40

Zahn-Waxler, C., 33
Zavitsanos, X., 22
Zimering, R., 209–229

Subject Index

Charles R. Figley, Ph.D., has edited many books focusing on psychosocial stress/post-traumatic stress disorder relations. He is also Founding Editor of the *Journal of Traumatic Stress*, Founding President of the International Society of Traumatic Stress Studies, and consultant to numerous mental health and treatment agencies and associations. He is Series Editor of the *Brunner/Mazel Psychosocial Stress Series*, and is the recipient of the 1994 Pioneer Award in Traumatology.